At the Glacier's Edge

Frontispiece. *Map of the Southern Part of the State of New York* [. . .], 1815. Courtesy of the Library of Congress, Wm. Damerum and Peter Maverick, *Map of the Southern Part of New York, Including Long Island, the Sound, the State of Connecticut, Part of the State of New Jersey, and Islands Adjacent: Compiled from Actual Late Surveys* (New York: Wm. Damerum, 1815). https://www.loc.gov/item/97683278/.

At the Glacier's Edge

A Natural History of Long Island from the Narrows to Montauk Point

BETSY McCULLY

RUTGERS UNIVERSITY PRESS
NEW BRUNSWICK, CAMDEN, AND NEWARK, NEW JERSEY
LONDON AND OXFORD

Rutgers University Press is a department of Rutgers, The State University of New Jersey, one of the leading public research universities in the nation. By publishing worldwide, it furthers the University's mission of dedication to excellence in teaching, scholarship, research, and clinical care.

Library of Congress Cataloging-in-Publication Data

Names: McCully, Betsy, 1950– author.
Title: At the glacier's edge : a natural history of Long Island from the
   Narrows to Montauk Point / Betsy McCully.
Other titles: Natural history of Long Island from the Narrows to Montauk Point
Description: New Brunswick : Rutgers University Press, 2024. | Includes
   bibliographical references and index.
Identifiers: LCCN 2023044607 | ISBN 9781978838918 (paperback) |
   ISBN 9781978838925 (hardback) | ISBN 9781978838932 (epub) |
   ISBN 9781978838949 (pdf)
Subjects: LCSH: Natural history—New York (State)—Long Island. |
   Natural history—New York (State)—Montauk Point. | Narrows,
   The (New York, N.Y.)—History.
Classification: LCC QH105.N7 M384 2024 | DDC 508.747/2—dc23/eng/20230921
LC record available at https://lccn.loc.gov/2023044607

A British Cataloging-in-Publication record for this book is available from the British Library.

References to internet websites (URLs) were accurate at the time of writing. Neither the author nor Rutgers University Press is responsible for URLs that may have expired or changed since the manuscript was prepared.

♾ The paper used in this publication meets the requirements of the American National Standard for Information Sciences—Permanence of Paper for Printed Library Materials, ANSI Z39.48-1992.

rutgersuniversitypress.org

For my husband and life partner, Joe

Contents

Preface

Since I was a young girl, I have been drawn to nature. The outdoors always beckoned me to come explore. My father, attentive to the budding naturalist in me, bought me Golden Guides to the natural world—butterflies and moths, trees, flowers, birds—little pocket-size books I have to this day. I not only wanted to be in nature, I wanted to understand the natural world. I wanted to know the names of the plants and animals that inhabited that world. I wanted to know the rocks and shells and stars. It was the beginning of a lifelong educational journey. I learned from my free forays into the field, observing, collecting, and simply reveling in the outdoor world.

I spent part of my girlhood in Lake Forest, Illinois, a leafy town on Michigan's North Shore outside Chicago. I moved there when I was four and left when I was eleven—a mere seven years, but formative ones. We lived in an old converted farmhouse where commuter trains whistled on the tracks behind our house. Between our house and the tracks was a wild field, a little prairie where grasses and wildflowers grew higher than my head. I was lucky to have such a world at my doorstep. In those days, the 1950s, I was free to wander at will, walking the fields, the woods, the ravines, and the nearby shores of Lake Michigan.

And wander I did. I am a polio survivor, so wandering—walking and exploring the land—gave me deep pleasure. I felt connected to the natural world. I could look at a bird on the wing and imagine its sensation of flight. I felt the bird's joy. Though at times I wished I could fly, I did not regret my lack of wings—I had my feet on the ground. I was glad for that. Early on, I came to know the place where I lived through my feet and all my senses. And though I did not understand it at the time, I was learning the importance of such place-based knowledge to our sense of self.

My father was a restless soul who uprooted our family many times over. As an adult, I continued the peripatetic life I was used to, moving every several years. By the time I came to New York in the 1980s, I was ready to put down roots. I settled into my then-husband's house in Manhattan Beach, Brooklyn, and there I spent the next seventeen years raising my son, teaching, writing, and, whenever I could, exploring the natural world wherever I could find it—beaches, city parks, botanical gardens, and my own postage-stamp backyard. Over the years, I recorded my observations in a series of nature journals. I became curious about how the place where I lived came to be. So I began delving into the city's natural history, from its geological formation eons ago, to the evolution of life in the region, to the arrival of the first humans at the end of the last ice age. A book grew out of those years of urban nature exploration, my first book, *City at the Water's Edge: A Natural History of New York* (Rivergate/Rutgers University Press, 2007).

When I remarried in the early 2000s, I moved to Nassau County on Long Island to live with my husband, Joe Giunta, in his neck of the woods. I never imagined I would find myself "out on the island"—at least that's how an urban New Yorker oriented to Manhattan saw it. It was common parlance— "Oh, I live out on the island." The funny thing is, I was always on Long Island! Brooklyn, like Queens—neither of which became a borough of New York City until the Consolidation of 1898—is on Long Island's western end. Once I moved "out on the island," my perspective of the place changed. I often set out with Joe, an avid birder, on birding trips that took us to many of Long Island's natural places. That's why I mention him many times in the book as my companion. I took nature walks on my own as well, equipped with my field guides, journals, and a camera to document what I observed. This book grew out of those forays into Long Island's natural world.

Long Island is an apt name. Stretching about 120 miles from the Narrows on its western end to Montauk Point on its eastern end, it's the largest island in the continental United States. Historically described as "fish-shaped," its "head" is bathed by the waters of New York Bay, and its forked "tail" juts out into the Atlantic. It is both a part of, and apart from, New York City. It has been very much affected by the city's growth, while at the same time retaining its sense of identity as a place apart. It comprises three human habitats: urban on its west end (the boroughs of Brooklyn and Queens); densely suburban in the middle (Nassau and western Suffolk counties); and rural to semirural on its east end, where farmlands have been giving way to suburban-type developments. Each kind of development has left its stamp on the land by altering, damaging, or outright erasing natural habitats. Yet, however fragmented and degraded they have become, the island still retains a mix of habitats that make it a rich subject for a natural history. It's surrounded by the sea, from the shallow waters of estuaries and bays to the deep waters of the oceanic abyss. It's watered by an extensive network of rivers, streams, ponds, springs, and large underground aquifers dating to the ice age. Its shores are fringed with acres of salt marshes and rimmed with miles of sandy beaches and dunes. Thanks to preservation efforts, it still retains large forested tracts. One of New York's largest forest preserves, the Central Pine Barrens, covers one hundred thousand acres in Suffolk County; within it grows the globally rare Dwarf Pine Barrens. Hither Hills State Park on Montauk Peninsula preserves one of the largest undeveloped expanses of maritime deciduous forest on Long Island, including the globally rare maritime oak-holly forest. Ecologically unique grasslands include the maritime grasslands of Long Island's South Fork and the Hempstead Plains Preserve in Nassau County, a remnant of what was once the largest prairie east of the Alleghenies. Some of Long Island's preserves, such as the coastal plain ponds, contain the highest concentration of rare species in New York State. Long a mosaic of natural and human habitats, Long Island offers us a perspective on how we have interacted with its nature—from depending on its natural resources, to depleting and damaging those resources, to remediating the damage and restoring the land and its waters. This book explores the island's diverse habitats, chronicling their natural and human histories.

Having lived on Long Island now some forty years, I've come to appreciate the value of growing roots in a place and coming to know it fully and deeply. Walking the land has been my way of coming to know a place. My walks have become shorter over the years, but whether I'm in the field for an hour or six hours (as I used to do), I am learning. I immerse myself fully. I hear the songs and calls of birds, I see the lilting flight of a butterfly, I feel the spongy moss underfoot, I taste the salt air of the sea and smell the pungent odor of a marsh at low tide.

Nature knowledge involves body, mind, and spirit. Bringing our bodies into nature, putting ourselves in the field, we gain a visceral knowledge. Through science—derived from *scientia*, "to know"—we gain an intellectual understanding. Through years of observation in the field, we reinforce what we observe with what we learn from the sciences, and conversely, we reinforce what we learn from the sciences with what we observe in the field. Our understanding grows deeper over time as we learn of the complex interactions of plants and animals in an ecosystem. In spirit, we feel our connectedness to the living web of the natural world of which we are a part. I come to nature to find solace. I come to nature to find that interconnectedness which I can only describe as love. I often feel joy to hear a bird singing or see a flower opening to the sun. Sometimes I come away feeling sadness, even grief, at all that has been lost, at the ways nature has been diminished—species declining and disappearing, habitats being degraded and destroyed—and I can only feel distress. For I know that the diminishment of nature, of which we are the prime cause, diminishes ourselves.

I hope you, my reader, will be inspired by this book to go out and explore the natural world yourself, wherever you are. If you're on Long Island, I hope this book will open up that world to you. Once you come to know a place in this way—the way of nature—you come to love a place. And out of that love, you will work to preserve and restore it.

At the Glacier's Edge

~

CHAPTER 1

Walking the Glacier's Edge

WHERE THE PAST IS PROLOGUE

On a winter's day I stand at the bluff's edge, cold wind buffeting my body, waves fifty feet below breaking on the narrow beach. Montauk Point is a wave-washed, windswept place at land's end, where North America's eastern flank slopes beneath the Atlantic and falls off into sunless depths. Beneath low clouds, the cobalt-blue sea is silvered in patches where shafts of sunlight break through. Wintering ducks—flocks of scoters and long-tailed ducks with scatterings of eiders, loons, and red-breasted mergansers—speckle the inshore waters. Farther out, black- and white-winged scoters fly fast and low in ragged skeins, shuttling in both directions. Above, gannets bank and turn, their white breasts catching the light, their long narrow wings tapering to black points. Where fishing boats trawl, gulls follow, perhaps interspersed with shearwaters. All is in motion: birds, waves, clouds, wind—and beneath the surface, schooling fish.

I have come here year after year for more than twenty years and have watched the bluffs give way to the onslaught of the rising sea. It has been rising since the end of the ice age, but its rate of rise is accelerating as we release more and more greenhouse gases into the atmosphere, elevating global temperatures and warming the seas. I have photographed the bluffs to chart their regress through the years as fissures cut ever deeper inland and their edges slump, disgorging boulders they held for thousands of years. From my vantage point atop a glacial moraine, looking out toward the horizon, I can mentally reconstruct the island's geological history and reflect on our human imprint.

Figure 1.1. Montauk Point Lighthouse on a winter day. The cliffs below the lighthouse have been bolstered with rip-rap and steel mesh. Photo by author.

The sea off Montauk Point—the easternmost point of land on Long Island and in New York State—extends 120 miles over the continental shelf, until it plunges to the oceanic abyss. During the height of the last glacial episode, some twenty-two thousand years ago, sea levels were 350 feet lower, and the coastline extended unbroken from Cape Cod southward. At the glacier's edge, a vast windswept tundra extended to the distant sea. The ice-free coastal plain was a "refugia," a refuge from the ice where tenacious species of plants and animals could survive, some of whose descendants populate the present-day East Coast, and many others that have become extinct. Both mammoth and mastodon teeth have been dredged up from the now-drowned continental shelf. A well-preserved tooth and partial skeleton of a mammoth were dug up from a mill pond in Queens in 1858 when the pond was being dredged to make way for a reservoir.[1] Woolly mammoths, musk ox, and caribou foraged on tundra grasses and sedges; mastodons, elk, and white-tailed deer browsed in black spruce swamps and patches of jack pine forest; and moose and giant beaver frequented glacial lakes and bogs. Fossilized spruce dated to twelve thousand years ago has been found in eroded bluffs on Montauk Peninsula, buried in ancient peat deposits from a freshwater lake.[2] The herbivores were stalked by carnivores—timber wolf, lynx, cougar, bobcat, and the now-extinct dire wolf. The omnivorous human hunter would soon join the predators, moving in nomadic bands across the landscape. The extinction of ice age fauna marked the end of the Pleistocene, and the spread of humans across the globe marked the beginning of the Holocene era.

A terminal moraine marking a glacier's farthest reach is buried beneath the sea several miles out from Montauk Point. Block Island, Nantucket, and Martha's Vineyard are all remnants of a moraine that extended from Cape Cod to Long Island's South Fork. During the ice age, Long Island was not an island but part of a vast plain. As the climate warmed, the glacier receded from the region, leaving recessional moraines in its wake and releasing torrents of meltwater. Montauk Point marks the stillstand of that glacier, the place where it paused in its retreat and melted out its load of rubble, an agglomeration of huge boulders, small cobbles, sand, and clay. A close look at the strata in the bluffs reveals lighter and darker colors in the layers, indicating more than one glacial advance: the darker grayish layers are Montauk Till, from an older advance interbedded with clay from a glacial lake that formed between the receding glacier and its terminal moraine; the lighter yellowish layers are outwash from a more recent advance. These layers are not neatly stratified but ripped up. When the younger glacier flowed over the older glacial sediments, it folded and ripped the strata, filling in the folds and surrounding the ripped blocks with outwash and sand as it melted out.[3]

Just how many glaciers advanced across Long Island and when they did so are matters of ongoing dispute among geologists, who have fiercely debated the questions for well over a century. Based on extensive fieldwork he conducted on Long Island for the US Geological Survey in the years 1902–1904, Myron Fuller concluded that four distinct glaciations traversed Long Island. With the publication in 1914 of his *Geology of Long Island*, Fuller's multiple-glacier hypothesis became the classic model for Long Island's formation. In 1986, the late geologist Les Sirkin proposed that the two moraines that define Long Island's backbone, the Ronkonkoma and Harbor Hill moraines, were deposited by two separate lobes of a single glacier, the most recent one, known as the Late Wisconsinan. According to his scenario, around twenty-two thousand years ago the Connecticut Lobe of the Late

Wisconsinan glacier surged down the Connecticut River valley, crossed Long Island Sound, and spread eastward across the South Fork, depositing the Ronkonkoma Moraine. The Hudson Lobe of the same glacier surged down the Hudson River valley to Staten Island and then spread eastward and westward, depositing the Harbor Hill Moraine. The region where the two lobes intersected he called the interlobate zone. Sirkin posited that the Roanoke Point Moraine, which extends from Port Jefferson to Orient Point on Long Island's North Shore, is a recessional moraine that is continuous with the Harbor Hill Moraine.[4]

In 1994, John Sanders and Charles Merguerian of Hofstra University challenged Sirkin's single-glacier hypothesis. In their scenario, based on the colors and layers of till and directions of grooves in glaciated rocks, the last glacier flowed in a northeast-to-southwest direction, crossed Long Island Sound, and covered Queens and Brooklyn only (see Fig. 1.2). They argued that two older, separate glaciers created the Harbor Hill and Ronkonkoma Moraines. The glacier that created the Harbor Hill Moraine flowed northwest to southeast across the Hudson River and spread eastward along the north shore of present-day Long Island. It deposited a reddish-brown till derived from the sedimentary rocks of the Newark Basin. The glacier that created the Ronkonkoma Moraine was far older and made three advances. The first left behind a terminal moraine that is "a now vanished and submerged terminal moraine," the second advance deposited the Montauk Till, and the third left behind the Ronkonkoma Moraine.[5]

In 2003, Bret Bennington of Hofstra University proposed a revised scenario based on a high-resolution digital elevation model of Long Island produced by lidar imaging, which renders the glacial geomorphology "with unprecedented clarity."[6] The model reveals the Harbor Hill Moraine to be a continuous linear ridge, clearly a terminal moraine. It shows no evidence of "discontinuities" that would have been the result of a separate lobe of the Late Wisconsinan glacier advancing down the Hudson River valley, as Sirkin proposed. Evidence of its being a terminal moraine, besides its clearly defined ridge, is its dissection by tunnel valleys, or meltwater channels that flowed beneath the glacier and deposited outwash in an elevated outwash plain south of the moraine. The tunnel valleys created the long narrow bays

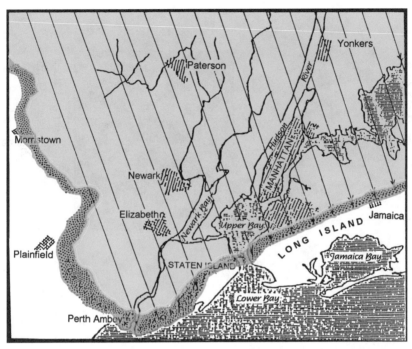

Figure 1.2. Rectilinear flow of glacier older than latest Wisconsinan, trending northwest to southeast across the Hudson Valley, depositing bouldery red-brown till and outwash across the New York City region and on the east side of the Hudson River. Adapted by Merguerian and Merguerian (2004) from Salisbury and others (1902). Courtesy of Charles Merguerian, Duke Geological Labs, 2023.

between the necks of western Long Island's North Shore (see Fig. 1.3). He defined the Roanoke Point Moraine as a "discontinuous kame moraine" that was "distinct" from the terminal Harbor Hill Moraine. Kames are conical hills of sediments melted out at the edge of a receding moraine. Bennington accepted the possibility, posited by Sanders and Merguerian, that the Ronkonkoma Moraine is a recessional moraine, and that the true terminal moraine is miles offshore from Montauk Point, as evidenced in the lakebed strata of the Montauk Till.[7]

What is indisputable is that Long Island is a creation of ice. All its topographical features, from its morainal ridges to its outwash plains, were sculpted by glacial advances and retreats. The zone where the Harbor Hill

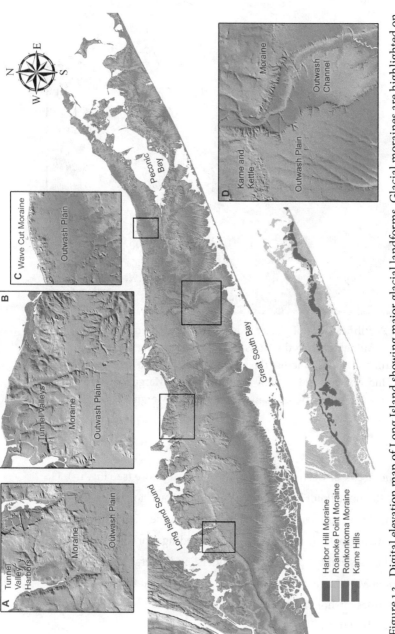

Figure 1.3. Digital elevation map of Long Island showing major glacial landforms. Glacial moraines are highlighted on the index map at the bottom. Map details highlight glacial landforms in different regions: (A) northwestern (Manhasset Neck) showing tunnel valley harbors, Harbor Hill Moraine ridge, and outwash plain; (B) north-central (Northport–Kings Park) showing tunnel valleys, Harbor Hill Moraine ridge, and outwash plain; (C) northeastern (Wading River) showing wave cut Roanoke Point Moraine and outwash plain; (D) southeastern (Yaphank / Carmans River) showing kame-and-kettle topography on the Ronkonkoma Moraine, outwash plain, and the wide glacial outwash channel occupied by the Carmans River. Figure by J. Bret Bennington, Hofstra University.

Moraine truncates (in geological parlance) the older Ronkonkoma Moraine is a hilly upland region in western Long Island, where place-names like Roslyn Heights describe the topography.[8] The rolling kame-and-kettle terrain of Long Island's northern half was shaped by a receding glacier as it melted back; where blocks of ice broke off and melted in place, they formed kettle holes, many filling with water and becoming the lakes and ponds that still exist today, like Ronkonkoma Lake in the island's center. Most of Long Island's rivers and streams flow in ancient glacial meltwater channels. The relatively flat terrain of Long Island's southern half is glacial outwash, overlain by glacial loess, a thick layer of mineral-rich soil that eroded from the moraines and deposited the fertile loam that today supports the potato and corn fields and vineyards of the South Shore. Cobbles exposed at low tide on any of Long Island's beaches are glacial drift, smoothed and rounded by water over time, the sands eroded grains of glacial rocks.

As the last glacier retreated northward around eighteen thousand years ago, glacial lakes formed between terminal and recessional moraines. Gardiners Bay, Block Island Sound, Long Island Sound, and Upper New York Bay were all filled with glacial lakes. Fed by glacial meltwater, these lakes rose, building up pressure against their morainal dams until the dams gave way.[9] During the ice age, the Hudson River had been diverted westward by glacial ice and dammed at the Narrows by the Harbor Hill Moraine. Glacial Lake Albany formed behind the dam, filling the ancient Hudson River valley. Around twelve thousand years ago, in what must have been a catastrophic flood, the lake breached the dam and the Hudson reverted to its ancient channel, draining the waters of the lake. According to the scenario reconstructed by Charles Merguerian, "a raging torrent of water" cut through two hundred feet of glacial drift and scoured the Narrows gorge down to bedrock.[10] Over the ensuing millennia, the river excavated an ever-deeper canyon as it coursed across the exposed continental shelf to the sea. The sea continued to rise, eventually drowning the river's mouth and creating the Lower Hudson Estuary. By around six thousand years ago, the sea more or less stabilized, and Long Island emerged as the largest island in the New York archipelago. Long Island Sound, once a valley dotted with glacial lakes, was now an arm of the sea separating Long Island from Connecticut. The Lower

Hudson Estuary now bathed Long Island's west end, and the Atlantic pounded the morainal bluffs of the east end. Sediments eroded from the bluffs and ferried by littoral currents built up the Napeague Isthmus, reconnecting Montauk Peninsula, and fed sand spits and barrier islands along the South Shore, creating a protected inshore lagoon, the Great South Bay.

———

Descending the steep trail from Garvies Point Museum, which overlooks Hempstead Bay on the North Shore, I take a trip down through the strata and back in time. To read the strata, I carry a copy of Les Sirkin's geology field guide.[11] Looking back up from the beach, I can make out a veneer of till at the top of the cliff overlying a thick layer of outwash, sediments that were deposited when the last glacier receded some eighteen thousand years ago. What lies beneath the ice age layers are what Sirkin describes as "large masses of clay and white quartz gravel," sediments far older than the glacial deposits.[12] The last glacier to reach Long Island excavated huge blocks of these sediments from Long Island Sound (then a valley) and thrust them into the moraines on

Figure 1.4. Sands Point Preserve on a winter day. Sands Point sits atop a recessional moraine overlooking Hempstead Bay on the North Shore. Photo by author.

the North Shore. Buried in these sediments are fossils that offer a window into the life of Cretaceous Long Island, when dinosaurs roamed the earth.

Long Island may well be a creation of the last ice age, its surface composed of glacial drift, but it lies on a thick bed of strata deposited at least 90 million years ago. The Cretaceous geological period lasted from around 145 million to 66 million years ago. During the mid-Cretaceous in our region, sediments eroded from the Appalachians were flushed by rivers seaward and deposited in deltas and flood plains on the coastal plain, accumulating in a two-thousand-foot-thick wedge of sand, silt, and clay at the edge of the continental shelf. Known as the Long Island Platform, the wedge is thickest on Long Island's South Shore (beneath Fire Island) and thinnest on the North Shore and west end.[13] It's all buried beneath the sea—except where it outcrops on the North Shore, thanks to the excavation work of the last glacier.

The clay layers are embedded with lenses of lignite, a kind of soft coal rich in Cretaceous plant fossil fragments, pollen, and spores (in fact, the fossil flora serve to date the age of the sediments). These index fossils testify to a subtropical forest of cycads, ferns, and early flowering plants when the region was the domain of dinosaurs, although no dinosaur fossils have been found on Long Island.[14] On the gravelly beach, one may find pieces of lignite eroded out of the cliff, as well as pyrite (fool's gold) and iron oxide concretions known as Indian paint pots—so named because these rock balls have interiors of reddish clay that may have been used by American Indians as pigment. What one finds on the beach are broken, hollowed-out hemispheres like pots or bowls that fit into the palm of one's hand. Slabs of siltstone and red shale are also found on the beach, formed in place out of cemented Cretaceous sediments. Embedded in these rocks, you may find imprints of Cretaceous plants—roots, branches, and even leaves—just as today we might see the imprint of a leaf in a cement sidewalk, though you may have to split open the rock to reveal the imprint.[15]

Fossils of Cretaceous flora found on Long Island and in adjacent regions are abundant, revealing an incredible diversity of plants. In 1906, paleobotanist Charles Arthur Hollick published a monograph detailing his collection of hundreds of fossils from Cretaceous beds in New Jersey and Long Island, identifying 222 species.[16] Many are plants that grow in subtropical conditions—eucalyptus, ficus, and cycads—but some we find in our own temperate forests today, including sassafras, viburnum, amelanchier, kalmia, magnolia, andromeda, laurel, and oak. And the gingko tree, which now we find only in our botanical gardens or planted as street trees, grew in the Cretaceous wild.

In the Cretaceous, the Long Island region was a subtropical zone with forests, swamps, and marshes covering a coastal plain. Many of the plants and animals that inhabited the region would be familiar to us, while many others are now extinct. We can reconstruct the plant life of Cretaceous Long Island because of plant fossils discovered here; however, to reconstruct the animal life we must look to fossil finds in New Jersey, where outcroppings correlate to those of Long Island.[17] The Raritan and Magothy formations, excavated from Raritan Bay southwestward, have yielded abundant animal fossils, both terrestrial and marine. Geologist William Gallagher of Rutgers University vividly describes the late Cretaceous world for us in his book, *When Dinosaurs Roamed New Jersey*.[18]

On the surface of a warm, shallow sea floated phytoplankton, dominated by the microscopic algae coccolithophorids, so thickly populating the waters that when they died and their minute shells drifted onto the seafloor, they formed deep chalk deposits over eons. At the base of the marine food web because of their ability to convert solar energy into carbon, the phytoplankton were consumed by zooplankton, dominated by shell-secreting foraminifera. The plankton were consumed by oysters, clams, and mussels, and in turn, these shellfish were consumed by skates, rays, and primitive sharks—and a new kind of gastropod, a carnivorous snail, the whelk. Other snails grazed the seafloor for algae, and lobsters and crabs scuttled about. Offshore, cephalopods propelled themselves through the water: prehistoric squids, the belemnites, housed themselves in hollow conical shells known to fossil collectors as squid pens; ammonites encased themselves in their coiled, chambered shells.[19]

The Cretaceous is known as the Age of Reptiles, and indeed reptiles dominated sea, sky, and land. Plying our waters were the first sea turtles; marine crocodiles, including a huge predatory crocodile known as the "terror crocodile," *Deinosuchus*, which lurked in tidal backwaters; long-necked, flippered plesiosaurs; and ferocious marine lizards, the carnivorous mosasaurs. In the skies glided the flying reptiles, the pterosaurs.[20] On land, hadrosaurs (duck-billed dinosaurs) browsed in the rich wetland flora along the coast, probably hunted by carnivorous dinosaurs. At least five species of dinosaurs inhabited the region at the end of the Cretaceous—on the eve of their demise.[21] But as put by Gallagher, "a modern fauna of animals was present under the dinosaurs' feet," so to speak—small mammals scurrying in the underbrush, frogs and land turtles dipping into the fresh waters of streams and swamps, the first true birds taking to the skies. Like those of plovers, the "small, hollow, fragile bones of these shorebirds are among the rarest of the vertebrate fossils found in the Marl deposits of New Jersey."[22]

———

If the geological history of Long Island offers us any lesson, it is that nature's edges are fluid. Glaciers have advanced and retreated, sea levels have risen and fallen, and lands have emerged and disappeared. The bluff where I stand on Montauk Point is now tumbling into the sea, eroding ever faster as the climate heats up. The old tarmac walkway that was laid twenty feet from the edge now skirts the edge, a portion of it having fallen with the bluff; I can see it continue on the other side of the gap, atop the hoodoos—those spires and columns formed by wind and water erosion. After every storm or wind event, those spires erode and crumble more, and the bluff wall releases more cobbles to the shore below. Clumps of grass and bayberry clasp the edge, and I wonder how long before they tumble down to the sea. Signs that once stood twenty-five feet from the edge, warning the unwary to stand back, have themselves tumbled down the eroding bluff face. New signs, placed farther landward, post the same warning. I look toward the Montauk Lighthouse, which was commissioned in 1790 by George Washington. The general, after conducting a survey of the site, known as Turtle Hill, declared it could withstand two hundred years of erosion—was he prescient? He may simply have calculated the erosion from natural causes such as storm surges and wind, but surely he could not have imagined a steadily rising sea and warming climate. When the lighthouse was completed in 1796, it stood 297 feet from the cliff edge; today, it is 50 feet. The base of the cliff has been armored with slabs of gray rock held in by wire, but the cliffs on either side have crumbled, and I speculate that in the not-too-distant future the hill and its lighthouse will be marooned.

As will we all.

CHAPTER 2

Shifting Sands and Walking Dunes

OUR LIVING SHORES

A winter day on Coney Island, the Anthropocene era. The uninhabited expanse of beach glitters with grains of quartz, feldspar, garnet, and mica. Gulls stand at the water's edge, facing the sun as if to concentrate its warmth in their white breasts. The water gleams like hammered pewter; clouds bank at the southern horizon, diffusing the rays of the sun. Here, where land meets sea, things are stripped down to the elemental. Wind whips the waves, sculpts the sand; water erodes the jetties, weathers rocks and bricks; sunlight bleaches wooden benches and fades the lettering on concession stands.

These natural processes shaped these shores long before humans came here, and they will continue long after. Waves sough over the sands, advancing and retreating in eternal cycles. Yet this shore is not eternal, but forever shifting. This is the water's edge at this point in time.

Twenty-two thousand years ago, when the last glacier reached its southern terminus, this was a vast windswept tundra laced with glittering ribbons of meltwater and dotted with glacial ponds, the shoreline some eighty miles distant, skirting the continental edge. In the ensuing millennia, the glacier retreated, its meltwaters disgorged tons of sediments that built up the coastal plain, sea levels rose hundreds of feet, and the ocean flowed around Long Island. By around six thousand years ago, sea levels reached their modern depth and stabilized—but that does not mean the shoreline became fixed. Daily tides and seasonal storms continually rearrange the sands. Winter northeasters and summer hurricanes strip the beaches of sand, depositing it in sandbars just offshore. In calm periods, waves transport sand from the offshore bars back to the land, rebuilding the beaches. It's a fairly balanced cycle of erosion and deposition, but sometimes, when storms are severe and storm surges high, powerful waves scour the beaches, depositing the sands in deeper water, where they cannot be reclaimed. Still, these are natural processes. But if one factors in the human-induced climate change that is accelerating sea level rise, and shorefront development that prevents the natural migration of barrier islands landward, barrier islands and beaches may simply disappear beneath the waves.

Such a fate for Coney Island was predicted as long ago as 1839, in Benjamin Thompson's *History of Long Island*. "The destructive effect of ocean storms has long been visible here, for much of what was once Coney Island has now disappeared," he wrote. "The exposed situation of this island subjects it to great encroachments of the sea, and to the probability that at some future (though perhaps distant) period it will be entirely destroyed." He continued, "In a terrible gale which occurred upon the coast on the 26th of January 1839, the whole of Coney Island, with the exception of a few sandhills, was completely inundated by the sea; the basement of the Ocean House [a resort hotel] was filled with water; the bridge was carried away, several small vessels were cast on shore, and one was driven a considerable distance towards Flatlands."[1] Thompson was describing a storm surge, a temporary phenomenon, but he also learned from old-timers that the sea was advancing on the island over time. He cited several anecdotal accounts, such as that of seventy-nine-year-old Court Lake, whose "grandfather, about 110 years ago, cut a quantity of cedar posts upon a part of Coney Island which is now two miles in the ocean; and that he himself cut fire-wood at a place now a mile and a half from the shore."[2] What Thompson seems to be describing is the gradual landward migration of the barrier island, confirming a natural process that is ongoing.

Coney Island is the most westward of five barrier islands that extend one hundred miles along Long Island's South Shore. The other four, going west to east, are Long Beach, Jones Beach, Fire Island, and Westhampton. Two spits—Far Rockaway on the western end (just across from Coney Island) and Southampton on the eastern end—complete the barrier system that girds the shoreline. The configuration of barrier islands enclosing bays characterizes the South Shore (and in fact the entire Atlantic coast from Massachusetts to Florida). These islands were formed over millennia, though it's not clear how they formed here. Possibly, they existed a mile offshore in fifty-foot-deep water, then began migrating landward around eight thousand years ago as sea level rise slowed.[3] Or sand bars dating to the last ice age merged with sand spits formed from eroding morainal headlands, creating barrier beaches. A strong longshore current (the littoral current) carries eroded sediments westward, feeding and replenishing the barrier islands. These islands are continually lengthening, migrating westward, and eroding; seasonal storms wash over them and cut inlets through them, and over time waves silt up and close the inlets. It's a continual process of erosion and deposition. Another scenario, based on analysis of the sand grains, posits that the barrier islands may have formed no more than five or six thousand years ago, fed by sediments that had accumulated in drowned river valleys and were dredged up and carried landward by natural wave action.[4]

The shores of Long Island are dynamic living places where land meets sea, described by ecologists as ecotones, edge environments where different ecosystems overlap.[5] They are at once places of water and earth, of marine and terrestrial life. Their shifting edges were never meant to be built on.

The entire South Shore was "almost entirely a line of hillocks," wrote Thompson, hills of "loose, drifting sand" like "drifting snow heaps."[6] Another native Long Islander, Daniel Tredwell, recorded his memories of the South Shore before it was heavily developed. Tredwell, who grew up on his father's farm in what is now Freeport, knew the South Shore intimately. He described "the continuous exchange of sand dunes and ocean strand" that he traversed on the eight-mile-long island of Long Beach, a place of dune and beach and marsh that he found beautiful. "The eye cannot penetrate the length of these dunes westward. They melt into the horizon and their magnitude is intensified with an endless variety of form. These sand hills have an individuality. They are unlike any other hills. They are miniature mountain ranges, as unstable as the waves of the ocean beating at their base. They encircle deep and watered valleys, having a soil and healthful vegetation."[7] The "deep and watered valleys" were the swales of the dunes, no doubt covered with bayberry, beach heather, and beach plum. The dunes themselves were covered

16 AT THE GLACIER'S EDGE

by dune grass, which dug its roots thirty feet deep, anchoring the dunes, as Tredwell noted. Here in this elemental landscape, "soothing in its silence and stillness," Tredwell found a sense of solitude.[8] Long Beach, separated by an inlet from Jones Beach, is now covered with houses, its landscape flat, its once-pristine dunes and buffering marshes gone.

If natural beaches are creations of water, then dunes are creations of wind. Wind sorts and sandblasts grains, blowing the sand downwind. On the beach, you can observe miniature dunes—rows of rippled sand. Where the windblown sand encounters an object—a blade of grass, a piece of driftwood, a fence post—it collects behind these "wind shadows."[9] The incipient dunes grow into elongated ridges perpendicular to the beach, and the ridges merge into a larger ridge parallel to the beach. The dune has taken on a classic shape, with a gently sloping windward side that rises to a crest and falls off into a steep leeward side. It is anchored by American beach grass, which sends down deep, extensive roots. Over time, clumps of beach grass spread from the dune to the upper shore, or berm, capturing more sand in their wind shadows, until another dune is formed. This seaward dune is the primary dune, and the more landward dune is the secondary dune; between them lies a hollow or swale. Where the hollow lies below the water table, bogs and marshes form. At higher elevations, maritime forests take root.

The most pristine and possibly the oldest dunes on Long Island are found on its eastern end, on the Napeague Isthmus. The name Napeague, a Montaukett name roughly translated as "drowned land," offers a clue to its ancient history, when the entire isthmus was submerged. Over millennia, longshore currents ferried sands from the Montauk and Amagansett morainal bluffs and deposited the sand between what was once Montauk Island and Amagansett. Layers and layers of sand accumulated over time to create the isthmus that connects Montauk Peninsula to the mainland. Now, as sea levels rise, it may once again become drowned by the encroaching sea. Dunes line both sides of the isthmus, the ocean-facing side (Hither Hills) and the harbor side. The Walking Dunes on the harbor side rise to forty feet, formed over thousands of years as prevailing northwest winds blowing off the harbor depos-

Figure 2.1. View of the Napeague Walking Dunes in early spring. Stunted
black cherry trees and pitch pines are half-buried in sand. Photo by author.

ited layers of sand in the lee of objects. They are known as the Walking Dunes
because they have been migrating in a southeasterly direction, responding
to the prevailing northwest winds. As they migrate, they alternately smother
and uncover maritime forests. In what is called a blowout, ancient tree
stumps may be revealed.

On a winter day, not worried about ticks, I follow a well-maintained trail
into the Walking Dunes on a circuit that allows me to experience its vari-
ous features: maritime woodland, wetland, bog, and of course the dunes
themselves, including one I can climb. But the dunes are protected, as well
they should be, and signs that instruct visitors to keep off the dunes or out
of a restoration area should be respected. From the top of the dune I am
allowed to climb, I can see a glorious landscape of creamy white dunes set
against a blue sky, and swaths of golden grasses. Portions of the dunes are
studded with gnarled, stunted trees and shrubs—oak, black cherry, beach
plum, bayberry, pitch pine. I visualize how the dunes will look come May
and June, when, for a brief time, beach plum blooms frothy white and golden
heather brightens the swales. That's when I venture into the dunes in search
of two orchids that grow in the bogs, rose pogonia and grass pink, though

Figure 2.2. Grass orchids grow at the base of a pitch pine in a boggy swale in the Walking Dunes on Napeague. Photo by author.

they are getting harder to find. Here, too, I may find cranberries in flower, their pale pink petals shaped into the pointy beak that gave the flower its original name of *craneberry*.

On the ocean side, Napeague Beach is one of only seven remaining undeveloped beaches on Long Island, harboring such rare species as piping plover, roseate tern, and seabeach amaranth—all listed under the federal Endangered Species Act.[10] The piping plover and roseate tern nesting colonies are cordoned off, protecting these vulnerable birds. Nonetheless, they are threatened by raccoons, feral cats, and unleashed dogs. And then there are the human disturbers. Though the beach itself is undeveloped, a cluster of houses abuts it, and residents are allowed to use the beach as long as they walk in. I have walked on the beach myself in years past, in search of the piping plover in spring. Now, after years of court battles pitting Napeague homeowners against East Hampton Town, the beach has been privatized, the result of a 2021 New York Supreme Court ruling that granted homeowners exclusive use of the beach and denied the public—primarily fishermen—the right to drive on what had become known as "Truck Beach." The town, advocating for the fishermen, asserted their traditional rights, citing an 1882 deed that conveyed one thousand acres on Napeague from East Hampton Town to Arthur Benson while reserving the right for local fishermen to land their boats and spread their nets. Unfortunately, the deed did not anticipate the car, and the privilege was abused by out-of-towners who were taking over the beach in summer.[11]

I find solitude on Napeague's harbor side, where another colony of piping plovers is protected; it's here that I've had the good fortune to see them. But here on this state beach, people are allowed to drive as long as they have a fishing license and beach driving permit, a privilege that has not been abused, unlike on the ocean beach. Still, the beach is corrugated by the heavy wheels of vehicles driven by licensed and therefore perfectly legal fishers and shellfish gatherers. They are doing what humans have been doing for thousands of years, fishing and gathering, and as long as it's sustainable, I respect it; the difference is the heavy vehicle churning up the sand. The beach is already narrowing as sea levels rise and high tides reach farther and farther

Figure 2.3. A piping plover on the Napeague Harbor beach. Piping plovers lay their eggs in shallow depressions in the sand, making their chicks vulnerable to predation. During breeding season, nesting areas are cordoned off to protect these endangered birds. Photo by author.

inland. The primary dune is simply crumbling away, and even the tough salt spray rose is succumbing to the sea's onslaught. I have observed and photographed these roses year after year and watched first one, then another blackened by the inundation of salt water.

OUR LIVING SHORES

I set out on a fall day to explore the Napeague Harbor Beach. I have timed my walk to low tide during a full moon, when the sand is packed down and easy to walk. Advancing and receding tides have sorted the sand grains from fine to coarse, distributing them like wavy layers in a sand painting: purple grains of garnet, charcoal grains of magnetite, yellow-gold grains of quartz. Rusted iron particles in the sand impart a coral tinge. The tides have also piled up mounds of pebbles—sandstone, quartz, granite, and granite gneiss—each telling a story of its glacial origin, when a river of ice transported the rock from distant lands. Their time in the sea has smoothed, rounded, and polished them. At the water's edge, cobbles are bright green and slick with algae.

The beach brims with life, though it's not immediately apparent to the eye. I pick up a pebble studded with stacks of slipper shells, inert and apparently lifeless as the rock, but in fact very much alive within their overturned shells. Slipper shells attach themselves tightly to hard substrates like rocks and carry out sexual reproduction: females are layered on the bottom and smaller males on top; in between are hermaphrodites, capable of switching gender as needed. I lay the pebble back down, leaving the slipper shells to be reclaimed by the tide. An exposed boulder bristles with the sharp cone-like shells of northern rock barnacles—again, inert and seemingly dead. As larvae, these crustaceans attach themselves to hard substrates head-first, secreting a strong glue to cement themselves firmly; once attached, they grow their shell houses—six chitinous plates that enclose them in a protective cone, and four plates at the end of the cone that open and shut like trapdoors. They close these four plates to conserve moisture when exposed to air, or to defend themselves against predators. When the tide washes over them again, they open and thrust their six pairs of feathery legs, or cirri, into the water to feed on plankton. Like the slipper shells, they are also hermaphroditic, possessing both male and female reproductive organs, but to reproduce they must cross-fertilize.

Here and there a knobbed whelk or a channeled whelk has been washed up onto shore. I search for whole unoccupied shells to collect, appreciating their spiraled form. The twisted axis, the columella, was highly prized by the original peoples of Long Island as the source of white shell beads for wampum. The shells of quahog clams provided the purple beads, and these are also here in abundance.[12] On occasion I've found a living whelk stranded by the tide and thrown it back into the water before a gull tore out its flesh— though I know the gull is simply feeding. Humans also enjoy whelk, which is known as scungilli, the commercial harvesting of which has begun to threaten the whelk's existence. The whelk feeds mostly on bivalves. Holding down its prey with its foot, it uses its own shell like a clam knife to pry the bivalve shell open, then inserts its radula-tipped proboscis to cut the flesh. It may also use its radula to drill through the shell, secreting a chemical that softens the shell. I don't find a whole whelk shell today, but I do find a whelk egg case, known as a mermaid's necklace, a string of papery disks that encase their eggs. I shake it and hear the rattle of dead miniature whelks inside the cases.

The receding tide has deposited a thick layer of wrack—seaweeds mainly, where live crabs may be entangled. Close by, a herring gull snatches up a glistening live blue crab in its bill, drops it, holds it down with its webbed foot, and picks at the succulent flesh. I stir the sea wrack with my foot, prompting beach fleas to jump out. These are amphipods, tiny shrimplike crustaceans that feed on decaying seaweeds and grasses, breaking them down and making their nutrients available to shore plants such as spartina grass. These herbivores make good snacks for shorebirds that forage through the wrack at low tide, like the pair of ruddy turnstones I observe using their bills to upturn pieces of seaweed that may harbor their prey.

I come to the mouth of the tidal creek that winds through the marsh in the dune swale and empties into the bay here. An exposed sand flat is covered by a thin iridescent film of water that mirrors a pair of piping plovers at the water's edge. I search for the sand burrows of hibernating sand fiddler crabs. In high summer, the flat is riddled with the holes excavated by sand fiddler crabs, which digest the sand for food and regurgitate processed pellets, stacking them beside the burrow openings like tiny cannonballs. They consume bacteria, algae, and detritus. Between the grains of sand throughout the year are millions of microscopic organisms—known as meiofauna—turning the sands, which only appear lifeless, into a living, breathing world. Even the minerals in the sand feed life, nourishing plants and the animals that feed on them.

We cannot re-create the living biome that is a beach. Break one strand in the life web and we can bring about a cascade of extinctions. Just as life feeds on life, life depends on viable, living habitats. As beaches diminish, so too do the plants and animals that spend all or part of their lives in these dwindling coastal strands.

Intertwined Lives

The Atlantic horseshoe crab is a creature of ancient lineage, whose ancestors evolved 450 million years ago. These are not true crabs but are more closely related to spiders. At Napeague Harbor, I've seen their myriad little shells, translucent as fingernails, cast off on the shore, especially where the creek empties into the bay. These are the molted shells of horseshoes, which molt many times as they grow. Occasionally I will see a large horseshoe shell turned up to the sky, its flesh eaten out by gulls. In spring, under a full moon, hundreds of these prehistoric creatures lumber ashore to mate. The spectacle along Long Island's shores may not be as impressive as on the shores of Delaware Bay farther south, where they come ashore in the tens of thousands, but witnessing this ancient spring rite performed by hundreds is no less moving. Carl Safina, in his book *The View from Lazy Point*, offers us an unforgettable description of this rite, which he witnessed at Napeague Harbor under a near-full moon at high tide: "Dark shapes appear farther out in slightly deeper water, like an approaching armada of landing craft," males clinging to the larger females, females clambering onto the beach to excavate nesting holes and lay their eggs to be fertilized by males "with a cloud of sperm." To Safina, the mating rite "is beyond reassuring: it's sacred."

He goes on: "Nothing is more venerable than the act of creating new generations of living beings—or more vulnerable. And that puts my heart on alert. Something in the pit of my stomach tells me that, after 450 million years, the only way to go from this feeling is down." His sense of foreboding is soon confirmed when a pickup truck, headlights beaming, pulls up to the beach. A man dressed in waders gets out, enters the shallow water, and scoops up horseshoe crabs handful after handful, tossing them onto his truck. The sight shocks Safina: "I've known that baymen use horseshoe crabs for bait. But knowing is not the same as seeing an ancient rite turned wholesale into flying junk." He is legal, he is licensed, and he has a limit of five hundred a day, Safina learns from the fisherman. Shocked again, he thinks to himself, "There aren't five hundred crabs here right now. That's the kind of limit that represents no limit." Later, Safina does his research: "In the year 2000 the state set its first quota: 366,000 crabs." But the fishermen took 628,000. The state cut the quota in 2004 to 150,000; the fishermen took 284,000. Obviously, enforcement is ineffective if done at all.[13]

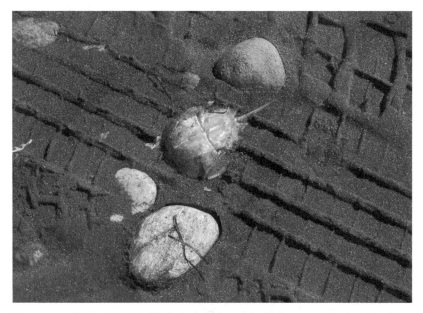

Figure 2.4. The molted shell of a horseshoe crab at Napeague Harbor beach. Horseshoe crabs will molt a number of times before reaching maturity. Photo by author.

Since the 1990s, fishermen have taken horseshoe crabs as bait for a burgeoning global market in conches (whelks) and eels, the take estimated to be in the millions—fifteen to twenty million between 1995 and 2000.[14] According to Deborah Cramer, horseshoe crab eggs—an important food for migrating shorebirds—covered the New Jersey beaches by the hundreds of thousands per square yard in 1991; by 2007, they had been reduced to a mere four thousand per square yard.[15] The decimation of horseshoe populations prompted the State of New Jersey in 2008 to declare a moratorium on harvesting horseshoe crabs for bait, a moratorium they upheld in 2014. In 2013, the Atlantic States Marine Fisheries Commission published its stock assessment on the horseshoe crab, which is under its management. While disclaiming the goal of its assessment study as anything other than the management of viable stocks, it does provide evidence of declining populations in New York and New England. Although the stocks of Delaware Bay appear to have stabilized, it states that "the status of horseshoe crabs in the New England region appears worse than what it was during the 2009 stock assessment." It suggests that "decreased harvest of the Delaware Bay population has redirected harvest to other regions, particularly New York and New England," and that such harvesting "is *not sustainable*" (emphasis added).[16] This comes from a government agency that oversees horseshoe crab harvesting and, according to some critics, protects special interests in setting its all-too-generous quota levels.

Cramer's book *The Narrow Edge* focuses on the interconnection between horseshoe crabs and red knots, two species whose fates are intertwined, as the crash of one pulls down the other. The red knot depends on horseshoe crab eggs to fuel its astounding migration from one pole to the other, traversing more than nine thousand miles. At one time not that long ago, Atlantic beaches, especially Delaware Bay, were literally covered with hundreds of thousands of shorebirds, knots among them, devouring millions of horseshoe crab eggs, an avian foodfest that none who have witnessed it will ever forget. Cramer cites the aerial survey carried out by Pete Dunne, Clay Sutton, Wade Wander, and David Sibley in May 1981 and 1982 during the spring peak of shorebird migration, which revealed staggering numbers of birds descending to Delaware Bay to fuel up before continuing their journeys northward. Of the 420,000 shorebirds they observed, 95,000 of them were red knots, and these were "just a portion of the shorebirds migrating through the bay each spring," estimated to be 1,500,000.[17] At the time of their survey, the knots, once hunted to near extinction, had rebounded, and the horseshoes, once decimated by the fertilizer industry, had also recovered (after synthetic fertilizers were developed). Still, the numbers of horseshoe crabs the surveyors observed were a fraction of their historical numbers. According to nineteenth-century accounts, horseshoes once numbered in the millions, "so thick," wrote ornithologist Alexander Wilson, they could be "shoveled up and collected by the wagon load." Wilson, who journeyed along the Jersey coast in 1810, described what he witnessed: "Their dead bodies cover the shore in heaps, and in such numbers, that for ten miles one might walk on them without touching the ground."[18]

Unfortunately, the rebound of both horseshoe crabs and red knots in the 1980s proved to be short-lived. Once it was discovered that the blue blood of horseshoe crabs could be used for biomedical purposes, they were again harvested without limits.[19] From 1989 to 2014, as their numbers plunged, the population of red knots dropped 75 percent.[20] The New Jersey moratorium of 2008 may have helped the knots' modest recovery from a low of thirteen thousand counted in 2004 to twenty-five thousand in 2012 (recall the ninety-five thousand observed in 1981–1982), but according to the American Bird Conservancy, this is not a viable population. In 2014, the US Fish and Wildlife Service listed the rufa red knot as threatened.[21]

The correlation between the overharvesting of horseshoes and the precipitous decline of red knots is clear—but does not tell the whole story. Red knots and other migratory shorebirds, like the creatures they feed on, also depend on the increasingly narrow, scarce strips of coastal beaches. In an opinion piece for the *New York Times*, John Gillis, author of *The Human Shore* (2012), claimed that 75 to 90 percent of the world's sand beaches are disappearing because of a combination of sea level rise, increasing storm action, and "massive erosion caused by the human development of shores." Not only beachfront development but the damming of rivers is depriving beaches of a steady supply of sand from upland sources. Moreover, sand-consuming industries—the cement industry chief among them—have

Figure 2.5. A migrating red knot forages on the beach. An increasingly rare visitor to our shores, this shorebird is threatened because of the decline in horseshoe crabs, whose eggs they depend on to fuel their nine-thousand-mile journey from their wintering grounds at the southern tip of South America to their breeding grounds in the High Arctic. Photo by author.

depleted inland mines and shores of sand. Gillis argues that sand itself should be considered "an endangered natural resource."[22] Without sandy beaches, where will the horseshoe crabs spawn and shorebirds feed?

THE HUMAN HAND

Where barrier beaches and dunes were once a line of defense against storm surges, buffering the relentless onslaught of the sea, we now have hard, human-made structures—buildings, streets, parking lots—all nonporous surfaces, unlike the sand they replaced and the dunes they erased. This hard development along the shores blocks the landward migration of beaches and barrier islands, short-circuiting the ancient process of erosion and deposition and halting the re-formation of beaches.

The human hand has both created and destroyed beaches, sometimes inadvertently. In the early 1920s, Robert Moses had 2.5 million cubic yards of sand pumped from offshore to widen the beach of Coney Island, one of the first beach creation projects.[23] In 1926, Moses literally created Jones Beach by dredging 40 million cubic yards of sand from the bottom of South Oyster Bay, connecting three original marshy islands into one and building up the barrier island's elevation to fourteen feet. By the time it was completed in 1929, Jones Beach had 6.5 miles of swimming beach out of 10 miles of shoreline. To construct his boardwalk, buildings, and parking lots, Moses erased the primary dunes, although he preserved some secondary dunes. Hardly a trace of the ancient marshes remains.

I have walked the Jones Beach boardwalk in the middle of winter, a biting cold wind whipping off the water, blowing the sands of the expansive white beach into incipient dunes that would form against the boardwalk and eventually engulf it—if not for the yearly bulldozing. I revel in the elements of wind, water, and sunlight. Gulls cry and alight on lampposts and rails, a peregrine falcon soars overhead, sometimes diving into a flock of pigeons, and wintering sparrows glean seeds in a scrubby dune skirted by the boardwalk. Leaving the main beach and boardwalk, I visit the older dune landscape preserved at the Theodore Roosevelt Nature Center, where a boardwalk winds through a beautiful swath of dunes and swales. Silvery bluestem and dune grasses shiver in the wind. The once-green leathery leaves of bayberries have turned bronze, their waxy berries long since stripped by birds. The goldenrods and golden-asters have gone to seed. Gazing over the sandhills, I can see the bright blue ocean in the distance. Even in a highly engineered landscape like Jones Beach I find nature, but it's not the nature that inspires me, as in the wilder landscape of the Walking Dunes.

The practice of replenishing beach sand is known as sand nourishment and is considered a "soft engineering" approach to preserving the shores. Over the decades, Long Island's barrier island beaches have been "nourished" in this way. It's considered by some a benign intervention that does not interfere with natural processes of erosion and deposition, in contrast to "hard engineering" such as sea walls, revetments, and groins that protect

Figure 2.6. The boardwalk at Theodore Roosevelt Nature Center winds through the ancient dunes of Jones Beach State Park. Photo by author.

communities (like Manhattan Beach and Seagate on Coney Island) but may starve the beaches. Coastal geologists Orrin Pilkey and Andrew Cooper, in their book *The Last Beach*, challenge the conventional wisdom on soft engineering of the shores. They raise pertinent questions: Where does the sand come from, and do we have enough? What is the impact of both sand dredging and nourishment on marine and shore ecosystems? Is it a futile, even destructive attempt to hold in place a shoreline that is by its very nature dynamic and shifting?[24]

Pilkey and Cooper consider beach nourishment to be a mere band-aid solution to the ongoing problem of coastal erosion in a time of rapidly rising seas. It's a costly form of remediation that must be done again and again to maintain the artificial beaches. As stated by Mark Mauriello, former chief of the coastal division of the New Jersey Department of Environmental Protection, "We can't just rely on beach nourishment to solve all our problems." He suggests that it must be complemented by a gradual retreat from the shore, to allow for natural landward migration of beaches and dunes.

Turn more and more of the shoreline into parks and preserves. Pilkey and Cooper detail not only the economic costs but also the environmental costs of beach nourishment. To replenish a beach, sand is dredged and pumped from offshore in a kind of slurry. Such dredging and pumping disturb the marine-bed ecosystem and bury the ecosystem of the existing beach—in effect smothering its life. Pilkey and Cooper describe the effects: "No foraging birds and crabs, no meiofauna to feed small crabs, no clams, nothing for fish to graze on, and, going up the chain, no mackerel and flounders offshore whose food has disappeared. . . . Replenishment makes the beaches resemble a small-scale movie version of a city abandoned as all residents are killed by a mysterious toxic cloud."[25] It's possible for beaches to recover after a few years, the authors concede, but continual replenishment interferes with the recovery of a healthy ecosystem. Offshore, dredging kills marine organisms and alters the sea-bed topography in ways detrimental to marine fauna—so much so that a planned replenishment project on Nantucket was stopped by a coalition of commercial fishermen.

The rising and falling of sea levels is as old as the sea itself, and shorelines advance or retreat in a continual process of erosion and deposition, landward and shoreward migrations that are "unpredictable and irregular." What Pilkey and Cooper call "the beautiful, flexible, and infinitely adaptable world that is a beach" is coming smack up against "the static, inflexible, urban beachfront world." The shores have nowhere to retreat to. "Many beaches have ceased to be the beautiful, self-sustaining ecosystems they once were. Instead, they have become long, narrow engineering projects sustained only by constant maintenance and ongoing expenditures."[26]

Unquestionably, both hard and soft engineering of beaches has altered Long Island's original shoreline. Engineers have constructed groins perpendicular to the shoreline to trap and hold sand for particular beaches, with positive results for those beaches. However, in some cases, the ill-considered building of groins to protect isolated communities from erosion has an adverse effect on adjacent communities down-current (westward) of the groins, which become starved of replenishing sand. At Long Beach, for example, forty-eight groins were built in the 1920s to trap and hold sand for their recreational beaches and protect their developments; in this case, there were no adjacent beaches affected. This was not the case on the barrier island of Westhampton: fifteen groins built by the US Army Corps of Engineers (USACE) between 1966 and 1970, intended to protect an isolated community on the east end of the barrier island (extending from Moriches Inlet on the west to Shinnecock Inlet on the east), trapped five million cubic yards of sand, starving down-current communities of replenishing sand. In the first year after the groins were built, the shore of the adjacent community of Westhampton Beach eroded twenty feet. No effort was made to artificially replenish the starved western beaches, despite continual erosion by storms both major and minor. The December 1992 northeaster generated a storm surge of eight feet, washing over the unprotected community, flooding homes and roads. The four-day storm breached the barrier beach, drowning eighty houses and damaging many more. Residents sued the federal government, the latest in a series of suits that began in 1966, and the upshot was that USACE rebuilt their community to make it more storm resilient. They used both soft and hard engineering to rebuild the beaches and buffer the communities of the whole barrier island. They filled in the breach, elevated the island above storm surge level, built an artificial primary dune of coarse sand dredged from offshore, and widened the beach to four hundred feet by pumping in coarse dredged sand (the use of coarser sand is believed to be more stable). They rebuilt the groins with heavier blocks and modified the groins so as to allow the longshore current to ferry sediments and replenish downstream beaches as they have for millennia. Such engineering solutions are well intentioned—restoring eroded beaches and dunes, allowing for the natural processes of erosion and deposition—but as effective as they may be in the short term, they require continual and costly maintenance and may not be enough to protect a coast from rising sea levels, which have accelerated since 1992.[27]

In 2012, Hurricane Sandy made a direct hit on New Jersey, New York City, and Long Island, and though downgraded to a tropical storm by the time it made landfall, its energy combined with a northeaster to generate a historic storm surge of more than thirteen feet (measured at the Battery), drowning low-lying coastal communities and washing over barrier islands. Beaches were severely eroded, dunes flattened. If the barrier islands had remained natural and undeveloped—places of marsh and dune—they might have protected the coast from the worst of the flooding. They might have followed their natural course of washover and landward migration in a fluid response to storm surges and rising seas. But the erasure of marshes and dunes, the construction of hard surfaces such as parking lots and roads, the building of erosion-buffering structures such as groins and sea walls, even the well-intended soft engineering solutions of sand nourishing and dune creation—all these feats of human engineering have increased the vulnerability of a shoreline already threatened by rising sea levels.

Long Beach was pummeled by the storm, the surge inundating shorefront houses and apartment buildings and burying cars in a sea of sand. Its boardwalk was demolished. No dunes, no marshes protected the community from the direct onslaught of the sea. Several weeks after the storm, once the streets were cleared of deep drifts of sand, I walked the Long Island beach, awestruck by the power of the storm surge that ripped up the boardwalk. To get to the beach, I had to traverse a sandy rampart where tall mounds of sand had piled up over the remnant boardwalk. The sea had done what it had always done during a storm surge, washing over the barrier island and pushing huge mounds of sand from offshore onto the beach. If there were no hard structures to obstruct the natural movement, the island would have migrated landward.

Just six years before, the Long Beach City Council rejected a proposal by USACE to construct a line of defense against future storms by building dunes and elevating the beaches. It was resoundingly rejected in favor of preserving shorefront views, the wide beach, and the historic boardwalk. As the *New York Times* reported, they would rue that vote. "The smaller neighboring communities on the barrier island—Point Lookout, Lido Beach and Atlantic Beach—approved construction of fifteen-foot-high dunes as storm insurance. Those dunes did their job, sparing them catastrophic damage while Long Beach suffered $200 million in property and infrastructure losses, according to preliminary estimates." The article quotes Joe Vietri, "director of coastal and storm risk management for the corps": "The difference was dramatic for areas with vital and healthy dune systems, which did better than those that did not."[28]

The assumption that artificial dunes are "vital and healthy" is open to question. It takes a long time for a dune to develop a self-sustaining ecosystem, anchored by grasses and shrubs like bayberry, yet fluid enough to migrate landward. Artificial dunes, even planted with dune grasses, easily erode in the track of storm surges. Moreover, if the core of the dunes is a hard structure, such as timber or rocks and sandbags, once that core is exposed by erosion at the base, it deflects wave energy seaward, accelerating beach erosion.

One such hard-core dune project was approved by the town of Montauk and State of New York in 2014. In the wake of Sandy, federal funds were available to rebuild the severely eroded beach. In the fall of 2015, USACE began constructing artificial dunes from a core of tall timber posts and sand-filled geotextile bags. Opponents to the project included surfers, who correctly claimed that the 3,100-foot-long dune—really a seawall fifteen feet high and fifty feet wide—would starve the beach. Citing the work of coastal geologist Orrin Pilkey, among others, they argued that the structure would behave no differently from a bulkhead or other hard structure. They also noted that the dunes, costing $9 million of federal money, would protect only commercial buildings—motels—built atop primary dunes in the 1960s and 1970s. Moreover, the dune project was a temporary solution before a more expensive sand nourishment project could be funded and implemented. Former Peconic baykeeper Kevin McAllister of Defend H2O, Thomas Bradley Muse, and Tom LaGrassa filed suit in the spring of 2014 to stop the project. McAllister stated in a press release that "the result of this shoreline hardening project is the inevitable loss of a coveted recreational beach."[29] He disputed the official line that geotextile sandbags did not constitute shore hardening. When the project went forward in the fall of 2015, several hundred protesters gathered on the beach in an act of civil disobedience to physically stop the construction; several were arrested. Despite the protests, the project barreled on, as engineers built a wall on the berm comprising fourteen thousand 1.7-ton sandbags to create a 3,100-foot dune. Then Hurricane Hermine spun up the coast in early September 2016, bringing high waves and a storm surge that severely eroded the beach in front of the artificial dune and exposed the sandbags—just as the critics predicted. As

Mike Bottini had written just a year before, "The bags will get exposed, because it's a bump-out into the ocean, and not where the dune wants to naturally lay."[30] In their defense, USACE claimed the revetment had served its purpose well, and that only a small portion of the sandbags had been exposed. Sue McCormack of the New York State Department of Environmental Conservation agreed: "Where we saw erosion is where we expected to see erosion. The project worked as designed. [It] kept the storm away from the foundations of the buildings along the shoreline."[31]

The Montauk project is part of a much larger beach-building enterprise. As far back as 1960, the Federal River and Harbor Act authorized what is known as the Fire Island Inlet to Montauk Point Combined Beach Erosion Control and Hurricane Protection Project, a project that came under the aegis of USACE. For decades the project languished for lack of funding and agreement on the roles for federal, state, and local agencies to play in a cooperative undertaking. When Sandy wreaked its havoc along the shores, the project took on greater urgency. At Fire Island alone, the storm surge erased more than half the beaches (measured in volume as 4.5 million cubic yards) and flattened or severely eroded dunes. A report published by USACE in June 2014 described "the dune and berm system along Fire Island" as "now depleted and particularly vulnerable to overwash and breaching during future storm events, which increases the potential for storm damage to shore and particularly back-bay communities along Great South Bay and Moriches Bay."[32] With funds from the Disaster Relief Appropriations Act of 2013, USACE expedited their shore-stabilization efforts. On Fire Island (the so-called Fire Island to Moriches Inlet Project), USACE began implementing their plan to stabilize nineteen miles of shore from Robert Moses State Park to Smith Point County Park. It involves conducting beach nourishment on a large scale—6,992,145 cubic yards of sand mined from "Borrow Areas" already designated offshore—widening beaches, elevating berms, building dunes, and in one area realigning dunes. This ambitious shoring up of our beaches has necessitated the relocation of 6 houses, the buyout of 41 other properties, and an easement affecting 411 additional properties. The breeding areas of the piping plover were also relocated to newly created habitats (termed "habitat offsets," as required by Section 7 of the Endangered

Species Act). The cost was estimated at over $200 million, financed by the federal government. Now here is the fine print, though it's stated clearly: "The project is expected to erode, and diminish in its protective capacity, eventually returning to a pre-project condition."[33] The project will essentially buy ten years of protection, perhaps another ten with successful removal of shorefront homes and other structures. Meanwhile, sea levels rise. Why not buy out all the properties on these islands and simply retreat from the coast? Sooner or later, coastal retreat will be a necessity.

Just before July 4, 2021, Ditch Plains Beach in Montauk—a prime surfing spot—was replenished with one hundred truckloads of sand that cost the local government $170,000. The surfers who had opposed the dune project of 2014, arguing that it starved the recreational beach of sand, got their coveted sand nourishment in time for the summer rush. This project was one of several in the Hamptons that year, totaling $1 million in local funds, as noted by Polly Mosendz and Eric Roston in "Unlimited Sand and Money Still Won't Save the Hamptons." Referring to the Fire Island Inlet to Montauk Point project, they estimated it would cost at least $1.5 billion in federal dollars over the next three decades—an infusion of moneys authorized by the CARES Act of 2020. They questioned how long such a temporary fix could be sustained, particularly as it benefited the wealthy few and did not address the very real problem of living on vulnerable shores. Alison Branco, coastal director for the Nature Conservancy of New York, told the authors, "Are we going to take this opportunity to re-envision the way we live with water, or are we just going to fight against it until we lose? You can continue to pour sand and build beaches. If your money is infinite and your sand is infinite. Of course, neither of these is true." State assemblyman Fred Thiele, a Hamptons native, concurred: "Putting sand on the beach continuously—is that a long-term strategy with sea-level rise and the changing climate?" The alternative? "Coastal retreat is going to have to happen," stated Thiele.[34]

Sand nourishment and dune creation may at least temporarily maintain wide beaches and protect shorefront communities from storms, but these so-called soft engineering solutions to coastal erosion merely postpone the inevitable. The sea will win. Sea levels in the New York bight, as measured at the Battery, have risen more than one foot in the last century and are projected to rise from another eight inches to as high as thirty inches between 2020 and 2050 (compared with eighteen inches between 1850 and 2017).[35] (The range between low and high estimates reflects the uncertainty of the rate of land-based ice melt on Greenland.) At Ditch Plains Beach and on Montauk as a whole, the sea is expected to rise as much as two feet above 1992 levels this century.[36] The New York region is a so-called hotspot, where the rate of sea level rise is higher than the global rate because of land subsidence and thermal expansion. The implications for coastal erosion and inundation are enormous.

———

In the 1840s, Walt Whitman often took long walks along the Coney Island shore, reveling in the solitude of sand and sea. In a reminiscence he wrote in 1882, he recalled his weekly sojourns forty years before on Coney Island's "long, bare unfrequented shore, which I had all to myself, and where I love, after bathing, to race up and down the hard sand, and declaim Homer or Shakespeare to the surf and sea-gulls by the hour."[37] Yet his evocation of solitude was deceptive, for already the island was becoming a popular resort—the place Thompson described—readily accessed by rail and bridge. By the time Whitman set down his reminiscences, Coney Island was becoming an amusement park and bathing beach.

The original Coney Island, like all the barrier islands along the South Shore, was a place of dune, marsh, and tidal creeks inhabited by waterbirds and other creatures such as the rabbits the early Dutch settlers called Coneys, for which the island is named. The Canarsee people called it Mannahanung, a Munsee word for "island." Most likely they visited the island to gather clams and oysters, perhaps to hunt waterfowl. It was a tidal place inundated by high tides, washed over by storm surges, unsuitable for settlement. After the Dutch settled the region, the island remained largely unchanged. Jaspar Dankers, a Labadist missionary visiting the region in the late 1670s, described Coney Island as a "low, sandy island" overgrown with bushes where settlers turned out their cattle to graze in the winter. Its marshes and meadows were threaded with creeks, its dunes "mostly covered with hollies"—a maritime woodland. The creek separating the mainland was abundant with good oysters that Dankers relished while camped out there.[38] One cannot imagine eating good oysters, much less finding them, in the trashed, polluted waterway Coney Island Creek has become.

I have seen storm waves surge under the Coney Island boardwalk and suck away the sand. Time after time. Year after year, winter northeasters pound the shores and scrape the beaches; and every spring, dredgers pump new sand from offshore to widen the beaches and bulldozers smooth them, erasing any incipient dunes, so that beachgoers may lie on them come summer. It's an urban beach made for people, a glorious place of sand and sea, boardwalk and amusement park, and it seems as if this world of human nature will go on forever. I walk the boardwalk, flowing through a sea of humanity. Immersed in a babel of voices—all the languages of the world, it seems—I can barely hear the swash and backwash of the waves on the shore. Yet the sea continues to rise, the waters sometimes lapping in gentle ripples, sometimes thundering in huge splintering waves. Groins trap sand in arcs, protecting the beaches. Where sea walls and revetments are built to protect communities like Manhattan Beach and Seagate on either end of the island, the beaches have long since disappeared, the waves lapping at the foot of the walls, or crashing over them—or breaching them entirely during storms like the so-called Halloween Northeaster of 1991, later named the "Perfect Storm," when the waters of the sea and the waters of the back bay united as one great water—drowning the island as they have for centuries. Then Sandy hit in November 2012, generating a huge storm surge that overtopped Long Island's barrier beaches and flooded shorefront communities, swallowing houses, drenching the streets with sand. It left in its wake unimaginable devastation.

The storm was personal to me. When the floodwaters subsided and the streets became passable, I visited Manhattan Beach, the community on the west end of Coney Island where I lived and worked for seventeen years, the place that inspired me to write about the natural history of the region. I knew from my research that Manhattan Beach, like all of the communities on Coney Island—Brighton Beach, Seagate, and Coney Island itself—was built on marsh and sand dunes, and I had personally witnessed the ocean overtopping the sea wall and running like a river down the street

Figure 2.7. Waves crash on Sagaponack Beach in Southampton the day after a hurricane. Photo by author.

during the 1991 Northeaster. The esplanade bore the scars of previous hurricanes that had buckled and cracked it. Still, I was not prepared for the devastation I witnessed. Huge concrete slabs from the esplanade and boulders from the revetment had been tossed onto lawns and into streets as if from a bomb blast—only the blast was the force of the ocean itself. Boulders and slabs were not all that were tossed onto lawns; boats and toilets and other debris from across the bay at Breezy Point were left high and dry like so much flotsam. I gazed across the water to Breezy Point, on the tip of Far Rockaway. Not only had it been flooded but wind-fueled fires had burned whole blocks to the ground, leaving nothing but charred rubble. Fire and flood, a biblical catastrophe.

Remarkably, in the wake of such devastation, most people returned to rebuild and repair; few chose to retreat. Who would buy their property? Where would they go? How can they give up the only community they have known (some for generations)? How can they let go of that connection to the sea that drew them here in the first place? It's a heart-wrenching dilemma, yet those shorefront strips are narrowing year by year as the sea advances, reclaiming the land we have reclaimed from the sea.

CHAPTER 3

The Blue Surround

FROM THE SHALLOWS TO THE DEEPS

One never has to travel far on Long Island to reach the water's edge. On a bright October day, I make my way from the top of a bluff at Montauk Point down to the shore, where a receding king tide—when the moon is at perigee, its gravity pulling the tides to their highest and lowest points—has exposed a usually submerged landscape. From a distance, I see blue tide pools reflecting the sky; on closer look, I see greens and reds through the clear seawater. These are seaweeds. Some are anchored to rocks and pebbles, others are epiphytic, growing on other seaweeds, like the delicate pink chenille weed that festoons a floating clump of Irish moss. At high tide line, sea wrack is strewn with desiccated seaweeds: blackened rockweeds, translucent purple ribbons of dulse, and long brown blades of kelp. The smell of decay is in the air. Here and there a skate has been stranded, its flesh stripped by gulls to reveal a pink-and-white skeleton. Now the flies continue the work begun by the gulls, and hidden from the eye, anaerobic bacteria break down detritus. Death and decay are part of the process of life here at the water's edge.

Walking back to the base of the bluff, I note how the last storm surge has eroded it, causing it to slump. The beach is a sea of pebbles washed out from the bluff. I find a boulder—an ancient glacial erratic—to sit on. Out in the water, half submerged, are other boulders. Each boulder harbors plants and animals adapted to their tidal zone. Just above the water line, rockweeds hang limply, their air sacs no longer buoyed by water. Above the seaweeds, firmly anchored to the rocks by byssal threads, blue mussels cluster in dense colonies, their shells clamped shut, conserving moisture; when submerged

Figure 3.1. Red and green seaweeds swirl in a tide pool at Montauk Point. Photo by author.

again, they will open their shells and filter the water for food. Above these, barnacles stud the rocks, seemingly inert but very much alive, ready to open their calcareous plates and sweep the water with their feathery legs for plankton. In the splash zone, cyanobacteria—the oldest form of life on earth—stain the boulders a dark blue green.

Offshore, microscopic phytoplankton drift at or near the surface, harnessing the sun's energy in the process of photosynthesis. The most abundant phytoplankton are diatoms, glass-like organisms encased in two silica valves that reveal their exquisite geometric forms only under a microscope. To the Victorian microscopists, they were works of art, which they arranged into designs like snowflakes and preserved in slides.[1] In nature, diatoms may link up to form chains that look like necklaces of Venetian glass. Come spring, diatoms will come to life, their cells dividing and multiplying into billions, staining the sea surface green.

Because of their ability to perform photosynthesis, phytoplankton are the primary producers of the sea, but they are not the base of the marine food chain as once thought. Smaller organisms inhabit the waters, the most abundant of which is *Prochlorococcus*, "the modern descendant of ancient earth's first photosynthesizing organisms," writes Deborah Cramer. As Cramer explains, if a phytoplankton is the width of a human hair, "these mere specks are one to two hundred times narrower."[2] Even smaller are bacteria and viruses such as anaerobic bacteria that consume detritus. Going up the food chain, herbivorous zooplankton graze on phytoplankton, such as tiny shrimplike copepods that consume ten times their weight in diatoms. In the warming waters of summer, the floating larvae of barnacles, worms, clams, mussels, oysters, and scallops also feed on phytoplankton. From bacteria and single-celled algae to multicellular vertebrates, all are links in a food chain. In the nutritional mathematics of the sea, as calculated by Cramer, "five thousand pounds of plants feed five hundred pounds of copepods," which in turn "feed fifty pounds of mackerel," and these in turn "feed five pounds of cod."[3] While convenient, the metaphor of a chain is somewhat simplistic; a web may be more apt, implying an interdependence and interconnectedness—myriad links that we may not always see or even yet fully understand. And we humans are part of that world, fishing the waters, gathering seaweed and shellfish, hunting seabirds and marine animals—the planet's seas and shores have sustained us for tens of thousands, perhaps hundreds of thousands, of years. Whether nomadic hunter-gatherers or more sedentary farmers and fishers, like any other animal we go where the food sources are, and the waters surrounding Long Island are rich.

The waters off Long Island range from the shallows of coastal estuaries to the deep waters of the abyssal plain. Biogeographically, Long Island lies in the Mid-Atlantic Bight between Cape Cod and Cape Hatteras, known as the Virginian zone, where the waters are warmed by the Gulf Stream.[4] On its eastern end, Long Island's North and South Forks jut like a whale's fluke into the Atlantic, and on its western end, its "head" is bathed by the Lower Hudson estuary. Known to the Lenapes as Muhheakantuck, "the river that flows both ways," the Lower Hudson is tidal, inundated by saltwater at high tide as far as Troy, while at the same time flushing fresh water and nutrient-rich sediments into New York Bay.[5] Harboring species adapted to a range of salinities—some thriving in freshwater, some in brackish, some in salt, some in both fresh and salt at different life stages—the Hudson estuary is a highly

productive marine ecosystem. At the end of the last ice age, the Hudson cut
a 100-mile-long channel through the exposed continental shelf before plung-
ing into a deep gorge. The now-drowned Hudson Canyon, which extends
350 miles beyond the continental shelf and reaches depths of over 2 miles, is
the largest submarine canyon on our Atlantic coast. Harboring a diversity
of sea life, from bluefin tuna and whales to deep-sea corals, it's now being
considered for designation as a National Marine Sanctuary.[6] The abundance
of marine food species—from shellfish and finfish that inhabit the estuaries
to deepwater fish and marine mammals—has attracted humans to the Long
Island coast for millennia.

For thousands of years since the last glacier receded, humans have
exploited this great marine ecosystem. Recent underwater excavations
have revealed a continuous human presence in the region for at least twelve
thousand years. People may well have been exploiting shellfish sources early
on, as ancient oyster reefs dating to 10,850 years ago have been found at depths
of sixty-five to three hundred feet off our present shore.[7] Oysters favor upper
estuaries and shallow bays, thriving in subtidal zones up to a depth of perhaps
ten feet. As sea levels rose and began to stabilize between six thousand and
four thousand years ago, people moved in to exploit the food-rich tidewater
and estuarial environments of the island. Numerous shell middens attest to
the presence of a more settled population, possibly numbering in the thousands, on the coastal plain. A shell midden at Stony Brook dating to the Terminal Archaic reveals the consumption of this important seafood source by
Native Americans around three thousand years ago.[8] Pits excavated in Marine
Park, Brooklyn, dating to the Middle and Late Woodland period (1,700 to
400 years ago) contain oyster, clam, scallop, and whelk along with deer bones.[9]
Finfish do not fossilize so well, so evidence of their consumption is scarce, but
a few fish bones and fishing implements have been found, including fish
hooks made of bone or bird claws and sinker stones used to weigh down nets.

It was the sea's bounty that first drew Europeans to the northeastern coast
of North America. Atlantic Cod was a lucrative commodity in medieval
Europe, a "cold food" allowed during days of fasting. It lends itself well to
salting and drying—indeed, the method enhances its taste—and can be preserved longer than salted herring, another "cold food." The long shelf life of

cod enabled seamen to sustain themselves on long voyages. Cod like to inhabit places where warm currents collide with cold currents, stirring up nutrient-rich phytoplankton. They will migrate along the front where warm and cold waters meet. They always migrate to warmer and shallower coastal waters to spawn, and their offspring tend to grow larger in warmer waters. Although able to tolerate freezing waters, cod are sensitive to even slight temperature shifts. During the Little Ice Age, which lasted from the 1300s to the early 1800s, schools of cod migrated farther west and south once the waters of their traditional breeding grounds in the Baltic and off Iceland became colder. Basque fishers followed the cod to the Grand Banks off Newfoundland and the Georges Bank off Cape Cod, Massachusetts—great shoals the cod found conducive to spawning. These fishing grounds were kept a guarded secret until 1497, when Venetian mariner Giovanni Caboto (Anglicized to John Cabot), piloting his ship *Mathew* along the coast of Newfoundland in search of a northwest passage to the Spice Islands, reported a vast cod fishery being exploited by the Basque. "The sea is covered with fishes," he wrote, "which are caught not only with the net, but in baskets, a stone being tied to them in order that the baskets may sink in the water."[10]

By the early 1500s, English, Spanish, Portuguese, and French fishing fleets joined the Basque on what came to be known as "the great fisherie."[11] The English had fewer ships by far, but the imposition of two fasting days a week in 1548, an ordinance that became strictly enforced in 1563, created demand for "cold food," and the Newfoundland fisheries became far more profitable. In 1578, based on Cabot's discovery, the English laid claim to the entire Newfoundland coast, challenging the customary usage by French, Spanish, and Portuguese fleets. In 1602, Englishman Bartholomew Gosnold, skipper of the fishing boat *Concord*, followed the coast southward from Newfoundland and rounded a cape on May 15, naming it Cape Cod for the abundant fish he encountered.[12] Gosnold's shipmate John Brereton, who recorded the trip, observed that "in the monthes of March, April, and May, there is upon this coast, [no] better fishing, and in as great plenty, as in Newfoundland: for the skulles of makerell, herrings, cod, and other fish, as we daily saw as we went and came from the shore, were wonderful; and besides, the places where we tooke these Cods (and might in a few daies have laden our ship) were but in

seven faddome water . . . where in Newfound-land they fish in fortie or fif-
tie faddome water."[13] Although he hauled in a load of cod, Gosnold was not
interested in the fish but in the roots and bark of the sassafras tree, a highly
lucrative commodity reputed for its healing properties, and this is what he
collected to fill the cargo hold.[14] But reports of man-size cod enticed English
merchants like George Weymouth, who sailed to Massachusetts shores in
1603 and confirmed Gosnold's report.

Each mariner, following the routes of fishers who followed the cod, provided charts and maps to serve the next would-be discoverer. Henry Hudson knew of Weymouth's journey and possessed his logs and charts, which
indicated a possible northwest passage at the top of Canada; he had also
heard from his friend John Smith, who suggested a potential passage farther
south, at around 40 degrees latitude.[15] In 1609, on his third voyage in search
of the Northwest Passage, Hudson sailed his ship *Half Moon* down the New
England coast from Newfoundland to Maine to Massachusetts, bypassing
Long Island as he sailed south to Virginia before heading north again, seeking the passage Smith so enticingly hinted at. Hudson never found the Northwest Passage, but his exploration of what he thought was the southern
route—up the river that would one day be named after him—opened the way
for the Dutch, who had sponsored his voyages, to secure the river as their
fur-trading corridor, establishing outposts first at Albany (Fort Orange) and
later at the tip of Manhattan, which they called Fort Amsterdam. They also
claimed Long Island as part of New Netherland, which was clearly mapped
by 1630, when Johannes de Laet, a founding director of the Dutch West India
Company, published his second edition of *The New World, Description of the
West Indies.*[16]

The story goes that the Dutch were familiar with ten of the fish they found
in the coastal waters, but after the tenth they assigned words that corre-
sponded to numbers for each new species they encountered—eleventh (*elft*)
for shad, twelfth (*twalift*) for striped bass, thirteenth (*dirtienen*) for drum,
and so on, not in the order in which they were "discovered" but in the order
in which they were seasonally abundant.[17] Cod, of course, was a familiar fish,
but apparently the Dutch did not make an industry of it, as noted by Adriaen van der Donck, a colonist in the 1640s. "Shiploads could easily and

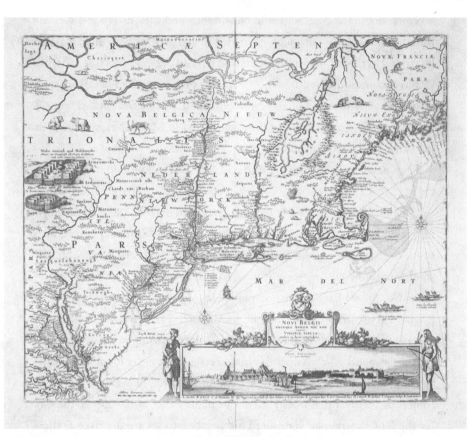

Figure 3.2. Map of New Netherland (Novi Belgii), Nicolaes Visscher, cartographer, about 1690. Long Island (Lange Eylandt) is clearly and accurately depicted. Lionel Pincus and Princess Firyal Map Division, New York Public Library. "Novi Belgii Novaeque Angliae nec non partis Virginiae tabula," New York Public Library Digital Collections. https://digitalcollections.nypl.org/items/510d47da-ef39-a3d9-e040-e00a18064a99.

cheaply be had nearby," lamented Van der Donck, who as a promoter of the colonial enterprise was quite critical of colonists who did not exploit the natural resources as fully as possible.[18] Van der Donck was intending long-term settlement and considered all resources potential trade commodities that would make New Netherland prosper. The Dutch West India Company preferred to trade in beaver pelts, timber, and wheat, but the colonists did enjoy consuming local seafood, especially the abundant oysters and the anadromous fish—striped bass, shad, and herrings—that were easily netted as they migrated by the millions from the ocean to spawn in fresh waters during their spectacular spring runs. To the colonists, it was inconceivable that such extraordinary abundance of fish as they found could ever be depleted.

SINGING THE BLUES

I recall the first time I witnessed the roiling of the waters. It was a spring day not long after I had moved into a house in Manhattan Beach, Brooklyn. In those days (the late 1980s), the ocean waterfront had not been blocked off by a padlocked chain-link fence and I was able to walk the esplanade all the way down to the beach. I loved to observe the changing moods of the waters, the shifting clouds, seasonal lights and shadows—and whatever life the bay harbored. In winter I would find rafts of scaup floating on the water, easily identified by their black-white-black bodies. Red-breasted mergansers dove and surfaced, and great cormorants flew in ragged lines over the water. These were the winter waterbirds. Come spring, terns would swoop in like swallows, flashing their pointed white wings and diving the waters for fish. One spring day, they were in a frenzy, shrieking and diving and bringing up fish in their bills. At first I thought they were roiling the waters, but as I scanned the bay, I realized that the waters were frothing white everywhere, and fish were breaching and leaping. It was the running of the blues.

Bluefish are voracious predators that will kill more than they will eat. Every spring, they migrate up the coast from more southern waters in large schools. They relentlessly pursue schools of baitfish like menhaden and alewives, often pushing them ashore, where they die in the thousands, stranded when the tide recedes. Bluefish, with their large mouths and sharp teeth, are formidable hunters. In what's known in fisher's parlance as a "bluefish blitz," they will snap their jaws and roil the waters to panic their prey, forcing the prey fish to leap out of the water in an attempt to escape; when they corral their prey, they bite into them, turning the waters red in a feeding frenzy. To the surfcaster angling for blues, this is a bonanza; to the recreational fishers on the boats that leave out of Sheepshead Bay, they are food and profit. Esteemed by those who have acquired a taste for the dark oily flesh, they will fetch a good price. Once I acquired the taste (I learned that freshness was key), I looked forward to the spring and fall runs, when I would go down to the Sheepshead Bay dock, buy a good-size fresh-caught bluefish, bring it home wrapped in newspaper, scrape off its scales, split and gut it, then bake it in foil with lemon and herbs.[19]

In the spring of 2015—and it was not the first time—tens of thousands of menhaden washed up onto the shores of the Peconic Estuary on Long Island's East End, forming deep drifts of decaying fish carcasses. Although fish kills occur every year—often the result of being driven ashore by bluefish and other predators—this looked unprecedented in its sheer volume. Veteran fishers blamed the blues, the usual suspects. Marine scientists blamed an algal bloom that consumed oxygen, leaving the fish literally gasping for air. Christopher Gobler, representing the Long Island Coastal Conservation Research Alliance, described a "massive mahogany tide" from a large bloom of the algae *Prorocentrum*.[20] And what caused the bloom? Now we get to the bottom of it: nitrogen runoff. In Suffolk County, outdated septic tanks and cesspools are a major contributor, followed by chemically fertilized grounds—agricultural lands, golf courses, and lawns. Even municipal sewage treatment plants contribute when they discharge nitrogen-rich water. Nitrogen overload is killing tidal wetlands and decimating scallop and clam harvests.[21] Bluefish, algal blooms, and nitrogen: everyone is right about what caused the fish kills; all these causes—natural and unnatural—are interconnected, and we humans are at the bottom of it. Our exploding population creates nitrogen overload; excess nitrogen in the waters triggers algal blooms, or explosions in their population; the algae feed on the nitrogen, and as they die and decay, they deplete the oxygen, driving oxygen levels down to zero in some zones (a condition known as anoxia); oxygen-breathing marine organisms literally suffocate, rising to the surface in massive fish kills; bluefish making their twice-annual runs as they have done for millennia pursue their prey to shore, but with these shallow inshore waters depleted of oxygen, the menhaden cannot breathe— and they die. Our sheer numbers are killing the waters that support the fish we depend on for sustenance.

It's hard to believe that a fish that migrates in schools covering tens of square miles of ocean, their runs marking the seasons for fishers, could become threatened. But their populations have begun to decline, prompting the National Oceanic and Atmospheric Administration (NOAA) Fisheries, the Mid-Atlantic Fishery Management Council, and the Atlantic States Marine Fisheries Commission in 2019 to declare the species overfished and initiate a bluefish management plan to rebuild stocks over seven years. The plan was revised and implemented in 2022.[22]

Had such a plan been in place, it might have staved off the crash of another predatory blue fish, the silvery Atlantic bluefin tuna.

These great fish have long inhabited our deeper waters. Robert Boyle, in his classic natural history of the Hudson, published in 1979, described abundant bluefins in the Mud Hole—a region of the submerged Hudson Canyon. It was there that fisherman Francis H. Low, so Boyle tells us, trolling in a twenty-two-foot skiff, caught a bluefin weighing 705 pounds in 1933—the largest at the time. When the marine explorer Finn Magnus, inventor of the plastic harmonica, dived into the Hudson Canyon in the 1950s, he found 500-pound bluefins associated with yellowfin tuna, dolphins, marlin, whales, and giant leatherback turtles.[23]

Bluefin tuna are powerful fish, their torpedo-shaped bodies designed for speed. They can retract their fins to reduce drag and achieve speeds of up to fifty miles an hour. They can dive down to four thousand feet, making them an elusive catch that excites the sport fisherman. Formidable sharp-eyed hunters, they pursue their prey in well-coordinated schools, forming a parabola that enables them to corral their prey, which can include bluefish. Bluefin can live up to forty years, grow up to ten feet in length, and weigh up to 1,500 pounds. The largest bluefin caught in our waters was off Montauk in

1977, weighing 1,071 pounds—still the record as of this writing.[24] In fall, they can be found from Montauk to Cape May, New Jersey, in depths of sixty to one hundred feet. And because they are warm-blooded, they can adapt to a range of water temperatures. Our western Atlantic population spawns in the Gulf of Mexico.

By the time Carl Safina wrote *Song for the Blue Ocean*, published in 1997, the Atlantic bluefin population had crashed. Safina likened the status of bluefins and other "magnificent creatures" of the sea to that of the buffalos in nineteenth-century America, their very existence as a species threatened by overfishing on the "rolling blue prairies" that are the world's oceans.[25] The opening pages of his book describe his mind-altering encounter with an adult bluefin. He was alone on his eighteen-foot boat at sunrise, drifting on a "molten, glassy sea," when the fish exploded through the surface "like a revelation": "A giant bluefin tuna, among the largest and most magnificent of animals, hung suspended for a long, riveting moment, emblazoned and backlit like a saber-finned warrior from another world, until its six hundred pounds of muscle crashed into the ocean like a boulder falling from the sky."[26] It was mind altering because he saw for the first time the creature in its wildness, "complete," worthy of being alive. He devotes the first hundred or so pages to the Atlantic bluefin, describing his attempts to follow its trail to see where it led and what it would reveal about changes on "Planet Ocean," seeking to understand why its population crashed—down 90 percent since the 1970s. In his interviews with tuna fishermen young and old, he found a divergence of opinion on the bluefin's status. The old-timers recalled days of better fishing, of course, while the young insisted that there were plenty of tuna out there, and that the scientists had vastly underestimated the numbers of this "elusive" fish. But the anecdotal evidence was compelling, from which Safina discerned a pattern of decline. He noted that a fish trap off the shore of Long Island that had been used to catch bluefins now caught none, according to the trap tender he interviewed. The trapper said, "In the sixties we'd sometimes have half a dozen of giant tuna in the trap" on a given morning, but for the past twenty years (before the mid-1990s), nothing. A captain of a commercial trawler from Long Island told Safina, "When I started tuna fishing in the early eighties it was pretty easy to catch giant tuna locally. Now you have to take your boat up to New England." Did the giants simply move north? Perhaps, but more likely it's "wishful thinking," concludes Safina.[27]

Like all tuna, the bluefin is highly migratory—populating the Atlantic and Pacific Oceans and the Indian and Mediterranean Seas—and therefore difficult to track and manage. Our western Atlantic population spawns in the Gulf of Mexico, and the eastern Atlantic population spawns in the Mediterranean, although recent geotagging of this species reveals that there may be considerable mixing of the western and eastern Atlantic populations.[28]

Paul Greenberg, in his book *Four Fish: The Future of the Last Wild Food* (2010), probes the causes for the Atlantic bluefin's decline. The oceanic abyss—the deep waters beyond the continental shelf—is "the final frontier of fishing and the place where the wildest things in the world are making the last argument for the importance of an untamed ocean," he declares.[29] In the last few decades, catches "have risen by over 700 percent"—and the prime catch is bluefin tuna. When the sushi craze took hold in the 1970s, bluefin were pursued with a frenzy that can only be explained by the price tag attached to a single giant fish. As Greenberg explains, the Atlantic bluefin are slow growers, taking seven years and more to reach the size of "giants"— five-hundred-pounders—that are the target of the sushi trade. Yet these giants are also the spawners, so their harvesting has led to their decline to the point that their populations may not be sustainable. He estimated that only nine thousand spawners were left in the western stock of the North Atlantic as of his writing.[30]

The year Greenberg published his book, 2010, the International Commission for the Conservation of Atlantic Tunas (ICCAT) and other marine conservation groups proposed an outright ban on fishing and trading bluefin tuna, but the Convention on International Trade in Endangered Species voted the proposal down. This typified the perennial lack of international cooperation or even agreement on what constituted a sustainable bluefin fishery, not to mention a lack of coherence on bluefin fishery management. As Greenberg pointed out, even ICCAT admitted its catch limits were not being respected.[31] In 2011, NOAA declined to list the fish as endangered, but in light of the disastrous *Deepwater Horizon* oil spill in the Gulf of

Mexico in 2010, which may have affected 20 percent of the Atlantic bluefin's spawning grounds, it added the bluefin to its list of Species of Special Concern.[32] In 2014, it imposed a ban on long-line fishing in the Gulf of Mexico during the peak spawning months of April and May (a ban on direct targeting of bluefin tuna in the Gulf of Mexico had been in place since 1982). Unable to ban bluefin fishing outright, ICCAT imposed a lower quota on Atlantic bluefin catches but in 2014 turned around and raised its quotas, to 14 percent for the western population, or two thousand tons, rationalizing its decision by citing recent tuna population growth. The Pew Charitable Trusts charged that larger quotas would just as likely reverse that positive trend, and moreover, ICCAT had delayed action on implementing an electronic tracking system to control illegal fishing.[33] ICCAT addressed the issue of quotas in a 2021 report on its management plan, claiming the quotas were working and citing as evidence the 9 percent increase in Atlantic bluefin tuna biomass between 2017 and 2021.[34]

At what point does a species reach that critical threshold when its populations are no longer viable, when the catch outpaces the species' ability to reproduce?

Some conservationists question whether quotas and fishery management can work, especially for a highly migratory species like tuna, if they have not worked in the past—which is why they propose an outright ban that allows the bluefin to recover. This too may be unworkable given the illegal trade in banned species (consider elephant ivory). Today, a single bluefin could fetch $1.75 million, a figure provided by the World Wildlife Fund. In a blog posted on his website in 2012, Carl Safina questioned a quota system that is based on supposedly sound science, when that science is open to question—namely, the concept of maximum sustainable yield (MSY).[35] As explained by Safina, the concept combines an idea and a number based on that idea: that we can take a certain number of a wild species without harming its population, but if we take more than a set maximum, the species cannot reproduce enough to outpace our extraction. The problem with this way of thinking about nature, argues Safina, is that it "wholly ignores food webs." He offers the example of herring: we set an MSY for herring that serves our own self-interest, but "where does that leave things that eat herring, such as tuna, whose own MSY can't be realized if we've already eaten much of their food?" Safina acknowledges that the concept has had some real application in reining in overfishing and setting limits. But enforcing regulations and quotas proves extremely difficult on a global scale. He puts forward a perhaps wiser solution: "Ban fishing in areas large enough to let fish populations recover." In other words, set aside marine reserves while at the same time allowing fishing elsewhere.[36]

Several decades ago, a neighbor of mine in Manhattan Beach, a teacher who looked forward to weekends out on his boat fishing, once returned with a yellowfin tuna, a migratory tropical fish that may enter the waters of the Hudson Canyon. It was a lucky catch. Having more than enough for his family, he generously offered a portion to my family gratis. Of course we accepted, and I set to work looking up recipes and preparing it. I had never had yellowfin tuna, either fresh or canned, though I might have had it as sushi. I did not know what to expect, but my first taste of the yellowfin was a revelation. It was the sweetest fish I had ever eaten, an awakening of my senses to the incomparable taste of fresh-caught fish from local waters.

It's a dilemma. Whether sports fisherman or consumer, there is always the allure of wild-caught fish. Who wants a plastic-wrapped piece of days-old or previously frozen fish from the supermarket when you can get one caught that day from local waters? And more and more, with the locavore movement growing in popularity, we want locally sourced, wild fish.

LEVIATHANS OF THE DEEP

Looking out from the Montauk cliffs, scanning the horizon, you might spot a whale breaching the surface. And if there is one, there are usually others.

Occasionally, these marine mammals wander from the deeper waters of the continental shelf into our inshore waters, entering our bays and sounds, breaching to the thrill of those lucky enough to encounter them. The year 2015 was a particularly good one for sightings of inshore whales. Three belugas and one minke wandered into Long Island Sound in May of that year—more than twenty years after the last sighting of any whale in the sound—and that fall, humpbacks were sighted on three separate occasions. Three humpbacks—an adult and two young—swam right beneath a recreational fishing boat, according to the captain. Thrilled at the unexpected sightings, all on board let go of their fishing poles for a few minutes to take videos of the whales as they breached.[37] The humpbacks were likely migrating from their feeding grounds in the Gulf of Maine to breeding territories in the West Indies. Whether the same individuals or different, a number of humpbacks returned in July 2016, nosing deep into the western corner of the sound. They were pursuing schools of menhaden, the same bottom-of-the-food-chain fish that attract bluefish to our inshore waters. The whales form "bubble rings" around the fish, frothing up the water, then plunge into the center with open baleen-fringed jaws to swallow the fish whole. Although humpbacks have made a comeback since they were listed as endangered in 1973, they are still just a third of their previous numbers. Despite this, our population (recently designated the West Indian population) was delisted as threatened by NOAA in 2016, although all humpbacks remain protected under the Marine Mammals Protection Act of 1972.[38]

Whales may also be sighted onshore, the unfortunate marine mammals stranded and, more often than not, dead. In 2015, five whale carcasses—two minkes and three humpbacks—washed up on Long Island shores. In April 2016, a humpback washed up in Napeague Harbor, and in late May of that year the bloodied carcasses of two pygmy sperm whales—mother and calf—washed up onto Shagwong Beach in Montauk.[39] That year, NOAA declared an "Unusual Mortality Event" for the West Indian population of humpbacks, and in 2023 it released data for the period 2016–2023, when a total of thirty-four humpbacks washed up on New York beaches, the highest of any state along the Atlantic coast. The causes of the mortalities are not fully understood, but about 40 percent were due to accidental vessel strikes—including whale-watching vessels—and entanglement in fishing gear. Other unverified causes include underwater sonar that may disorient the whales; habitat change such as expanded recreational marinas in their calving grounds; natural toxins in the food chain; food shortages caused by overfishing of their prey; ingestion of plastic; and climate change, which may disrupt their northern feeding grounds. Or in some cases it may simply be natural causes such as disease and death.[40]

Whales have always beached. They are part of the lore and ritual of Native Americans on both the Atlantic and Pacific coasts of North America. Based on colonial accounts, the Indians of Long Island practiced a ritual to honor the whale spirit, consuming the tails and fins of a beached whale in a ceremonial feast.[41] The Shinnecocks and Montauketts of eastern Long Island continue this ritual to this day, a right protected since colonial times, presumably carrying on an ancient tradition. A carved mica tablet from Brookhaven, most likely dating to the Middle Woodland period (around two thousand years old), depicts an image of a horned sea serpent with three feathers in the center surrounded by tails and fins as if swimming in a pod of whales.[42] The feathers may represent the sky world and the horns the earth world, the serpent thus connecting all three worlds. In Algonquian lore, a spirit called Abomacho, a sea serpent, possessed great healing powers.[43] In his *Chronicles of the Town of Easthampton*, first published in 1840, David Gardiner (a descendant of one of the original colonial Long Island settlers, Lion Gardiner) described the Montaukett ritual in language that reflects the ethnic bias of the observer:

> The most savory sacrifice made to their great deity was the tail or fin of the whale, which they roasted. The leviathan from which it was taken was at times found upon the sea shore, and a prolonged pow-pow, or religious festival was held. At these festivals great efforts were supposed to be necessary to keep the evil one with-out the charmed circle of their incantations. His presence, it was supposed, would defeat the pow-pow in the procurement of the favor and particular regard of the good deity. Violent gesticulations, horrid yells, and laborious movements of the limbs and body, with distortions of the features, were continued until the excitement produced madness. When the evil spirit was supposed to be subjugated, the dance and the feast commenced.[44]

The right to beached whales was so important to the Natives that clauses in land deeds spelled out the boundaries of that right—or its loss. In 1648, Montaukett sachem Wyandanch and other sachems of eastern Long Island negotiated with the English the boundaries of East Hampton (east to Napeague) when it was being established. While trading away their right to access beached whales on English lands, they ensured their ancient right to the fins and tails of beached whales was protected. In 1658, Wyandanch, acting alone, handed to Englishmen Lion Gardiner and Thomas James the right to beached whales on Napeague Beach without stipulating in the contract "ancient rights." Instead, according to John Strong, he secured for himself and "his successors" the right to receive payments for each beached whale after the first—in effect trading away his people's ancient rights for personal monetary gain.[45]

———

During colonial times, the North Atlantic right whale was the species most likely to be seen and hunted offshore, as they frequented inshore waters where they preferred to feed. The origin of their name is uncertain— perhaps they were the right whale to hunt because of their valuable oil, or because they were relatively easy prey, being slow swimmers and surface feeders.[46] These enormous marine mammals—next to the blue whale the largest of cetaceans—can grow up to fifty-two feet long. Their life-span averages fifty years, and some individuals may live as long as seventy years or more, although human-caused mortality has reduced their life-spans to an average of forty-five years for females and sixty-five years for males. Females do not calve before they are about ten years old, and gestation can take twelve months. Once calving every three years or so, they now calve every six to ten years as a result of human-caused stresses, mainly entanglement. Between December and March, the whales migrate to coastal waters off South Carolina, Georgia, and northeastern Florida to calve, and in spring they return to the waters off New England and as far north as Canada to feed. Instead of teeth, these whales have baleen, parallel plates of keratin extending from the upper jaw like bristly combs; these enable them to simply open their mouths wide and sieve the water for zooplankton.[47]

For centuries before colonization, Europeans had exploited right whales. Baleen was a valuable commodity, used for stays in skirts and for brushes, but even more valuable was the whale's copious oil, considered a superior luminant and lubricant. Like cod, whale meat was also considered a "cold food" that could be consumed on holy days, a product that came into high demand as the number of holy days increased to 166 a year.[48] The Basque had long hunted these whales in the eastern Atlantic (possibly since the seventh century), but by the mid-1500s, they were taking right whales off Labrador and Newfoundland during their fall migrations, dominating what was becoming a profitable commercial enterprise. Perhaps as many as a thousand Basque fishermen were engaged in the hunt, killing between three hundred and five hundred whales each season and producing an estimated five hundred thousand gallons of oil a year in the 1560s and 1570s. Between 1530 and 1610, it's estimated they killed twenty-five thousand to forty thousand whales, depleting the stock to the point where they had to hunt farther north.[49]

It's possible that the Algonquians adopted Basque hunting techniques in the 1500s—the Basque used small boats and harpoons—but it's also possible they had already been hunting the whales. English explorer George Weymouth, sailing off of Maine in 1605, observed an Indian (presumably Abenaki) hunt: approaching in "a multitude of boats," they "strike him with a bone made in fashion of a harping iron fastened to a rope," then circle him, shooting him with arrows as he rises out of the water, until they kill him; then they tow him to shore and "call all their chief lords together, and sing a song of joy."[50] Certainly, by the mid-1600s on Long Island—just as the Montauketts were giving up their beach use rights—eastern Long Island Indians, principally Shinnecocks and Montauketts, were being recruited as whalers, valued for their superb whaling skills. Shore whaling took place from November to April, when the seas could be rough and waters frigid. Equipped with iron-tipped harpoons—eight-foot oak or hickory shafts topped with two-foot-long barbed iron shanks—the men set out in open boats made of double-sided cedar, each about twenty-eight to thirty feet long and six to eight feet wide at the center. As a rule, two boats, each carrying a crew of six—four oarsmen, a steersman, and a harpoonist—would approach a whale, and when they came within fifteen feet of the animal, they would harpoon it, sometimes repeatedly until the whale died. This could take anywhere from an hour to half a day. Then they would tow the beast into shore, a long, laborious haul from miles out. A nineteenth-century account describes a crew killing a whale ten miles out and taking twelve hours to tow the carcass to shore. They had to time the landing to the tide, so that they could anchor the whale in the tidal flats as far above low tide line as possible. Once landed, they set to work butchering the whale and stripping its body of blubber, a process that could take three days. They carted the strips of blubber to a tryworks, where they cut the blubber into chunks and boiled them in 250-gallon kettles to render the valuable whale oil. The whole process, from killing to rendering and barreling the oil, could take up to a week. It was a smelly affair indeed. The oil was then shipped out to European markets. The Indian crew were paid in trade goods rather than cash and were granted their customary rights to the tails and fins.[51]

The first commercial whaling enterprise on the northeast coast (aside from the Basque enterprise far to the north) began in Southampton in 1650, when John Ogden received the first whaling license. Sagaponack was the whale-boiling station. Southampton was settled in 1640 by English colonists from Lynn, Massachusetts, and already by 1644 they had "discovered"—probably from the example of the Montauketts—the value of beached whales. They organized a community enterprise to exploit this resource: they divided the town into four wards of eleven people each, assigning by lot two people from each ward to cut up the whale. The cutters got a double share and the rest was divided in equal shares among the town residents over sixteen years of age. Just a few years later, enterprising townsmen in both Southampton and East-hampton (now East Hampton) launched the live whaling industry.[52]

As shore whaling grew and thrived, companies competed for whalers, driving up the price of their labor. Unfortunately, they were often persuaded by offerings of liquor and guns. To regulate such practices, towns began requiring labor contracts. By 1670, Indian whalers got half the market share—but again, not in cash. Instead, they received their pay in the form of a credit line, similar to the system of sharecropping—which in effect placed the Indians in perpetual debt to the companies. A whaling account book kept by William "Tangier" Smith of Brookhaven between 1696 and 1721 illustrates how the system worked. It was customary for whalers to sign a contract for a season. Typically, at the start of the season, they would already be in debt for more than they would be able to pay back at the end of the season. Of Smith's thirty-two whalers, all remained in debt to his company no matter how long they worked for him. John Strong, in his history of the Montauketts, provides several examples: Abraham worked as a whaler for eleven seasons and owed ten pounds at the end; Sacutacca worked as a whaler for ten seasons and owed more than six pounds at the end.[53]

Although Southampton was displaced by Nantucket as the center of the New England whaling industry, Long Islanders continued to engage in shore whaling. Shore whaling peaked between 1670 and 1725 or so. The highest recorded number of whales killed was 111 in the year 1670, which yielded four thousand barrels of oil; a year later, the number of whales killed is not recorded, but a mere six hundred barrels were yielded. This may not have been indicative of decline, as numbers fluctuated year to year—in 1687, for example, two thousand barrels of oil were produced.[54] Up until 1820, records were incomplete and inconsistent, the measurable quantity of oil perhaps reflecting a dramatic decline in the numbers of whales frequenting the shores, or the size of whales caught. For example, in 1708, the governor of New York reported that "A Yearling will make about forty Barrils of Oyl, a Stunt or Whale two years old will make sometimes fifty, sometimes Sixty Barrils of Oyl, and the largest whale that I have heard of in these Parts, Yielded one hundred and ten Barrils of Oyl, and Twelve hundred Weight of Bone."[55] Moreover, beached whales, which may have included those whales injured but not caught by shore whalers, might not have been counted in the tally but may have accounted for a portion of the oil production. But overall, the decadal trend was downward, as shore whaling reduced populations of right whales up and down the northeast coast. Whaling outfits that designed larger boats capable of undertaking longer voyages to pursue whales farther out to sea—like those of Nantucket—would edge out those who continued to employ small boats within ten miles of shore. But whoever dominated the industry, the pattern was the same: depletion of stock. In fact, as Eric Dolin argues, they were victims of their own success: "Like the Long Islanders before them, the Nantucketers' success proved to be their undoing, as the whales near shore became scarcer with each passing year." In 1726, eighty-six whales were taken, marking "the high point for shore whaling"; by 1760, "the era of shore whaling on Nantucket had come to an end."[56]

Right whales continued to be hunted into the twentieth century, when their numbers may have dropped as low as fifty in the western North Atlantic.

The last right whale taken off Long Island was in 1924.[57] In 1931, the Convention for the Regulation of Whaling imposed a moratorium to protect the declining whales, reasserting it in 1949; Japan and the Soviet Union refused to sign. Obviously, the whale must still have been overhunted, as their increasing scarcity prompted the Endangered Species Conservation Act to list the North Atlantic right whale as endangered in 1970, a status that still holds under the Endangered Species Act. A recovery plan was published by NOAA in 1991 and revised in 2005. Recovery efforts include reducing the chances of ship collisions by mandating speed restrictions in "Seasonal Management Areas" and rerouting shipping lanes; reducing the chances of entanglement in fishing gear through regulations and restrictions on fishing gear; protecting critical habitats; continuing the international ban on commercial hunting; and rescuing entangled and stranded live whales. By 2010 they began to recover—increasing from their low of 270 individuals in 1990 to 483—but then continued their decline.

Today, the population is 350 individuals. Only fifty-seven calves were born from 2017 to 2023, and births are not outpacing deaths. Like the humpback whale, the right whale has experienced an unusual mortality event. During the period 2017–2023, ninety-four individuals were found dead, injured, or sick—a significant portion of the population. Thirty-five of these were documented deaths, and it's thought they represent only a third of the mortalities. Vessel strikes and entanglements took their toll, if not killing then maiming the creatures, but many died from unknown causes. This is a serious setback for their recovery.[58]

If there has been a moratorium on commercial hunting since 1924, then what is pushing these leviathans toward the brink of extinction? Right whales breed, calve, and feed in shallow coastal waters—the very habitats that are subject to anthropogenic environmental disturbances. They must navigate congested shipping channels, communicate with their fellows over the noise of boat engines and sonar, run a gauntlet of gill nets and other fishing gear. As Deborah Cramer notes in her book *Ocean: Our Water, Our World* (2008), "Fishing gear entangles more than three-quarters of North Atlantic right whales at least once in their lives." She describes the hazard: "Hundreds of feet of line, crisscrossed around their flippers, looped around their bodies, or caught in their mouths, impede swimming and feeding and, if the line is embedded, expose them to infection."[59] They may also be exposed to oil spills, toxic chemical effluents, and possibly neurotoxins from increasing algal blooms. Autopsies conducted on stranded whales found organochlorines, PCBs (polychlorinated biphenyls, a group of toxic manmade organic chemicals), and bromated flame retardants (used in boat maintenance) in their bodies. Ship collisions and gear entanglement remain the top causes of mortality, as documented by Cramer: "at least twelve right whales died from fishing entanglements and ship strikes" between 2001 and 2006 alone, and this out of a population of four hundred. Now, she adds, climate change may be affecting the distribution and composition of zooplankton in their feeding grounds, with unpredictable consequences.[60]

PAILS FULL OF BIVALVES

When Jaspar Dankers, a Dutch Labadist missionary who toured New Netherland in 1679, visited Gouanes, now the site of the infamous Gowanus Canal (on Long Island's west end), he was warmly welcomed as a houseguest with a "pail-full of Gouanes oysters, which are the best in the country."[61] His hosts roasted them on the fire, to Dankers's immense gustatory enjoyment. "They are large and full," he wrote, some not less than a foot long. Some were smaller varieties. A century later, they were still plentiful. In 1748, Swedish naturalist Peter [Pehr] Kalm attested to the excellent quality of New York oysters, which were harvested from prolific beds "in view of the town" (Manhattan). He described the processing of oysters for export, when they were boiled, seasoned, pickled, and packed into glass or earthenware jars. He noted how the discarded shells piled up in huge mounds to be burned into lime, which the colonists used to whitewash their houses, and the whole shells spread onto their wheat fields. And although the former inhabitants of the island did not burn the shells, they similarly piled them up in mounds that could be seen everywhere. Kalm, who was most attentive to any signs of overfishing or overhunting, described nothing but abundance in regard to oysters.[62]

More than a century after Kalm's visit, in 1804, Reverend Timothy Dwight noted the sad state of Long Island's oyster industry, particularly at Blue Point (part of Brookhaven). Once a seemingly "inexhaustible" source, he wrote, the oysters from these famous beds "have become lean, watery, and sickly, and have declined still more in their numbers than in their quality. Formerly they were large and well flavored; now they are scarcely eatable; and, what is worse, there is reason to fear that they will soon become extinct."[63] In his traveler's guide to Long Island, published in 1807, Samuel Latham Mitchill confirmed Dwight's findings. For thirty years, he reported, Blue Point oysters were harvested in "enormous" quantities, but now the beds had collapsed.[64]

Ernest Ingersoll, a naturalist who was a protégé of Louis Agassiz, attempted to account for the decline in numbers and size of Long Island oysters, publishing a census and history of the American oyster industry for the US Fish Commission in 1881. Historically, the famous Blue Points were renowned for their huge size; once "large, crooked, heavy-shelled, elongated," they were now "small and round."[65] He quoted an 1853 article in the *New York Herald*: "At one period, when they might be regarded as in their prime, they attained a remarkable size; but now their proportions as well as their numbers, have been greatly reduced." He also cited a survey undertaken by Count Pourtales of Cambridge in 1873. In his report, Pourtales described one of the oldest beds off Patchogue, where "tongs bring up large quantities of dead oyster-shells of great size." These old shells were the substrate for living oysters, "about three years old . . . intended for planting at Rockaway." He noted that the Patchogue beds had declined significantly in productivity due to overfishing. Ingersoll explains the practice that he felt had led to overfishing and decimation: "For a hundred years no one had thought anything like protection to the beds, or even moderation in raking, necessary. . . . There seemed no bottom to the mine. . . . All at once young oysters began to be hard to get, and the increase seemed to be almost at an end. The young men had little knowledge of the great armies of infant mollusks which the old men had seen speckling the gravel beaches and rocky shoals all over the bay a few years previous. . . . The oystermen of the present generation suffer a scarcity that their grandfathers would have thought it impossible should ever occur." How had this come to pass? Oysters were simply being harvested too early, before they were four or five years old, before they had even spawned, which Ingersoll compared to digging up a plant before it had set seed. And with the increasing scarcity of native oyster beds such as those in Brookhaven bay, there was precious little seed to harvest for starting and renewing domesticated oyster beds.[66]

At the time of Ingersoll's report (1881), domesticated beds were cultivated from Jamaica Bay to Patchogue on the South Shore and from the East River to Mount Sinai on the North Shore. Ingersoll speculated about when the practice of seeding beds began. The earliest instance of transplanting natural oysters to staked-out tracts offshore may have been in the Harlem River, but oystermen on City Island (located in the western corner of Long Island Sound, just off the Bronx) developed it into a successful enterprise. In the early 1800s, the City Island oysters were still natural, but by the early 1840s, their planted beds were becoming a main source of New York City's oysters.[67]

While Ingersoll attributed the decline of the oyster beds to overfishing, he also acknowledged the impact of pollution in some parts of New York's waters. The East River between Great Neck and Hell's Gate, he wrote, hosts "very persistent natural beds of oysters," but "in the lower part of the river the oil and deposits from the petroleum refineries at Hunter's Point [Newtown Creek] have injured or wholly destroyed the beds."[68] He found a similar situation in New York Bay, where "sewage and waste pollution of the factories of Jersey City have corrupted the shallow water along the Bergen shore."[69] In the decades following his census, pollution would become so noxious that a number of oyster beds had to be closed, especially after outbreaks of typhus from eating polluted oysters. By 1920, oysters had disappeared from New York Harbor, and by 1921, commercial oyster harvesting from New York City waters was banned, a ban that holds today.

Like their bivalve cousins, clams and scallops, oysters inhabit inshore waters, up to a depth of ten feet, making them quite vulnerable to pollution— this despite the fact that they are filter feeders that help keep the waters clean. A few years before Ingersoll published his report, the *New York Times* reported, "The oystermen say that all that they can rake up . . . is from four to eight inches of stinking garbage, and that every oyster, seedling and all, has been killed."[70]

New York Harbor had long been used as a dumping ground for the city's garbage, including human and animal wastes. As the urban population grew, these wastes literally piled up in alleys, gutters, and streets. The installation of a sewer and water system in both Manhattan and Brooklyn in the mid-1800s represented a huge advance in sanitation—but while flushing filth from gutters and those houses outfitted with plumbing, the sanitary system simply shifted the pollution to the waters. Raw sewage turned the harbor into a cesspool. The earliest sewage treatment plants were built on Long Island—the first on Coney Island in 1887, and the second at Sheepshead Bay in 1891—but these were woefully inadequate, as became obvious in the 1920s, when the metropolitan population soared to ten million. According to a study conducted by the Regional Plan Association in 1929, over a billion gallons of raw sewage poured into the harbor every day. Massive fish kills covered the bays, the casualties of oxygen-depleted waters. People were dying of typhoid and dysentery from eating contaminated shellfish and swimming in polluted waters. New York had truly become, as a Public Health Committee report declared, "a body of land entirely surrounded by sewage."[71]

Such gross pollution of the harbor would be remediated by the building of sewage treatment plants throughout the region during the twentieth century. However, even treated sewage pollutes the waters in ways that were not understood until recently. The discharge of treated wastewater creates a condition known as nitrogen overload. In Jamaica Bay alone, four wastewater treatment plants discharge 240 million gallons of wastewater and fifty thousand pounds of nitrogen into the bay every day.[72] Excess nitrogen encourages algal blooms, which consume oxygen when they die and decay. Animals that live in shallow water, like oysters, are deprived of oxygen.

Today, the eastern oyster is considered "ecologically extinct" in the Hudson-Raritan Estuary (the regional waters that include New York Bay and Jamaica Bay on Long Island's west end).[73] The only bivalve to build reefs, it is a "keystone species," an "ecological engineer" that creates habitat for other species.[74] Besides this service, it filters up to fifty gallons of water a day, consuming algae and plankton and absorbing pollutants. Experimental oyster beds constructed in turbid waters have shown that the oyster improves water clarity to the point that sunlight reaches the seabed, supporting the growth of eelgrasses—essential habitat for its cousin bivalve the bay scallop. Moreover, as a reef builder, it provides a buffer to tidal and storm surges in a time of rising seas. Because of the vital roles this humble bivalve plays in the estuary, its restoration is deemed vital.

In 2009, the New York/New Jersey baykeeper and the New York–New Jersey Harbor and Estuary Program formed the Oyster Restoration Research Partnership. That same year, the US Army Corps of Engineers published their draft restoration plan, in which they called for establishing two hundred acres of oyster reefs in the Hudson-Raritan Estuary by 2020 as part of their overall plan.[75] By 2010, six pilot reefs were constructed under the aegis of the Oyster Restoration Research Partnership—Governors Island, Soundview lagoon, Hastings-on-Hudson, Staten Island, Bay Ridge, and Dubos Point in Jamaica Bay, the last now solely managed by the New York City Department of Environmental Protection (NYCDEP).[76] The Staten Island and Bay Ridge reefs proved difficult to manage, but the others showed promise for the long term, especially Soundview. Here, at the confluence of the Bronx and East Rivers in the western corner of Long Island Sound, they laid down 125 cubic yards of shell as substrate "to create the largest expanse of subtidal habitat in the Lower Hudson Estuary" (about one acre). Such expansion would increase the chances of attracting wild oysters to the reefs, viewed as a positive development.[77]

At Jamaica Bay, oysters planted in 2010 at Dubos Point and in Gerritsen Creek have survived, grown, and reproduced. Such positive results have encouraged the NYCDEP to expand its seeding area by half an acre. In 2014, it received a $1 million grant from the Sandy Resiliency Grant Program, indicating a recognition of the reef builder's value in enhancing coastal resilience. The oyster reef program is an integral part of an overall plan to protect the watershed of Jamaica Bay. The NYCDEP also began upgrading sewage treatment plants to reduce nitrogen overload, reducing it by an impressive 30 percent since the 1990s (as of 2014). In its 2018 status update, nitrogen levels continued to decline, then began ticking upward in 2016.[78]

On both the North and South Shores of Long Island, oysters are being commercially harvested, but nowhere near the scale of the nineteenth-century harvests. On the Great South Bay, for instance, where the industry was centered at West Sayville, it's estimated that at its peak in the 1880s, seventy thousand barrels a year were harvested, most from baymen working small cultivated beds they leased from the towns. These small family-run businesses were bought out by Sealshipt Oyster Company in 1912, later known as Bluepoints, which employed hundreds of harvesters, paying them low wages to work long hours under contracts that stipulated they sell their catch only to the company. The oyster beds of the Great South Bay were decimated first by the hurricane of 1938, then again by the massive brown tide (a harmful algal bloom) that infected the waters surrounding Long Island in 1985. Sealshipt closed its doors in 1999, when another brown tide poisoned the waters.[79] Baymen continue to harvest oysters, however: the Great Atlantic Shellfish Farms, for example, manages seed oyster production for seven small farms, each leasing three-to-five-acre plots of a ninety-five-acre underwater farm. Oyster populations in the Long Island Sound were also devastated by the brown tide of 1985, recovering somewhat in the 1990s before being hit by a parasitic disease known as MSX. Habitat restoration in the sound, coupled with expansion of cultivated beds, enabled the oyster population to quadruple between 2012 and 2014. Wild oysters still inhabit these waters (mainly in western Long Island Sound and Huntington and Northport Bays), and baymen harvest them, but the oysters that are commercially harvested for the restaurant trade come from cultivated beds. Frank M. Flower and Sons of Oyster Bay, for example, have been in the oyster business since 1887; they started their first hatchery in the 1960s and are now cultivating oysters on 1,800 acres of leased underwater beds.[80]

The success of cultivated oysters is paralleled by that of the cultivated bay scallop industry. Like oysters, bay scallops depend on healthy inshore waters and are highly sensitive to pollutants and algal blooms. In the past, the harvesting of wild bay scallops in the Peconic Bay "contributed more than $10 million to the local economy"—the fishery alone valued at $2–$4 million—and supported more than "400–600 full-time baymen."[81] The 1985 brown tide decimated these wild stocks. In 1986, local baymen initiated scallop restoration efforts to save both the scallop and their livelihoods, enlisting the help of Cornell Cooperative Extension and Long Island University. The *New York Times* described the reintroduction efforts as a kind of triage to save the life of the industry. Overseen by Christopher Smith of the Suffolk County Seagrant Program in Riverhead, several million scallop spat were shipped from New England beds and transplanted to Northwest Harbor, Orient Harbor, and Flanders Bay.[82] After they successfully rebuilt the stock, the 1999 brown tide destroyed them, and for the next decade the harvest was down 99 percent compared with historical levels. But efforts to restore them have been persistent, and in recent years spectacularly successful, despite recurring seasonal algal blooms. In 2005, the Cornell Cooperative Extension Marine Program, Long Island University, and the Southold Project in Aquaculture Training partnered in an ambitious restoration project with a grant of $2 million from Suffolk County, again overseen by Smith. By 2009, the scallop population at Orient Point, the center of the spawning sanctuary, increased 5,000 percent, with dramatic increases in other planting beds as well. In total, they planted over eight million scallops from 2006 to 2018 and continued to plant and harvest despite a massive die-off of scallops in the years 2019 and 2020 from undetermined causes. It's thought that a combination of factors—warmer and more acidic waters, low dissolved oxygen levels, a parasite, and possibly a new predator, the cownose ray, that has migrated from southern waters—all may have contributed to the recent decimation of Long Island scallops.[83]

A key ingredient to the success of bay scallop seeding is the reestablishment of eelgrass beds, which serve as protective cover for both juveniles and adults. The spat attach themselves by threads (byssus) to eelgrass blades until they are mature enough to swim. The association of eelgrass and scallops is an example of two species whose fates are intertwined; when the brown tides of the 1980s and 1990s killed off eelgrass (by blocking sunlight), bay scallop populations also plummeted. Any bay scallop restoration project must include restoration of eelgrass meadows.[84]

―――

Discarded bay scallop shells are piled high on the landing at Napeague Harbor, where a host of gulls scavenge the remains, and flies feast on decaying flesh. The baymen have already been out and brought in their haul, shucking them onsite, just as the colonists did three centuries ago and, before them, the original inhabitants, leaving their shell mounds for archaeologists to delve millennia later. Nearby are stacked metal baskets used to plant spat. Despite the fetid smell, my mouth waters, as I think of the sweet succulent meat of bay scallops, so unlike the larger sea scallop. It's the height of bay scallop season, which lasts from late fall to early spring, and if the harvest is good, I will be able to get these little bivalves from my local seafood store, shucked and ready to cook. I see the scallop barge out on the water and recall my going out on it a few years ago, courtesy of the South Fork Natural History Society, to observe the seeding of spat in the harbor when the reseeding program was just beginning. The tiny spat were being lowered into the water in lantern nets that were strung on long lines floated on buoys, the nets pulled up and checked periodically to observe scallop growth and monitor their health. It was wet and slippery on board, where the mollusks, encased in their fingernail-size shells, were kept damp in shallow trays of saltwater until they were lowered into the bay. Water sloshed onto the boat, misting my skin; I tongued the salt from my lips. It felt good to be there, observing people engaged in restoring other creatures to their native habitat.

From the landing I walk along the beach, curving around the point. Scattered in drifts over the upper beach are dry ribbon-like strands of eelgrass—a sign of a healthy harbor. The shore is littered with empty scallop half shells, their ribbed sides revealing subtle and varied striated colors. I pick one up and rub my thumb over the corrugated exterior and its smooth nacreous interior. It is still damp, with grains of sand clinging to it. Left on the beach, it will break down and add its grains to the beach.

I think of the living creature that once grew the shell, layer by layer. Arrayed along the scallop's mantle are thirty or forty glittering blue eyes through which it perceives light and shadow, and most importantly predators like sea stars before it becomes prey. On spying a sea star, the scallop, which lacks a foot, propels itself away by clapping the two sides of its shell together to force out water through its mantle, enabling it to bounce up and across the surface. The shell serves a dual purpose, to propel and protect. If you pick up the live scallop it will clamp its shell shut. This does not deter determined scallopers who know the art of shucking and shelling, for a reward well worth the effort: the sweet morsel that is the little muscle that

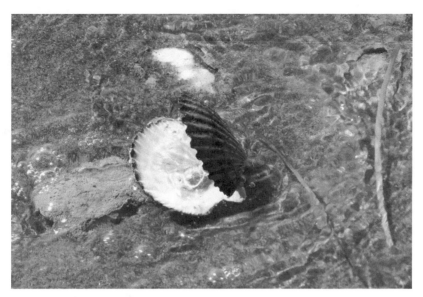

Figure 3.3. A bay scallop shell in the waters of Napeague Harbor. Photo by author.

holds the two sides of the shell together. And when we taste the meat we taste the sea—sweet, briny, mineral.

In efforts to restore and rebuild the populations of both finfish and shell-fish, a new paradigm has been emerging. As stated by the Nature Conservancy in 2006, historically, the emphasis has been on restoring populations of species for fisheries; now, the primary goal is "the rebuilding of natural capital—reefs and robust spawning populations capable of sustaining both fisheries and the health of coastal ecosystems."[85] Local economies become tied to local ecologies. To me, restoration is about more than protecting livelihoods, or planting and harvesting a crop for our consumption, vital as these things are; it is about healing the damage we have caused to marine ecosystems, and in the process healing and restoring ourselves.

CHAPTER 4

Seas of Grass

OUR GLORIOUS SALT MARSHES

In the fall of 1842, a teenage boy set out from his farm in Freeport with five farm hands to go marshing in Hempstead Bay, a time-honored communal tradition of cutting and curing salt hay from the offshore marshes to provision their cattle in winter or to sell to large farmers for profit. Twenty-five years earlier, his father had received a patent to a cluster of little islands on Shell Creek known as Mud Hole Hassock. They arrived on the second Monday of September, to be in place when marshing started at sunrise on Tuesday. Although they held patent to the place (unlike most farmers, who simply staked out their claim for the season), they still erected a rake and a pair of poles to mark it. Such claims were absolutely respected. They built their hut on a slightly elevated mound by Shell Creek, and as soon as all was in place, they dined on their provisions of ham, beans, bread, hard tack, and pies. As the days went on, they would avail themselves of the marsh's bounty, consuming eels, clams, fish, and game birds such as snipes, all cooked up in a big iron pot and served on pewter plates. That night they slept fitfully, emerging from their shelter to look at the moon and stars, "reflected in flickering zig-zag lines upon the rippling waters."[1] The next day the marshing would commence, as all hands swung their sharpened scythes through the grasses. They cut enough each day to load up a boat or two and float it on high tide back to their mainland landing place, where it would be cured.

The boy was Daniel Tredwell, a Long Islander who wrote a memoir of his days growing up on Long Island. In *Reminiscences of Men and Things on Long Island* (1912), Tredwell described a landscape that had disappeared

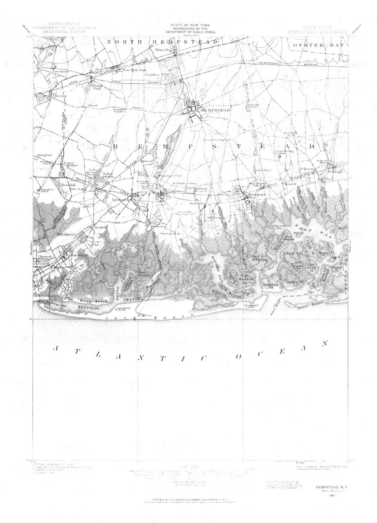

Figure 4.1. Topographic map of Hempstead Harbor, survey year 1897.
Courtesy of United States Geological Survey, USGS Historical Quadrangle
Scanning Project, 2023.

in his lifetime. The marshes of the Great South Bay he estimated to be
50,000 acres, of which 8,300 were considered the common lands of the
Town of Hempstead. Since the incorporation of the town, noted Treadwell,
these commons, along with the adjoining Hempstead Plains, had been a
bone of contention between those who wanted to divide and privatize the
lands, and those who wanted to preserve them as a commons in perpetuity.[2]

In recollecting the long-gone days of marshing, Tredwell recalled them like "a hazy daydream with no recognition of time," a memory of immense pleasure in a landscape "unlike anything else in nature. And the creeks, the waterways, are labyrinthian and present novelties at every turn unknown to the most noted rivers of the world."[3]

The Marine Nature Study Area in Oceanside sits in a neat suburban enclave of pastel and stucco houses, where street names point to the neighboring golf course: Slice Drive, Links Drive, Bunker Drive, Trap Road. On a muggy June day, I drive through the labyrinthine streets, following the brown signs toward the nature preserve. I park in the little lot next to the headquarters and, donning binoculars and camera, head out into the salt marsh, walking a berm. The marsh is a sliver of fifty-two acres set aside as a preserve in 1970, a tiny fragment of what was once a vast coastal wetland. It's threaded by a little creek, Walls Point Creek, and bordered by a larger creek, Bedell Creek, both of which empty into the Great South Bay; at high tide, the creeks flush the marsh with salt water, and at low tide they drain it, exposing mud flats that attract waders and shorebirds. A shelly beach edges the marsh, and just across the water, a salt marsh island like that where Tredwell cut salt hay shimmers through the hazy air in colors of green and gold.

I have come to observe and photograph the breeding birds here. Since Superstorm Sandy, the boardwalk and berm have been beautifully rebuilt, offering an easy walk with ample photo opportunities. Several photographers have mounted their cameras on tripods, adjusting the long lenses on their subjects; I prefer to travel light, using a pair of binoculars to scope the marsh and a point-and-shoot camera with a good zoom lens to capture my subjects. A pair of glossy ibis pick their way through the grass, their humped backs iridescent in the light, and a yellow-crowned night-heron pokes his head up now and then as he feeds. A female osprey sits on the platform nest while the male wheels above her, whistling. The manic cries of laughing gulls rend the air and common terns shriek and dive-bomb the water for fish. From elevated posts—a reed or nest box—male red-winged blackbirds display their red epaulets like flags, calling "konk-la-ree!" A song sparrow trills. All is sound and motion, full of life.

Besides the yellow-crowned night-heron, three other herons and two egrets breed here: black-crowned night-heron, green heron, great blue heron, great egret, and snowy egret. I easily pick out the tall, long-necked great blue in the distance. Closer to me, the two egrets strut and stalk the marsh, their plumage bright white against the green sea of grass. Like the great blue, their long necks and legs have adapted them to shallow aquatic environments. The snowy riffles the mud with his golden feet to stir up prey. The great egret extends his neck and keeps his eye out for fish in the creek, ready to spear one with his heavy bill. I zoom in on his eye to see its golden orb and green lores. Often, I don't have to zoom far: this egret is so bold he struts on the boardwalk or roosts on top of one of the kiosks. He was probably not so bold in the days when his ancestors and those of the snowy were hunted for their plumes, much sought after in the late 1800s and early 1900s to adorn ladies' hats. The plume trade pushed these beautiful waders to near extinction; in fact, the movement to protect them led to the formation of the Audubon Society and the setting aside of bird preserves. They rebounded—until faced with a new threat, DDT, which was sprayed on

Figure 4.2. A great egret stalks the marsh of the Marine Nature Study Area in Oceanside. Photo by author.

marshes to eradicate mosquitoes; the pesticide accumulated in the tissues of predators like egrets and ospreys and eagles, causing their eggshells to thin and nesting to fail. It has since been banned—largely as a result of Rachel Carson's articles in the *New Yorker* and her book *Silent Spring*, published in 1962—but new pesticides and the continued practice of mosquito spraying pose new threats, as we will consider later.

Unintentionally, I approach near a willet's nest, flushing the male bird, who cries out his signature "will-will-willet" call and flashes his white wing stripes in a noisy display. The willet constructs a nest by bending down grass stems to form a hollow; after the eggs hatch, the female absents herself and the male attends the hatchlings for several weeks. By flying away, the male hopes to distract me from his precious young, but they are safe from passersby, out of sight in the grasses. The willet is one of the few shorebirds who breed on Long Island; most shorebirds are migratory, stopping to feed in coastal marshes in spring and fall. They leave their northern breeding grounds as early as late July, so it's possible to see both breeding and migratory shorebirds here at once.

On a late July day I have seen flocks of migratory dunlin descending to the marsh near shore, rising again in concert, wheeling out over the water, and returning to alight again, not far from where they first lifted off. This behavior once made them easy targets for gunners, who could take a dozen or more in a single shot. They were known to hunters of the nineteenth century as "black-breasts," but in their nonbreeding plumage they lack the black belly.[4] On a good migration day, if you visit at low tide when the mudflats are exposed, you can observe hundreds of shorebirds. The little sandpipers (peeps) are not so easy to distinguish without a scope and expertise with identifying shorebirds, but the greater yellowlegs stands out. It's a large sandpiper with long yellow legs, and if that's not enough to give him away, he has a distinctive three-note call. The yellowlegs was known to hunters as the "Telltale Tatler," because it will give alarm if a predator is near, its loud call alerting fellow shorebirds to scatter.[5] Unlike dunlin, greater yellowlegs do not forage in flocks, a behavior that made them not worth the hunter's shot. The greater yellowlegs was one of the shorebirds exempt from the hunting ban established by the Migratory Bird Treaty Act of 1918 (the others were black-bellied and golden plovers), until all shorebird hunting was banned in 1928.[6]

Less conspicuous than waders and shorebirds are two species that inhabit salt marshes exclusively and are known to breed here: the salt marsh sparrow and clapper rail, both of which have declined significantly as their habitat has dwindled or become degraded. The salt marsh sparrow secretes itself in the marsh grasses, no sooner seen than out of sight—but on the day I visit, this lovely sparrow with its buffy face shows itself at the top of a grass stem, long enough for me to snap a photo or two. I also observe one scurrying like a mouse across the path as he moves from one side of the marsh to the other—although, given its behavior, it might be the more secretive seaside sparrow, also known to breed here. Both sparrow species feed on grass seeds, snails, amphipods, insects, and spiders. The clapper rail is more elusive, and on this hot sunny day he does not show himself to me, though I have seen him here in the past.

Figure 4.3. A salt marsh sparrow briefly reveals himself atop a snag at the Marine Nature Study Area in Oceanside. This endangered sparrow breeds in the salt marshes here. Its leg is banded to keep track of this rapidly declining species. Photo by author.

To see a clapper rail, a cloudy day at high tide is best, when they are more likely to emerge at the edges of the marsh, although low tide at dusk may bring them out to feed in the exposed mud, where they forage for snails and worms to supplement their diet of small crabs. The expression "thin as a rail" refers to its ability to melt back into the grasses. John James Audubon's description of the clapper rail is memorable: "They have a power of compressing their body to such a degree as frequently to force a passage between two stems so close one could hardly believe it possible for them to squeeze themselves through."[7] But even if you cannot see one, you might listen closely for their clacking calls. They construct their nests in hummocky cordgrass stands, bending dead stems down to form a fibrous dome, something like an inverted conical basket that protects the bowl-like nest. The king rail, usually a denizen of brackish to freshwater marshes and rare on Long Island, has also been spotted in this marsh. Remarkably, these rails are successfully interbreeding with clapper rails here.[8] In the 1800s, when clappers were far more abundant on Long Island, especially the South Shore, they were shot for meat by hunters, who called them meadow hens, and their eggs were relished as "exceedingly delicate eating." The hunters tracked them during extreme high tides, when the spartina was submerged, leaving the rails nowhere to hide.[9]

Though I enjoy the outing at the Oceanside preserve, I feel sad for the degradation and erosion of the once-vast coastal wetlands of the Great South Bay, of which the marsh is but a scrap wedged between a too-green golf course and suburban houses, each with its manicured green lawn—and I think of all that nitrogen washing into the bay, no doubt mixed with pesticides and herbicides in a toxic brew. There's such a thing as too green. But I appreciate that this marsh exists at all, preserved by caring people, serving as a nature center to educate schoolchildren about the value of a salt marsh and its wonderful diversity.

THE MAKING OF SALT MARSHES

The Long Island South Shore Estuary Reserve extends about seventy miles from Hempstead Bay on its western end to Moriches and Shinnecock Bays

Figure 4.4. A salt marsh on the Great South Bay in winter. The dormant grasses wear a golden hue; by summer, they will become a green sea of grass. Photo by author.

on its eastern end, its centerpiece the Great South Bay, "the largest shallow estuarine bay" in New York State.[10] These shallow bays, enclosed by barrier islands, encompass 173 square miles. As in all estuaries, fresh water draining from the watershed mingles with salt water from the ocean. Geologically, estuaries are rare ecosystems formed five to six thousand years ago when sea levels began to stabilize; they are dynamic ecosystems, continually shaped by forces of wind and water. The balance of fresh and salt water is critical to maintaining healthy estuaries; now, as sea levels rise, that balance is disrupted. For thousands of years, the shallow-water bays of the South Shore Estuary have been ideal for the formation of extensive salt marshes. Today, rising sea levels are drowning marsh islands, and the formation of new coastal marshes is blocked by extensive shoreline development.

Salt marshes grow along shorelines behind sand spits and barrier beaches, places protected from direct wave action. Sediments ferried by longshore currents or by creeks and rivers accumulate to form mudflats in the intertidal zones. Seeds of salt-marsh cordgrass wafted by winds or whole plants rafted by tides take root in these flats, spreading rapidly through underground rhizomes to form dense colonies. They may spread seaward, wherever fresh sediments have been deposited, or landward in response to sea level rise. The rhizomes stabilize the sediments, and the leaves trap sediments, gradually elevating the marsh in a process known as accretion. Decaying rhizomes and roots build a peat bed that over time raises the level of the marsh, allowing less salt-tolerant plants to flourish. Salt meadow hay, a finer grass than cordgrass, colonizes the higher ground, forming thick, matted swaths of an expansive grassland. Unlike the stiff, coarse blades of cordgrass, the blades of salt meadow hay are wiry and its bases weak, the plants easily flattened by winds and spring tides so that they look swirled. This is the salt hay that was cut by Treadwell during marshing.[11]

Spartina grasses are the foundation of the estuarial ecosystem, the basis of the food chain. They are known as primary producers because they can convert sunlight into carbohydrates in the process of photosynthesis. They are not the only primary producers; single-celled microbes also play the same role, as they have since the beginnings of life on earth. In salt marsh muds at the roots of grasses, photosynthetic sulfur bacteria break down sulfates and release hydrogen sulfide as they decompose dead marsh grasses, generating that familiar rotten-egg smell exuded by marsh muds exposed at low tide. On salt pans—extremely saline patches—colonies of microalgae form pinkish mats. The work of these and myriad other microbial decomposers is essential to the healthy functioning of a marsh as they release carbon dioxide and other chemicals for reuse by the growing plants. It is a self-sustaining cycle of life and death, growth and decay.

Looking closely into the green world of cordgrasses, you may see marsh and possibly common periwinkles scraping algae from the blades with their radula. Common periwinkles are not native to the region but were introduced in the last century, possibly in ship ballast; they prefer rocky shores, but on Long Island's sandy South Shore, rock structures such as jetties, groins, and revetments may provide grazing for periwinkles. At high tide, you may observe dozens of air-breathing salt marsh snails crawling up grass stems to avoid the reach of saltwater; these snails forage on dead cordgrasses. Grooved trails etched in mud lead you to a group of eastern mud snails, or dog whelks, which feed on the surface of marsh mud, grazing on microalgae and seaweeds as well as detritus, and scavenging animal remains.

I have observed hundreds of these herding in the shallows of a tidal creek where they grazed the mudflat. Scanning the edges of a tidal creek, you may see a colony of ribbed mussels anchored in marsh peat, attaching themselves to cordgrass roots with strong threads called byssus, in effect binding the marsh together. At high tide, they open their shells and filter the water for plankton, detritus, and bacteria; if a large group is present, they can filter all the water flowing through a marsh in a tidal cycle. Besides cleaning the water, they also fertilize the cordgrasses with their nitrogen-rich wastes.

Tidal creeks are like the arterial system of the salt marsh, daily tides flooding and flushing, cleansing, and nourishing the wetland ecosystem. In summer you may observe myriad little fish milling in the shallows, which offer some protection from larger marine predators. These include Atlantic silversides, sheepshead minnow, and mummichog and other killifish. Non-migratory mummichogs are the most abundant, most likely because they can tolerate fluctuating salinities and polluted water. They eat salt marsh snails, amphipods, grass shrimp, insect larvae, algae, and detritus. In late spring they begin their reproductive cycle, the males spawning at full and new moon during high tides, the females depositing their fertilized eggs on spartina leaves or in mats of algae in the upper marsh. The eggs hatch during the next spring tide, the larvae taking shelter in upper marsh pools until they are large enough to survive in tidal creeks. In winter they hibernate by migrating up tidal creeks and burrowing in the mud of tidal pools. Tidal creeks also provide sheltered nurseries and feeding grounds for juvenile fish that will return to the open sea in winter, including shad, striped bass, and bluefish—all carnivores that will eat the smaller fish. In late summer, if you stand quietly at the mouth of a tidal creek at low tide, you may observe these juveniles flipping and flashing their silvery sides, riffling the water.[12]

All these smaller denizens of the marsh are food for larger creatures—turtles, raccoons, and birds. The diamondback terrapin, for example, is the only reptile whose exclusive habitat is the estuary and salt marsh. It feeds on periwinkles, snails, crabs, worms, and mussels; its eggs and hatchlings provide food for raccoons, foxes, crows, and gulls. Our only beach-nesting turtle, the female lays her eggs in ocean dunes above the high tide line. Soft engineering projects that pump offshore sand onto beaches and flatten dunes pose a threat to these turtles. They are also threatened by toxins in the estuaries. In the spring of 2015, about a hundred dead diamondback turtles washed ashore at Flanders Bay, Long Island, likely from food poisoning. Kevin McAllister of Defend H2O speculated that the turtles died from ingesting toxic shellfish. It's known that the Peconic Bay and other inshore waters of eastern Long Island are contaminated with saxitoxin, a poisonous microorganism associated with algal blooms, which have been increasing in recent years. These turtles, once hunted to near extinction to meet market demand for terrapin soup, are now threatened by habitat degradation and loss.[13]

Diamondback terrapins play an important role in sustaining coastal ecosystems, according to a study of the Jamaica Bay population conducted by Alexandra Kanonik and Russell Burke of Hofstra University in 2009. According to Kanonik and Burke, their eggs provide nutrients for plants "in an otherwise nutrient-poor environment" and food for predators such as raccoons, which consume 93 to 100 percent of the eggs.[14] The turtles also eat periwinkles, which, if not kept in check, would overgraze salt marsh cordgrass. Habitat destruction, such as filling in Idlewild marsh and disrupting tidal creeks to build Kennedy Airport in the 1940s, coupled with shore highways and roads, blocks the transit of turtles back to their traditional nesting grounds. At Kennedy Airport over the years, hundreds of sexually mature terrapins have tried to cross Runway 4L, heading for their ancient nesting site on the adjacent beach there—an uncounted number in 2009, eight hundred in 2012, four hundred in 2013, and three hundred in 2014, according to the *New York Times*.[15] As noted by Kanonik and Burke, the wetlands of Jamaica Bay National Wildlife Refuge constitute "1% of their pre-1700 coverage."[16]

The Unmaking of the Salt Marshes

For thousands of years, Long Island's tidal wetlands supported an abundance of species, including human hunters, fishers, and shellfish gatherers who used it sustainably. In the past century, the great seas of grass that graced our shores were severely fragmented, and they continue to be threatened by pollution, coastal development, and climate change.

The vertical accretion of salt marshes has historically kept pace with sea level rise and will maintain equilibrium if that rise is within four to ten inches a century as in the past. But as emphasized by Judith Weis and Carol Butler in their book *Salt Marshes: A Natural and Unnatural History* (2009), climate change is altering that equation, as thermal expansion of the oceans and melting of glaciers accelerates the rate of sea level rise in the twenty-first century.[17] A warming climate is just one of many pressures exerted on salt marshes; development has taken a huge bite out of the coastal wetlands, from sheer destruction—draining, dredging, filling, and building—to contamination from pollutants.

When Tredwell wrote his memoir, tidal wetlands in Nassau and Suffolk Counties had already been severely reduced. An account on Long Island's topography published in 1839 estimated that Long Island salt marshes covered over seventy thousand acres (more than one hundred square miles), of which Suffolk County comprised over fifty-five square miles, and Queens County forty square miles (Nassau County was not yet carved out of Queens County).[18] By 1900, the salt marshes of Nassau and Suffolk Counties covered about forty-eight thousand acres. Between 1900 and 2004, they were reduced to twenty-four thousand acres, with the greatest losses in Nassau County.[19] This is not surprising, since Nassau County in particular has undergone extensive suburbanization since the early 1900s. Before the passage of the state's Tidal Wetlands Act in 1973, many of these shoreline marshes were simply filled in, and sooner or later developed. Hard development in wetlands prevents the natural landward migration of salt marshes as the sea level rises. As stated in a preliminary report on the state of New York City's wetlands drafted under Mayor Michael Bloomberg in 2012, "In New York City, the highly urbanized edge of many of our tidal wetlands prevents inland migration to adjacent upland or freshwater zones. Development before the adoption of federal or state regulations often occurred directly up to or on wetlands, leaving no transition area."[20] In New York City, which includes Kings and Queens Counties on Long Island, tidal wetlands have diminished by 90 percent over a period of 130 years.

The story of Jamaica Bay typifies the fill-and-build pattern of growth that has characterized New York City since the colonial era, when the Dutch drained and filled marshes and built out shorelines to create taxable real estate. The salt marsh islands that once turned this estuary into a sea of grass remained relatively untouched (except for by hay cutters, wildfowl hunters, and fishers) until the early twentieth century, when private developers and city planners began to put forward schemes for transforming the bay, from turning it into the largest deep-water port in the world—which involved destroying the wetlands and dredging the bay—to reclaiming wetlands for suburbs, to using it as an industrial and sanitary landfill site. All of these fill-and-build schemes were carried out to one degree or another.

The first threat to the wetlands occurred when a consortium of private developers put forward a plan to turn Jamaica Bay into a great maritime port. The port scheme was never realized—New Jersey would displace New York as the region's primary port facility—but much dredging, filling, and bulk-heading was done with the goal of making it a premier port. Most of this work was carried out by private developers, but by 1912, with an infusion of state and federal funds, the city's Department of Docks began to develop the bay. The city dredged Rockaway Inlet to accommodate ships and constructed fourteen piers between Barren Island and Mill Basin. By 1924, Gerritsen and Mill Creeks had been bulkheaded and dredged, creating Kimball and Mill basins. Between 1913 and 1923, Flatbush Avenue was extended to Rockaway Inlet, connecting Barren Island to the mainland.[21]

Disdainful of the port development scheme, which he characterized as a "slick real estate promotion," Parks Commissioner Robert Moses published his own plan for Jamaica Bay in 1938, proposing waterfront and island parks in place of shipping terminals.[22]

To create Marine Park, Moses built on the legacy of Frederic B. Pratt and Alfred T. White, who, alarmed at the encroachment on a once-pristine wetland, donated 140 acres for a park preserve in 1917; Moses expanded the original parcel to 1,844 acres in 1937, and this would become the basic building block of the future Gateway National Wildlife Refuge. In the early 1950s, Moses designated the central portion of Jamaica Bay (including Broad Channel) as a bird preserve. Sand dredged from Jamaica Bay was used to form dikes on the east and west sides of Cross Bay Boulevard, creating two impoundments of fresh water—one of forty acres (the West Pond) and one of one hundred acres (the East Pond)—to harbor migratory waterfowl, historically reported to have numbered in the tens of thousands at the height of migration. The impoundments, according to a New York City Parks (NYC Parks) report of 1964, attracted previously rare species such as glossy ibis, first observed in 1960. In 1974, the city transferred 1,024 acres of this parcel to the National Park Service to create Gateway.[23]

The apparently benign creation of a wildlife refuge, with coastal wetlands and uplands preserved from development, nonetheless entailed hard development. To provide auto access to his parks and suburbs, Moses constructed highways and bridges, including the Belt Parkway (first called Marginal Boulevard), built in 1938, and the Marine Parkway and bridge. These autoroutes facilitated access not only to the parks but to new commuter suburbs like Marine Park, created from fill in the 1940s. Continuing a time-honored New York tradition, Moses used sewage sludge as part of the fill for Marine Park. When residents got wind of it, they sued the city in 1948; the city removed the offensive fill and replaced it with sand.[24]

Factories had already made inroads into the bay since the mid-1800s. On Barren Island, for example, where fish oil and fertilizer were rendered, daily scows would deliver their loads of dead horses, cows, dogs, and cats—hence the name Dead Horse Bay. Moses cleared these noxious industries, but at the same time, he created new dump sites beginning with Mill Basin in 1933. In 1949, Moses designated a section between Belt Parkway and Jamaica Bay for two so-called sanitary landfills, the Fountain Avenue and Pennsylvania Avenue landfills, the largest at the time (they are now being turned into parks). Moses may have thwarted a scheme for a maritime port in Jamaica Bay but could not prevent the construction of an airport, a pet project of Mayor Fiorello La Guardia. For the site of the airport, the city secured almost five thousand acres of wetlands that included a golf course named Idlewild, after which the airport was named. The airport was built on landfill dredged from Grassy Bay. Opening in 1948, Idlewild would continue to expand over the salt marsh, becoming the John F. Kennedy International Airport in 1963.

During the period of aggressive fill-and-build development (1924–1974), 75 percent of Jamaica Bay's marshes was lost.[25] Jamaica Bay is an estuary comprising salt marsh islands, mud flats, and tidal creeks covering about twenty-six square miles. Based on historical maps, it's estimated that Jamaica Bay originally had 16,000 acres of salt marsh. Between 1924 and 1974, dredging and filling alone erased 780 acres of marsh, and another 510 acres were lost due to "other reasons," likely erosion and eutrophication.[26] Despite federal and state regulations passed in the 1970s to protect Jamaica Bay's wetlands, that loss has accelerated. Aerial images show that between 1974 and 1994, 526 acres of marsh islands were lost, a yearly average loss of 26 acres; and between 1994 and 1999, 220 acres were lost, a yearly average loss of 44 acres. What was causing these losses? According to the US Army Corps of Engineers, "There is no consensus among ecological experts."[27] Storm surges, erosion, offshore dredging, and eutrophication each play a role, but climate change has been recognized since 2001 as a primary cause.[28] Sea levels are rising, drowning marsh islands—and with shoreline hardening they cannot migrate inland as they have historically done. And it is precisely because of sea level rise that coastal cities need the buffer zones provided by healthy marshes. In response to this reality, from 2006 to 2012 the US Army Corps of Engineers restored about 160 acres on five islands—Yellow Bar Hassock, Elders Point East and Elders Point West (once a single island), Black Wall, and Rulers Bar—using sand dredged from Ambrose shipping channel. They transplanted hundreds of thousands of marsh plants adapted to different zones of the marshes—including cordgrasses and salt hay—and broadcasted seed. In a feasibility report published in February 2017, they proposed restoring five more islands, a project still underway. The corps declares that, "left alone, the marshes could vanish by the year 2025." In 2022, they received $19 million in federal funding to continue the work.[29]

———

One of the ways humans have altered our marshes is mosquito ditching, whereby parallel grids of ditches are dug to control mosquito breeding. Ditching had been practiced since colonial times to support the growth of salt marsh hay, which prefers a lower saline environment, as well as to drain marshes, deemed to be sources of disease, although the mosquito was not yet recognized as a vector. Once it was understood that mosquitoes were the vectors of many potentially deadly diseases, mosquito control became paramount. Cutting ditches to control mosquitoes began in the early twentieth century and was carried out on a large scale in the 1930s, when the Civilian Conservation Corps was set to work digging them by hand. By the 1940s, nearly all the coastal marshes, including marsh islands, were ditched, as revealed in historical aerial and present-day satellite photos of Long Island marshes.[30]

As described by Weis and Butler, ditching as it was historically practiced had dramatic ecological effects, both negative and beneficial, depending on one's perspective. The concept behind ditching was to eliminate the stagnant pools of water mosquitoes breed in; yet the practice also removed the favored habitat of killifish, which eat mosquito larvae. The steep sides of ditches discouraged the growth of cordgrass, the base of the ecosystem. In its place, marsh elder took root in the diked-up banks, and rushes grew in the dried-out soil—providing habitat for birds such as willets that favor elevated portions of the marsh. This could be seen as beneficial, but in fact, as Weis and Butler conclude, bird populations are reduced in ditched marshes, likely a result of the loss of pools and reduction of invertebrates. Invertebrates cannot thrive in steep-sided ditches and dried-out soil.[31] Since the 1960s, a new approach to mosquito control has been implemented, known as open marsh water management. The goal of this approach is to maintain and create open pools of sufficient depth to provide habitat for mosquito-eating fish, encouraging them to remain in the pools throughout tide cycles. This approach has been quite successful, reducing the need for mosquito spraying.

Unfortunately, spraying marshes with pesticides has been common practice since the development of organochlorine chemicals in World War II. These pesticides, composed of carbon and hydrogen, were considered desirable for agricultural use because they do not dissolve in water and persist in the soil—the very qualities that allow them to build up in the environment and in the food chain to the point of toxicity. In the 1940s and 1950s, DDT was sprayed extensively on farms to control agricultural pests and on marshes to control biting flies and mosquitoes—until mosquitoes began to develop resistance. Rachel Carson raised the alarm about DDT and the myriad other toxic chemicals—pesticides and herbicides—being sprayed with abandon in the United States, which were building up in animal tissues, including our own bodies. Carson died of breast cancer in 1968 and did not live to see DDT banned nationwide in 1972 (it was banned on eastern Long Island in 1966). Despite this victory, the persistent use of chemicals to eradicate noxious insects and plants would surely have dismayed her. Marshes continue to be sprayed, and though the pesticides break down quickly, unlike DDT, they continue to serve death sentences to animals other than the targeted pests. As Weis and Butler point out, organochlorines were replaced by organophosphates, which are composed of the same chemicals as nerve gas—another wartime legacy—and as a result "can cause convulsions and respiratory paralysis and ha[ve] caused death in fishes and birds."[32]

The Long Island marshes of Suffolk and Nassau Counties today are being sprayed by a liquid form of methoprene, which inhibits mosquito larvae from growing into adults.[33] It's sprayed solely on South Shore marshes where human populations are low, an indication that aerial spraying is not exactly benign for humans and other nontarget animals. In fact, in a 2009 Nassau County document explaining their mosquito control program, an appendix lists wetland and shore birds that are affected by such spraying, including herons, egrets, and terns.[34] In New York City, the Long Island boroughs of Queens and Kings Counties are sprayed by Anvil 10 + 10 (as of September 2022). Despite the assertion by local governments that these pesticides pose "no significant risks to human health," the public must be warned when and where spraying is to take place, and they are encouraged to stay indoors and close windows and vents during and for a time after the spraying, remove clothes and toys from outside before the spraying, and wash any exposed skin.[35] All these precautions seem to contradict their assertions that the chemical spraying is safe for humans. From a public health viewpoint, the rationale for spraying is based on weighing the risks to human health from spraying versus the risks to humans from West Nile virus. West Nile virus can kill, but the mortality rate is low. Between 1999 and 2021, there were 55,443 cases nationwide, with 2,683 deaths, or an average of 5 percent.[36] Most develop "mild, flu-like" symptoms, but less than 1 percent develop "severe neuroinvasive disease," such as meningitis and encephalitis, which, if it does not kill, will disable the victims.[37] The health effects of Anvil, a synthetic pesticide used by New York City, have been shown in studies that revealed that in large doses its central ingredient, Sumithrin, may affect the central nervous system and disrupt the endocrine system, acting like estrogen in promoting the growth of cancerous tumors.[38] Methoprene, in contrast, does not show estrogenic effects, nor does it promote cancer. All well and good for us—but what about other animals? What about the marsh ecosystem and its inhabitants? Weis and Butler state in their 2009 book that there are few known toxic effects on nontarget species, but they express concern about the potential harm to crustaceans. The National Pesticide Information Center went further in its 2012 paper, stating that methoprene is toxic to fish, in some species highly toxic, moderately toxic to crustaceans, and highly toxic to freshwater invertebrates, accumulating in tissues.[39] Sound like DDT? What happens when you get to the top of the food chain, when birds eat the crustaceans, fish, and invertebrates?

I always return to Carson's *Silent Spring*, that touchstone environmental work, where she made the eloquent case that it is not about just one chemical but the buildup of the myriad chemicals we are exposed to in our lifetimes, or in a particular place we frequent, the accumulation in our tissues, the unknown synergistic effects of multiple toxic chemicals wreaking havoc within the cellular environment of our bodies. Writing in 1962, she noted that over two hundred chemicals had been created since the mid-1940s to kill animals and plants deemed "pests": "Can anyone believe it is possible to lay down such a barrage of poisons on the surface of the earth without making it unfit for all life? They should not be called 'insecticides,' but 'biocides.'"[40]

THE REMAKING OF THE SALT MARSHES

On a warm spring day, I meander around the Salt Marsh Nature Center in Marine Park, following the well-maintained walkway. Crossing the green painted steel bridge over the creek, I look out to the pilings that indicate where Gerritsen's mill once stood. Looking beneath the bridge, I see ribbed mussels anchored into the mud at the foot of marsh grasses—a sign of a healthy creek. The area is fenced off to protect it from those who would trample or trash it. Still, discarded plastic bottles and aluminum cans pollute it, though they will be cleaned up by vigilant volunteers. Out on the pilings, double-crested cormorants literally hang out, drying their wings. A great egret wades in the shallows and a yellow-crowned night-heron forages in the grasses. My eye follows the creek as it winds toward Jamaica Bay; in the distance, the Marine Park Bridge is visible through the haze. Nearby, at the creek's edge, a male osprey stands sentinel on a post, guarding his mate as she sits on the nesting platform, incubating eggs. Male red-winged blackbirds chortle noisily in the reeds and flash their scarlet epaulets, proclaiming their territory. I think I hear a clapper rail in the grasses. Following the walkway as it curves around the marsh, I come to a large puddle, where a spotted sandpiper forages by itself, reflected in the pollen-dusted water, bobbing its tail. I hear the unmistakable song of a prairie warbler, rising in a crescendo, a hopeful music. Perhaps he will stay and breed here. But the music is interrupted by the roar of a jet overhead, flying low, as it takes off from Kennedy Airport. I photograph it as it looms, heavy-bellied, over the marsh—a reminder of the extensive development that has transformed this region since the last century.

In its natural state, this marsh was part of an extensive wetland system that fringed the Jamaica Bay shore. It is threaded by Gerritsen Creek, a freshwater stream; the portion that flowed north of Avenue U was buried beneath fill and converted into a stormwater drain when Avenue U was constructed in the early 1900s. Across the street from the nature center is the Marine Park ballfield and parking lot, once the site of Ryders Pond. Here, on higher ground, stood an ancient Indian village—the largest in Brooklyn—that was at least six thousand years old when the Europeans arrived. When they laid out Avenue U, workers uncovered a dozen or so graves covered by oyster shells. Archaeologists who excavated the area after the turn of the twentieth century found hundreds of spear points, arrowheads, and potsherds—and significantly, objects that reflected European contact: metal arrowheads, spoons, and broken glass from rum bottles.[41]

Long before European contact and for a little time after, the original inhabitants, known to the Europeans as Canarsee, exploited the wetland's abundant food sources: they set up weirs at the mouths of tidal creeks to trap anadromous fish like shad on their spring runs, gathered shellfish from mudflats and shallow waters, netted or shot waterfowl with their arrows, and

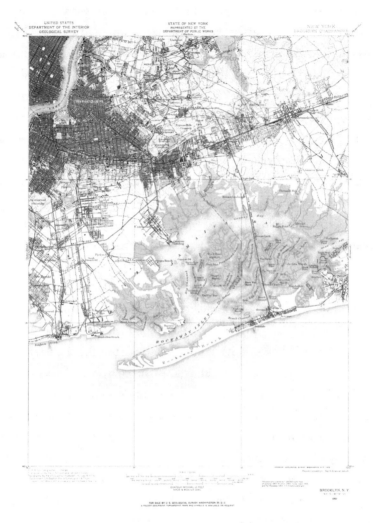

Figure 4.5. Topographical map of Brooklyn, based on 1897 survey. The map shows Jamaica Bay, its then-extensive marsh islands, Idlewild before the airport was built, the Rockaways, and the eastern portion of Coney Island. Marine Park and the Belt Parkway did not yet exist. Courtesy of United States Geological Survey, USGS Historical Quadrangle Scanning Project, 2023.

took deer and other game animals in the maritime grasslands. Once they adopted farming, they raised crops of maize, beans, and squash. Quahog clamshells found along the creeks also provided a source of wampum, the currency used to trade with the Europeans. Ryders Pond was fenced off as a Canarsee reserve in 1665, but by 1684, the colonists had bartered with the Indians—represented by Annenges, Arrenopeah, and Mamekto—to transfer the tract called Makeopac, including Ryders Pond, to the town of Gravesend. One of the first Europeans to settle here was Hugh Gerritsen, who got a land grant from the Dutch West India Company in 1645. He built a tide-water gristmill and dam in 1688, which stood until it burned down in 1935. The pilings from the old mill are exposed at low tide. The area was relatively unchanged for centuries, home to farmers and fishermen, remaining rural until the late 1800s.[42]

Today, Marine Park is a densely settled suburb in the heart of Brooklyn, a region of well-kept rowhouses and heavily trafficked tree-lined streets bordered by Kings Plaza, a huge shopping mall on Flatbush Avenue. The park that gave the neighborhood its name is the largest in Brooklyn, spanning 798 acres, including underwater lands. Designated by NYC Parks as one of New York City's "Forever Wild" places, it comprises salt marsh, grassland, and an ecologically unique maritime woodland spanning 531 acres on the banks of Gerritsen Creek. In 2016, a large-scale habitat restoration project was launched by NYC Parks in concert with the Natural Areas Conservancy, the Nature Conservancy, and the Jamaica Bay–Rockaway Parks Conservancy. Volunteers, many of them neighborhood youth, worked under the auspices of the Student Conservation Association to restore the maritime eco-communities of salt marsh, grassland, and forest.[43]

The work that goes on here reflects a growing environmental awareness of the vital role played by wetlands in the ecosystem. A strong grassroots movement to give people access to our shores and restore or re-create wetlands has gained strength and traction over the last several decades, bringing to a halt the inexorable and previously unquestioned fill-and-build pattern of development. Any plans to harden or fill in the waterfront or wetlands are met with public challenges and subjected to environmental reviews. This change in approach to waterfront development is indicated by a report on

"Gerritsen Creek Ecosystem Restoration" produced by the US Army Corps of Engineers in 2003. The engineers recognized the profound disturbance of the ecosystem caused by human activities in the Jamaica Bay watershed, particularly dredging, filling, sanitary landfill, and coastal hardening. These activities had "severely degraded" the coastal estuary and disturbed and fragmented critical habitats, creating "a significant disruption to the area's entire inter-connected coastal ecology."[44] Their plan was to restore sixty-seven acres of maritime grasslands and tidal wetlands. They acknowledged this was a mere "fraction" of what once existed, but their project would be part of a string of restoration projects on Jamaica Bay.

On July 20, 2005, Mayor Michael Bloomberg signed a law (LL 71) requiring the New York City Department of Environmental Protection to devise a comprehensive watershed protection plan for Jamaica Bay.[45] As part of Bloomberg's PlaNYC, the city published a document in May 2012 outlining its "wetlands strategy." The authors of the document estimated that the wetlands of New York City—most extensive in Jamaica Bay, the shores of Staten Island, and around Long Island Sound—covered between 5,600 and 10,000 acres, representing a decline of 85 percent of the city's coastal wetlands over the course of the twentieth century. Their specific goal, worked out with state and federal agencies, was "to restore or create over 146 acres of wetlands." The goal was based on the principle of "no net loss of wetlands," which accords with federal guidelines established in the 1980s. But they went beyond the stated quantitative target "to improve the quality of the city's remaining wetlands and maximize their ecological functions to the greatest extent possible."[46] To that end, NYC Parks was restoring White Island, in Jamaica Bay, "through shoreline stabilization, invasive species removal, and plantings of marsh grasses." They had already placed 150,000 cubic feet of clean sand on this island, and at Gerritsen Creek they had restored twenty-two acres of wetland and coastal grassland.[47]

These are modest goals, of course—whether it is even feasible to expand or recover wetlands to precolonial or even pre-twentieth-century levels, given the extent of coastal development, is nowhere considered, except in the statement of the obvious: "Urbanization has contributed to the drastic decline in New York City wetlands from pre-colonial times." They elaborate: "The dredging of channels and the construction of bulkheads, pierheads, and hardened shorelines have significantly altered tidal wetlands, shoreline, sub-surface and aquatic habitats, and hydrology. Today, the city's high marsh areas and accessible low marshes are either completely filled or confined to narrow strips in the landscape. The upland edges have been filled and hard-ened for urban development."[48] The target goal of "no net loss" implies that coastal development will continue but will be "balanced" by wetlands pro-tection and creation. In other words, development projects that destroy wet-lands must be offset by creating or restoring wetlands elsewhere in the region. What this report does signify is, in its authors' own words, "a shift in thinking over the past twenty years," one that "has led to an increasing recognition of the importance of regional planning for habitat protection and restoration." Simply put, the flow of water and migrations of species recog-nize no municipal and state boundaries—and to protect these natural resources, regional cooperation is a necessity.[49]

Jamaica Bay and Long Island Sound are part of Long Island, yet New York City's wetlands plan extends only to their municipal borders. The Long Island Sound Study, a coalition of federal, state, and local stakeholders that has been active in restoring the health of the sound since 1984, came out with its wet-lands plan in 2015, enlarging the goals to include twelve coastal habitats, from tidal wetlands and eelgrass and shellfish beds to coastal forests, grass-lands, and river corridors. Of tidal wetlands, their goal was to restore 515 acres by 2035, adding to the 985 acres restored since 1998. Among their priority sites were Alley Creek and Little Neck Bay, both part of Queens—therefore indicating regional cooperation. Volunteers removed invasive species; replaced dirty fill with clean fill; planted species native to coastal forest, tidal wetland, grassland, and riparian corridor habitats; and incor-porated green infrastructure.[50] By 2019, they had completed restoration of 410 acres of coastal habitats, including salt marshes, along Long Island Sound.[51] The coalition's revised goal, as stated in its 2022 work plan, is to restore 1,000 acres by 2035.[52]

The Long Island Sound Study recognized that habitat restoration alone will not save the sound; the problem of pollution had to be addressed head-on. Healthy wetlands depend on clean waters. A primary source of pollution is nitrogen runoff from combined sewer and stormwater overflows (CSOs). In 2011, the New York City Department of Environmental Protection built a new CSO retention facility in Bayside, Queens, which collects five million gallons of CSOs during rain events that would otherwise discharge into Alley Creek and Little Neck Bay, halving the CSOs from about 246 million gallons to 112 million gallons a year. The year before (2010), the department had restored sixteen acres of tidal wetlands and native coastal grasslands to further absorb stormwater runoff and improve tidal flushing. In 2019, it restored another 1.9 acres.[53]

The authors of the 2015 Long Island Sound Study plan acknowledged outright that we cannot return "to a pristine past," but we can restore the Long Island Sound's ecosystems to a state of health and abundance, an "'Urban Sea' . . . where humans can enjoy both a healthy environment and a thriving economy." The connection the authors drew between a thriving environment and economy went further than the language of the 2012 PlaNYC report in that it did not try to "balance" development goals against eco-restoration goals but instead asserted that "the health of the Sound and the waters that drain into it is inextricably tied to the health of an economy that supports the people living in the watershed."[54] Ecology and economy—as indicated by their shared linguistic root, eco- (ancient Greek, oikos, meaning "house" or "household")—are integrally connected. As economy involves the management of one's household finances, ecology implies not merely a scientific understanding of natural systems but management of ecosystems. The human hand plays an essential role in both. But unlike an economy in a free-market world, where the "invisible hand" regulates the system, ecosystems, once damaged or unbalanced, cannot restore or rebalance themselves.

CHAPTER 5

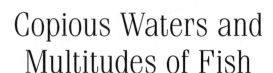

Copious Waters and Multitudes of Fish

The river of ice begins its slow retreat. As the last glacier melts back, it releases torrents of meltwater ferrying tons of silt and gravel across the outwash plain. Fresh water flows into glacially carved channels and ancient river valleys. Where chunks of ice have broken off and melted in outwash, myriad ponds fill with water. Huge lakes rise behind morainal dams until they breach the moraines and release their pent-up waters to the sea. The permafrost thaws and the rains fall, soaking into the porous ground, percolating down into underground reservoirs, century after century. Springs bubble up from the aquifers, welling up through gravel and sand, replenishing ponds and feeding rivers and streams with pure filtered water.

COPIOUS WATERS

On a somewhat sultry day in mid-June, Joe and I drive the near-empty back-roads of the Peconic River headwaters region, where flat pinelands are interspersed with fields of grass in a patchwork. We're exploring Calverton Ponds, a 350-acre preserve that contains a rare coastal plain ponds complex. We pull into a small parking lot and walk a short trail toward the Prestons Pond, passing a gnarled Atlantic white cedar tree, a relic of what may have been an ancient stand. The little pond shimmers like a blue jewel set against a green expanse of freshwater wetland. At our approach, two painted turtles basking on a log eye us warily, the larger of the pair lifting his head to reveal his green-and-black-striped neck and yellow plastron, beautifully

Figure 5.1. A painted turtle lifts his head at Prestons Pond in the Peconic River headwaters region. Photo by author.

reflected in the still water. He slowly turns and raises his front leg, his extended claws lightly touching the other's carapace in a protective gesture. A green frog rests half-submerged in the water, his round golden eyes protruding, watchful for a passing insect that might be his meal. Dragonflies and damselflies dart and hover, flashing their iridescent colors in the sunlight. One perches on a waterlily. We linger awhile in the cool of an overhanging oak tree, appreciating just how special this place is.

After the last glacier receded from Long Island some eighteen thousand years ago, its meltwaters formed chains of hydrologically connected ponds south of the recessional moraines. The ponds of the Calverton Ponds Preserve in the Central Pine Barrens and the so-called Paternoster of the Long Pond Greenbelt on the South Fork are two beautiful examples. Their water levels fluctuate season to season and year to year, mirroring the rise and fall of the water table and rates of precipitation, drying up completely in times of drought. Some are merely vernal pools, magically filling with water in spring—just in time for spring peepers and other frogs to begin their mating rituals. The plants growing on these pond shores are adapted to cyclical fluctuations in water levels. During dry periods, seeds of annual herbaceous plants can germinate and grow in the exposed substrate; during wet periods, invasive woody species are drowned and kept at bay. The zones of shoreline vegetation range from sedges, grasses, and herbs on the upper shore to floating aquatic plants like bladderworts in the permanently flooded zone.[1]

Coastal plain ponds dot the Atlantic Coastal Plain in both glaciated and nonglaciated lowlands, but the outwash plain of Long Island harbors rare pond shore communities of plants and animals—more than three dozen species considered rare in New York State.[2] These include plants such as the slender blue flag, which emerges in June with its stunning purple flowers, and two fish species, the colorful and diminutive banded sunfish and equally small swamp darter, all listed as threatened in New York.[3] Female American eels, a globally endangered species, mature in the ponds before eventually making their way back to the ocean to breed. Long Island is the only breeding territory in New York of the regionally endangered tiger salamander, and the coastal plain ponds are its primary habitat. The salamander is extremely loyal to its natal waters and will return year after year to the same pool, whether a pond or mudhole. The adults emerge from their underground burrows on a rainy night in early spring to mate.[4] Another regionally rare creature, the spotted turtle, may also be found here; once a common turtle on Long Island, it is now a Species of Special Concern in New York State.[5]

The coastal plains ponds of the Central Pine Barrens, like all of Long Island's freshwater ponds and streams, are fed by springs that are connected to a vast underground aquifer, Long Island's most important source of fresh water. The Magothy Aquifer supplies all of Nassau County and half of Suffolk County with potable water—water stored in a natural underground reservoir that dates to the Cretaceous geological era, a layered sand-and-clay formation extending from Long Island to New Jersey and Maryland. Beneath the Magothy, separated by a clay layer, lies an even deeper and older aquifer, the Lloyd Aquifer, which plunges eighteen feet below ground and overlies bedrock. Its water is over five thousand years old. To preserve this precious resource, the state placed the Lloyd Aquifer under moratorium.[6] That leaves the Magothy as the major source of Long Island's water, supplemented by the Pleistocene-era Upper Glacial Aquifer; only Kings and Queens Counties draw from the upstate reservoirs that supply New York City. According to the US Geological Survey, based on a study of water use on Long Island between 2005 and 2010, around 500 million gallons a day on average are drawn from the aquifers, 75 percent coming from the Magothy. That compares with an average daily recharge of 1,500 million gallons from different sources, principally precipitation.[7]

Long Island seemingly has no shortage of the groundwater its people depend on for their water supply, but its long-term viability is threatened by a multitude of factors, from saltwater intrusion to toxins to overbuilding. As the sea level rises, the water table also rises, which allows for saltwater intrusion farther inland and up into the groundwater. An increasing population strains the water infrastructure, as wells pump harder to meet growing demand for fresh water, potentially depleting more water than can be recharged. Moreover, large-scale sewer plants siphon away potential recharge water to flush treated effluents into the bays. Development that paves over naturally porous surfaces, replacing fields and marshes with hard surfaces, does not allow rainwater to seep down into the water table and recharge it. What seeps into the ground may be contaminated by agricultural and industrial toxins. Historical data collected by the US Geological Survey, Suffolk County Health Department, and Suffolk County Water Authority document 117 pesticide-related chemicals detected in Long Island's drinking water aquifer system. These chemicals include herbicides and fungicides as well as pesticides applied on farms, lawns, gardens, golf courses, and parks. Superfund sites dot Long Island, the legacy of defunct aerospace industries that left toxic chemicals that still persist in the soil, infiltrating into the groundwater. Protecting and preserving the lands that lie above the aquifers is clearly essential; the protection given the core Pine Barrens region has unquestionably kept the Magothy Aquifer pure (see chapter 7, "Falling Trees").[8]

———

I reach the kettle lake by car, staying on the backroads when I can. To best experience the kame-and-kettle terrain of Long Island's glacial landscape, I take the old Vanderbilt Motor Parkway, or County Road 67, which climbs the Ronkonkoma Moraine. This portion of the historic parkway, from Nichols Road to Lake Ronkonkoma, was completed in 1911, the last segment of a forty-five-mile-long motor parkway built by William Kissam Vanderbilt expressly for cars when the North Shore was still predominantly rural and great estates sprawled along the fabled Gold Coast, the setting for *The Great Gatsby*. The highway now runs through modest suburban neighborhoods, curving and dipping as it ascends the moraine.

Ronkonkoma Lake is known as a water-table lake; it's not actually at the top of the moraine (that would be a perched lake) but in a kind of basin, formed when a block of ice buried in till melted. Seen in a satellite photo, Ronkonkoma Lake appears as a roundish blue blob, somewhat broader at one end than the other—a perfect example of a kettle pond. At ground level (or water level), I feel I am looking across the water through a fish-eye lens. Sixty-five feet at its deepest and two miles in circumference, the lake is fed by underwater streams, its level rising and falling irregularly. According to local legend, it's a bottomless lake with an unfathomed hole at its center that connects in a subterranean tunnel to Long Island Sound or to hell, depending on who tells the tale. No doubt these myths are fed by annual drownings of unwary swimmers who go out of their depth, so to speak. I find the place vaguely depressing, knowing perhaps too much—that bacteria levels are so high swimming is often banned, that oxygen levels are so low that fishing at depths greater than fifteen feet is unproductive, no doubt from nitrogen runoff from the surrounding communities. Yet this lake is a prime fishing ground, populated by large-mouth bass, small-mouth bass, yellow perch, white perch, and walleye. Its name is of Algonquian origin, probably meaning "boundary fishing place." In precolonial times it was home to four Algonquian groups—the Setaukets, Nissequogues, Unkachogues, and Sekatogues—who shared its shores and the bounty of its waters.[9]

Leaving the lake, I take Vanderbilt Motor Parkway back to Nichols Road, descending the south slope of the Ronkonkoma Moraine. The intersection of Vanderbilt Motor Parkway and Nichols Road roughly marks the headwaters of the Connetquot River, now buried beneath the roadways. This river originates in the south slope of the moraine around sixty feet above sea level and meanders south across the outwash plain to Nicoll Bay. On the moraine's north slope at the same elevation, the Nissequogue River rises and flows north to Smithtown Bay.[10]

———

Seeking the headwaters of the Nissequogue—and not incidentally to chase the elusive red-headed woodpecker birders had reported in Blydenburgh County Park—Joe and I set out to explore. It's a week after a blizzard dumped more than two feet of snow on Long Island, and days of extraordinarily warm temperatures have melted much of the snow, leaving the ground slushy and muddy. Hardly anyone is here, except for an occasional dog walker. We gingerly make our way down the wooden steps and along the edges of Blydenburgh Pond to the boarded-up millhouse, to scan for wintering ducks. Despite the thaw, a skim of ice still coats the surface, inviting two daredevil boys to test the edge, but the slushiness keeps them back. The old dam sluices the pond waters into a small waterfall, which tumbles into a slow-moving stream where mallard ducks collect in eddies, sometimes upending themselves to feed in the cold water. The pond itself is empty of bird life except in a far ice-free corner, where Canada geese gather with gulls and a few ducks—too far away for us to identify them. In the shrubs along the pond edge a ruby-crowned kinglet flits. In the trees, a hairy woodpecker gives his sharp squeaky call as he hitches up a trunk, and an American robin surveys the lake, his orange breast brilliant against the blue of sky. The red-headed woodpecker finally shows up, calling and flying from one tree to another, then landing on a horizontal branch; he's a juvenile just beginning to acquire adult plumage, his red feathers catching the light. In time he will acquire a fully red head and the black-and-white plumage that has earned the woodpecker the nickname "flying checkerboard." He's a special find, a species that has sharply declined (down 70 percent from 1966 to 2014) because of loss of forest habitat and traditional food sources. Red-headed woodpeckers, like all woodpeckers, are cavity-nesting birds that need snags and old trees for nesting holes. At Blydenburgh, he was in a favored habitat of riparian deciduous woodland.[11]

Blydenburgh County Park is located in the headwaters of the Nissequogue River. More than eight miles long, the Nissequogue flows through lands that have largely been preserved from development—half the river corridor and most of the wetlands are parklands. The park is a preserve of 627 acres where the mill and dam (circa 1798), miller's house (1802), farm-house (1820), and farm cottage (1860) that once belonged to the Blyden-burgh estate still stand, meriting the site a listing on the National Register of Historic Places. Connected to Blydenburgh Park is another undeveloped tract of 543 acres, Caleb Smith State Park Preserve, created in 1963. Together, the two parks form 1,170 contiguous acres of riparian woodland and fresh-water marsh.

Caleb Smith Park got its name from the original landowners, the Smith family, whose roots in the region went back to the mid-1600s, when Rich-ard "Bull" Smythe founded Smithtown (just north of Hauppauge) in 1663 on land purchased from Lion Gardiner, who had in turn been gifted the land by the Montaukett sachem Wyandanch. Richard's grandson Daniel and great-grandson Caleb built a house on the estate in 1758, which still stands in the park, albeit extensively altered through subsequent generations. In 1798, Caleb Smith II, Joshua Smith II, and Isaac Blydenburgh, cousins by marriage, together built a dam and mill complex, jointly operating it until the son and namesake of Caleb Smith sold it to the two sons of Isaac Blyden-burgh. Besides powering the gristmill, the twelve-foot-high dam backed up the river into its three tributaries, creating a broad, shallow reservoir that in time became a renowned trout-fishing pond. One hundred acres of forest had to be cut down to create the pond, earning it the sobriquet "Stump Pond" from the leftover stumps that surprised the unwary fisherman who waded out into the shallows casting for trout. Apparently the pond was so popular it became nearly depleted of trout by the late 1830s, prompting the owner to limit catches to ten fish per person on a given day, with only three days allowed to any fishing party. In 1888, the Blydenburghs sold the estate to the Brooklyn Gun Club (renamed the Wyandanch Club in 1893 to honor the Montaukett who originally conveyed the land to Lion Gardiner). They built a clubhouse and turned their domain into a private resort for their wealthy members, a trend that typified the privatization of coveted fishing and hunt-ing grounds throughout Long Island. It proved to be a blessing in disguise, preserving riparian corridors from suburban development and the trashing of the commons.[12]

The Nissequogue River is wilder in some of its stretches than any other river on Long Island. The late sportswriter and angler Nick Karas devoted an entire chapter to Long Island's trout streams in his classic book on brook trout. Of the Nissequogue he wrote, "In stark contrast [to the Connetquot], the Nissequogue River has in places ill-defined banks that lens into adjacent spring-fed swamps; in others its waters are forced to rush wildly, squeezed between banks of glacially sorted gravel. The river ranges greatly in character, from broad outflows of ankle-deep water, to alternate rushes of fast water, to deep, dark, sullen pools."[13] Karas attributed its preserved character to the fact that colonial settlers dammed portions of the headwaters to power their grist mills, creating trout ponds as a bonus, while leaving the rest of the river alone. Hikers on the Long Island Greenbelt Trail can trace the Nissequogue from its headwaters to its mouth, beginning at Blydenburgh County Park and ending at Sunken Meadow State Park on Long Island Sound, where 1,287 acres at the river's mouth are preserved from development.[14] One could argue that the park itself, built by Robert Moses in his inimitable style, is itself a development, replacing sand dunes and marshes with parking lots and ball fields. Still, there are unspoiled dunes, forested bluffs, a tidal creek, and marshes.

On a Thanksgiving weekend in 2015, Joe and I visit Sunken Meadow, joining joggers and other walkers on the boardwalk. The weather's so warm everyone is shedding their jackets, and we do the same. We walk to the boardwalk's west end, where I take photos of the Harbor Hill Moraine, which rises as a wooded bluff above silvery dunes and a crystalline beach. Leaving the boardwalk, we cross the parking lot and walk along the banks of Sunken Meadow Creek, which meanders between a line of dunes and the bluff before joining the Nissequogue River at its mouth. Upstream by the footbridge, buffleheads dive into the water and resurface; downstream, black ducks emerge from tall marsh grasses, and a great egret stalks prey along the river's edges. We walk around the curving beach to the river's wide mouth, where fresh water pouring into Long Island Sound paints a light blue swath against the darker blue of the saltwater bay.

The Nissequogue, Connetquot, Peconic, and Carmans are Long Island's four major rivers. More appropriately classified as streams, they are not great roaring rivers fed by mountain snowmelt and myriad tributaries, not rivers

Figure 5.2. The mouth of the Nissequogue River at Sunken Meadow State Park. Photo by author.

of tumbling falls and swift rapids, but mostly quiet, meandering rivers fed by groundwater and springs. They all have their origins in the last glacial retreat, but the Peconic is the only river on Long Island to flow west to east.[15] Classified in *Ecological Communities of New York State* (2014) as "coastal plain streams," the rivers are "slow-moving often darkly stained," characterized by "abundant submerged vegetation"—pondweed, waterweed, bladderwort, and duckweed—and inhabited by freshwater fish such as redfin pickerel, pumpkinseed, and the aforementioned swamp darter and banded sunfish.[16]

Winding twelve miles from its headwaters to its mouth, the Peconic is the longest river on Long Island.[17] It originates in the heart of the Central Long Island Pine Barrens near Ridge; flows eastward to Riverhead, where it becomes estuarial; and meanders through an eight-hundred-acre wetland before emptying into Flanders Bay. The headwater region, still relatively undeveloped, harbors rare natural communities including the Atlantic Coastal Plain ponds, Atlantic white cedar swamps (the largest occurring in Cranberry Bog State Park), and the Long Island Pine Barrens. In 1987, New York State designated two portions of the Peconic "scenic" and "recreational" under the National Wild, Scenic and Recreational Rivers Act of 1973, although a ruling in 2010 by New York State Department of Environmental Conservation (NYSDEC) commissioner Alexander Grannis allowed development in the town of Riverhead on portions designated within the "recreational" segment as "communities," where development already existed at the time of its designation as a scenic and recreational river.[18]

From its colonial farming days through its industrialization in the mid-1800s, the Peconic River at its mouth has long been developed. In its farming days (and farming, like fishing, would continue even through industrialization and postindustrial suburbanization), the Peconic was mined for bog iron, a valuable commodity before the iron seams of Pennsylvania were discovered in the mid-1800s. Bog iron was valued because it was rust resistant and heavy, considered essential to the maritime industry. It was smelted to make hollowware—pots and pans and other domestic goods—as well as farm implements. Iron was dug from the river sediments with tongs and transported by boat along the river to an iron smelter, or "bloomary," essentially a furnace located in heavy pine woodland, where trees could be cut to feed the furnace. In the late 1700s, a smelter was located in Patchogue and an ironworks in Riverhead.[19] By the mid-1800s, there was a soap factory, a fertilizer works, a woolen mill, and wood molding and planing mills located in Riverhead. All these industries drew their power from the Peconic, beginning with the first dam, built in 1659 to power a sawmill.[20]

The least developed portion of the Peconic is in its upper reaches, though even here the river was dammed in the mid-1700s to create cranberry bogs.[21] Besides hosting rare plant and animal communities such as those found in the coastal plain ponds, the protected grasslands, wetlands, and woodlands associated with the river in its upper reaches host breeding birds that include the grasshopper sparrow, as well as wintering species such as the short-eared owl, once common birds now "in steep decline."[22] In 2006, New York State designated the Peconic Headwaters a Natural Resources Management Area covering about four thousand acres in the Calverton Ponds region.[23]

Long Island's rivers have historically been renowned for their fishing, particularly brook trout. Nineteenth-century naturalist and avid fly fisherman Henry William Herbert, whose pen name was Frank Forester, waxed poetic, even rapturous, in his descriptions of trout fishing on Long Island: "I am clearly of the opinion that for very early fishing in March and April there is no place on this continent at all comparable to Long Island, where along the south shore they can be taken in numbers almost innumerable, in every pond, stream, and salt creek, until the end of July, when they cease to bite freely."[24] In his book *Frank Forester's Fish and Fishing*, published in 1859, he takes the reader on a journey across Long Island from Williamsburg on the west end, through Jamaica and the Hempstead Plains in its center, and down to the South Shore: "Now we are in the land of Trout streams, baymen, and wild fowl. The rippling dash of falling waters catches our ear, at every half-mile as we roll along, and every here and there, the raised bank on our left hand with its line of stunted willows bent landward by the strong sea-breeze, the sluice-gate, and the little bridge, with the clear stream rushing seaward under it, tell us that we are passing a Trout pond."[25] Of all the trout fishing sites on the South Shore, the Connetquot and Carmans were, by sound reputation, the two best. Several decades before, in 1837, a reporter for the *Spirit of the Times* described "the never-to-be-sufficiently praised Connetquot Hotel opposite Fire Island, of Liff Snedeker's. . . . You can almost throw a fly from his door into his pond, and a famous one it is."[26] The anonymous writer noted that 3,300 trout were reportedly taken the season before, and 2,000 during the season of his visit.

Liff Snedecor's (a spelling variant) Connetquot Hotel was located near Oakdale right on the stagecoach route between Manhattan and Montauk, fronting the trout-filled river. Since 1825, the inn had hosted both sports fishermen and deer hunters on its extensive grounds. When Herbert visited Snedecor's, fishermen were limited to a dozen fish per person per day in the pond, where they were allowed to fish from their boats, although no limit was placed on fish caught by fly-fishing along the banks of the stream.[27] With fish stocks dwindling, wealthy sports fishermen anxious to keep their favorite fishing holes well stocked formed a consortium and eventually bought out the Snedecor lands in 1866. They became the South Side Sportsmen's Club, whose founding members included a number of wealthy Manhattan men—Samuel Barlow, Andrew Carnegie, Lorenzo Delmonico, August Belmont, James Gordon Bennet Jr., Abram Hewitt, Oakey Hall, George M. Robeson (Bureau of Fisheries), and George Bird Grinnell. They built the first

Figure 5.3. Kayakers on the Carmans River at Wertheim National Wildlife Refuge. Photo by author.

fish hatchery on the Connetquot in 1868, which was not successful because the water was too warm for brook trout. The club's third try, a hatchery built on the main river in 1897, proved a success, hatching brown, rainbow, and brook trout.[28] In 1973, after the club sold the land to New York State, the property became Connetquot River State Park, designated in 1987 as a wilderness preserve. The privatization of the lands as a hunting and fishing preserve for a century ensured that the riverfront and its adjacent forest were not developed, even as suburbs pressed against it.[29] Today, there are stretches of the river that offer the fly fisherman an experience of wild solitude and fine trout fishing.

The Carmans River was once called the West Connecticut (and the Connetquot the East Connecticut), its name derived from a Munsee word for a river that is tidal in its lower stretches. The river rises as a stream in Middle Island, within Cathedral Pines County Park, and flows southward for ten miles through pitch pine–oak woodlands and red maple swamps, emptying into the Great South Bay. Just below Sunrise Highway on the South Shore, the river becomes tidal in its last two miles. The best place to fish in the heyday of trout fishing, the early to mid-1800s, was in its tidal waters at what was called the "crossing-over place," a reference to the highway crossing (then South Country Road, now Montauk Highway). A mill and dam complex was built in the mid-1700s just above the crossing-over place, and it was here, around 1821, that Sam Carman Jr. turned his father's house into an inn. Sam Carman's became famous among anglers for its trout fishing. Herbert described it as "very decidedly the best Trout river on Long Island": "In Carman's River the largest fish in America are, I think it will be allowed, mostly caught, running often quite up to five pounds weight, and I fully believe that if it were fished patiently and resolutely, especially at gray twilight, or in the shimmering moon-shine quite down to the bay, through the salt meadows, with a small Trout on good spinning-tackle with three swivels, or with a very large gaudy fly, sunk by means of a shot to several inches below the surface, fish might be taken of seven or eight pounds weight."[30] More commonly, fish of two pounds were taken, less often up to four pounds, but the right timing and technique might snag a larger fish. Herbert described the best way to fish this river:

> The course of Carman's stream lies chiefly through open salt meadows, and the banks are entirely destitute of covert, so that very careful and delicate fishing is necessary in order to fill a basket. Even with ground bait it is desirable to keep completely out of sight, walking as far from the bank as possible, and to avoid jarring the water, so wary and shy are the larger fish. It is also advisable to fish downwind. Trolling is very successful in this water, the same precautions being taken, and the bait-fish dropped as lightly on the surface, as if it were a fly, as to create neither splash nor sound.[31]

Brook trout are also known as sea trout—or salters, if they are taken in tidal waters—and these were the trout taken in both the Connetquot and Carmans Rivers. Brook trout are euryhaline fish, equally at home in fresh and salt waters, swimming upstream in fall to spawn. They are not true trout but rather North American charr, a species that thrives in cold water and shuns warm water (above 70 degrees Fahrenheit). They also shun stagnant water and will seek fresh running streams (but not rapids) with gravelly beds

Figure 5.4. *The American Brook Trout* (Salvelinus fontinalis), artist J. L. Petrie, 1898. General Research Division, New York Public Library. "The American Brook Trout, Salvelinus fontinalis," New York Public Library Digital Collections. https://digitalcollections.nypl.org/items/510d47da-68e2-a3d9-e040 -e00a18064a99.

to spawn. The spring-fed rivers of Long Island are ideal, keeping cool even at the height of summer—though climate change is now affecting temperatures (see the discussion later in this chapter). The brook trout is Long Island's only native trout, and its abundance in Long Island's waters was legendary. As noted by Samuel Latham Mitchill in his classic *Fishes of New York* (1815 edition), "The lively streams descending north and south from their sources on Long-Island, exactly suit the constitution of this fish."[32] By the time Tarleton Bean published his *Fishes of Long Island* in 1902, Bean found that "few of the natural brook trout streams of Long Island now furnish good trout fishing, except those which have been restocked."[33]

Karas ascribed the historical decline of wild brook trout less to overfishing than to deforestation. Stripping the watersheds of forest cover and managing urban land use poorly have caused the river waters to warm to temperatures above what brook trout can tolerate. "Brook trout have been likened to canaries in mines to detect deteriorating air quality. When brook trout disappear from a stream it's a sign that water quality has deteriorated and the stream is in trouble."[34] Since Karas published his book in 1997, global warming has certainly influenced water temperatures. John Waldman, in *Running Silver* (2013), writes that global warming has "pushed out" native brook trout from its lowland waters, although they persist at higher elevations. Other factors have contributed to their decline, including the introduction of nonnative trout, dams that block upstream passages, landfill, and conversion of headwater regions to create cranberry bogs (Waldman mentions Cape Cod as an example, but this also occurred in the headwaters of the Peconic).[35] But he also holds out hope that due to the "ecologically plastic" nature of these fish, which have adapted to glacial and postglacial eras by moving into saltwater habitats, for example, our native brook trout will persist, even though they move northward from our region.

The decline of brook trout, already obvious to anglers in the mid-nineteenth century, motivated wealthy New York enthusiasts to privatize the best fishing grounds. Daniel Webster, who had reportedly caught a fourteen-and-a-half-pound brook trout in the Carmans pond in 1827, paid Carman an annual rent for exclusive rights to a portion of the river above the dam, which he shared with friends Philip Hone, John and Edward Stevens, Walter Brown, and Martin Van Buren. Many of the same men who purchased Liff Snedecor's bought out Sam Carman. In 1858, August Belmont organized the Suffolk Club, whose members included John Van Buren (Martin's son), Peleg Hall, W. Butler Duncan, Watt Sherman, and Joseph Grafton. These men bought out all twenty owners of riverfront lands, fifteen hundred acres in all, leaving Sam Carman the house.[36] They built a clubhouse, established a private preserve, and added a hatchery. Unlike the South Side Sportsmen's Club, which had one hundred members, this more exclusive club was limited to fifteen members. One of the guests was Theodore Roosevelt, who visited on May 14, 1915, and caught seven trout, releasing one.[37] The club was dissolved in 1923, when Anson W. Hard and his wife, Florence, bought out his fellow club members' shares, adding seven hundred acres to the original six hundred for use as a private preserve. His son and heir Kenneth leased out a portion of the property to a fishing club in 1936, and in 1950 he developed it as a commercial preserve for hunters and fishermen (the Suffolk Lodge game preserve). As in the case of the Connetquot club, rising taxes and costs forced him to sell the property to the county in 1962. The county turned the land into Southaven County Park in 1964, now a park of 1,356 acres.

Over the decades, purchases of lands along the Carmans River corridor have helped preserve it from development. The mouth of the river became part of the Wertheim National Wildlife Refuge when Maurice Wertheim gifted 1,600 acres to "the people of America" in 1947; the refuge now covers 2,550 acres, offering significant protection to the river's watershed and estuary. The NYSDEC has managed the waters since 1964. In 1977, largely as a result of the advocacy efforts of naturalist Dennis Puleston, the state designated the river a Wild, Scenic, and Recreational River and a Significant Coastal Fish and Wildlife Habitat, designations that have helped keep the waters clean.[38] The Carmans holds an original wild population of native brook trout. In 2010 and 2011, the NYSDEC stocked upper portions of the river and its lakes (Upper Lake, Lower Lake, and Hards Lake—all created by dams dating to the mid-1700s) with ten thousand brown trout and rainbow trout, both hatchery species tolerant of warmer water than the native brook trout.[39] It continues to stock the river annually with two to three thousand trout.[40] In addition, it has been making efforts to improve passage of migratory fish that have been blocked by the numerous dams and culverts. In 2008, for example, the state Department of Transportation constructed "an Alaskan steep-pass fish passage" over the dam at Hards Lake just north of Sunrise Highway.[41] The latest fish ladder was completed at Lily Lake Dam in early 2023, described in a National Public Radio news report as "the first unrestrained route for fish in over 260 years."[42] Kevin McAllister of Defend H2O, the advocacy organization that had pushed for the fish ladder, stated that fish ladders not only open up migratory routes but also mitigate the effects of climate change on water temperature. Quite simply, still water behind the dam heats up and flows downstream, negatively affecting brook trout. "Flowing water is cool water," he stated. McAllister envisions a future when such dams would be deconstructed, allowing a freshwater wetland to grow.[43]

According to Martin Van Lith, Brookhaven town historian and chair of the Open Space Council in 2009, the Carmans is the "cleanest" river on Long Island.[44] Of course, "cleanest" is a relative term, simply meaning it is the least polluted. Van Lith made the claim in 2009; in 2013, the Town of Brookhaven undertook a comprehensive study of the river that assessed water quality among other indicators of health and viability. It recommended the river set a short-term "non-degradation" goal to reduce nitrates and a long-term "restoration" goal to recover water quality. The Carmans is fed primarily by groundwater from the Upper Glacial Aquifer, and if chemicals such as nitrates have seeped into the aquifer, they may migrate into the river, though the mechanism is not well understood. Like all the rivers of Long Island, the Carmans has elevated levels of nitrates, though it is hard to determine how much is from stormwater runoff or groundwater. None of the river water is suitable as drinking water, and some portions are off-limits to swimming because of contaminants.[45] And contaminants affect not only us humans but other animals of the river community.

AND MULTITUDES OF FISH

The abundance of fish in colonial North America was legendary, described by one chronicler after another in terms that seem apocryphal if not mythical. Perhaps the most dramatic exhibitions of Edenic plenty were the spring runs of anadromous fish—the striped bass, shad, and river herring that migrated from salt to fresh waters to spawn. The seething spectacle invited John Bunyan–like exaggeration, describing the fish as so thick a man could walk across on their backs. Thomas Morton, for instance, described striped bass in "such multitudes, that I have seene stopped into the river close adjoining to my house with a sand at one tide, so many as will loade a ship of a 100 Tonnes. Other places have greater quantities in so much, as wager have bin layed, that one should not throw a stone in the water but that he should hit a fishe. I my selfe at the turning of the tyde, have scene such multitude passé out of a pound, that it seemed to mee, that one might goe over their backs drishod."[46] William Wood described the striped bass of New England to be as large as four feet in length. "At some tides a man may catch a dozen or twenty of these in three hours," he wrote in 1634. He explained the best method of catching them—by hook and line from spring to fall, and by long seine nets during their upriver spring runs, at which time they could seine two or three thousand in a draught. Wood called the striped bass "one of the best fishes of the country," of which men never tire of eating. The head, with its rich bone marrow, was particularly esteemed, so that they would eat it fresh and salt the rest for winter. [47]

Atlantic striped bass have historically entered the waters surrounding Long Island from New York Harbor to Long Island Sound, running up the Hudson River in spring to spawn above the brackish line, then returning in summer to feed in the bays and harbors. Zoologist James De Kay, cataloging New York fauna in the 1840s, noted that not all striped bass were migratory: "The larger individuals, called Green-heads, never ascend fresh water streams. Along the coast they enter creeks and inlets at night with the flood tide, in order to feed, and return with the ebb. Advantage is taken of this circumstance by stretching a seine across the outlet, when great numbers are taken. As the weather grows colder they penetrate into bays and ponds connected with the sea, where they embed themselves in the mud. Near Sag Harbor I noticed one of these ponds which was a source of great annual profit to the owner."[48] John Waldman states that nonmigratory striped bass inhabit waters south of Virginia, but migratory populations spawn in the Delaware and Hudson Rivers, and in the tributaries of the Chesapeake, their "major spawning ground," according to Waldman. Those found in waters around Long Island are migratory.[49] Tarleton Bean, who cataloged the fish of Long Island in 1902, stated that "it is a permanent resident in Gravesend Bay" and "moderately abundant in Great River [the tidal portion of the Connetquot], where it is reported to occur almost throughout the year."[50] Waldman describes the striper as "the consummate urban species, flourishing in metropolitan harbors such as in Boston, New York, and Baltimore, where it ambushes baitfish prey from behind manmade pilings, or at night at the shadow lines of bridges."[51] The running of striped bass off Montauk Point in fall, as they migrate out of Long Island Sound into Atlantic coastal waters, is legendary among surfcasters, who find their bliss casting off the rocks of Montauk Point. Waldman quotes Long Islander Peter Matthiessen, the late writer and naturalist: "The unseen quarry and mysterious dark water, the pleasure taken in the strong and skillful cast, the sound and smell of sea and weather, the healing solitude, and the suspense, are reward enough for the true sportsman who seeks no profit from the hobby, and surfcasting for striped bass probably claims more fanatics than any other form of saltwater fishing."[52]

To early colonists, for whom the brutal New England winter often meant the starving time, the spring fish runs seemed providential. The alewife's spring appearance in the Taunton River, for example, was described by an early Massachusetts colonist as "a sort of fish appropriated by Divine Providence to Americans and most plentifull afforded to them so that remote towns [far upriver] have barreled y'm up and preserved them all winter for their relief."[53] Commonly known as river herring, alewives arrived in the rivers "in such multitudes," declared William Wood, "as is almost incredible, pressing up in such shallow waters as will scarce permit them to swim, having likewise such longing desire after the fresh water ponds that no beatings with poles or forcive agitations by other devices will cause them to return to the sea till they have cast their spawn."[54]

What Wood recognized, in an almost empathetic way, was the instinctive and powerful urge to migrate and spawn that characterizes the little alewife (and indeed all migratory fish species). Centuries later, in 1959, John Hay memorialized the fish in his book *The Run*: "Fragile they are, and powerful, a wonderful work of which so many are made as to afford them death as well as life."[55] Bean reported young of the year taken in Gravesend Bay, Peconic Bay, Mecox Bay, Shinnecock Bay, and parts of the Great South Bay in the late summer and fall of 1897 and 1898. He found young alewives abundant in the fresh waters of Long Island, particularly in streams emptying into the Great South Bay such as the Swan River.[56] Paul Greenberg, in his book *Four Fish*, paid tribute to herring and other prey fish such as menhaden as "the silver coin of the realm," a reference to their ecological role as keystone species in the marine food web, linking fresh- and saltwater systems and serving as an important prey fish to larger food fish predators.[57]

Shad was another anadromous fish whose spring runs were spectacular in the colonial era and were still impressive in 1770. In April of that year, the *New York Journal* reported "a remarkable number of shad fish" taken at the Verrazano Narrows, on Long Island's west end: "One of the seines, as it was drawn toward the shore, was so filled with fish, that the weight pressed it to the ground, whereby great numbers escaped. A second seine was then thrown out around the first, a third around the second, and a fourth around the third. . . . The number of shad that were taken by the first net was three thousand; by the second, three thousand, by the third, four thousand; and by the fourth, fifteen hundred; in all, eleven thousand five hundred!"[58] In the same shad run, the narrows, Peter Cortelyou (descendant of the first Cortelyous to settle Bay Ridge, or Nyack) trapped an estimated sixteen thousand shad in balloon-like fyke nets, and through the next six spring runs an estimated total of one hundred thousand.[59] The shad crashed in the 1820s, down 96 percent by Cortelyou's reckoning.

The thrashing multitudes of silvery fish on their spring runs in colonial America throw into shadow another fish that was also a vital food source. Long before the European colonists trapped them, the humble American eel was a mainstay of the Algonquians, who smoked them for an oily, nutritious winter food source. They used every part of the eel, including its skin, which could be dried and used like string, and its fat, which was used to waterproof leather, oil the hair, and protect the skin from sun, wind, and insects. In contrast to the anadromous fish that spawn in fresh waters and then migrate to the sea, the catadromous eel spawns in the sea and migrates up rivers and streams before returning to its natal ocean waters. These remarkable creatures spawn in the Sargasso Sea south of the West Indies. The transparent, willow-leaf-shaped larvae, called leptocephali, drift on the Gulf Stream for up to a year until they reach the continental shelf, when they metamorphose into the next phase, glass eels, so named for their lack of pigmentation. As they gradually attain pigment, becoming elvers, they swim into bays, estuaries, and rivers along the western Atlantic coast. Fully pigmented eels are called yellow eels, the most long-lasting phase of their development, when they feed and grow. This phase can take anywhere from three years to over thirty years, with females growing larger and living far longer as a rule than males, likely because of the females' freshwater habitats. Male yellow eels inhabit brackish waters such as estuaries and tidal creeks, whereas females migrate up rivers and into headwater streams. They have been found far upstate from the Adirondacks to the Great Lakes, inhabiting almost any fresh water, from swamps and ponds to springs, streams, and rivers, in shallow waters and deep. They can traverse high falls (although the Niagara Falls stop them) and tolerate high altitudes and extreme cold. In winter, immature eels burrow into muddy or silty water bottoms and stay torpid, while mature eels—the males mature much faster than females—migrate back to their natal waters, traversing thousands of miles to reach the Sargasso Sea to spawn and begin the cycle anew.[60]

When active in spring, immature eels may migrate from fresh to brackish or salt waters to feed, their slimy coating enabling them to slither over dirt or grass. On a spring walk at Long Pond on the South Fork, I found an eel beached up one of the streams. The snakelike fish looked desiccated and appeared dead, until gently prodded with a stick. When it responded, I nudged it back into the stream, where it swam an S-curve until it came to rest beneath oak leaves in the bottom of the shallow stream.

Eels have suffered the same fate as other diadromous fish, experiencing severe declines from their historical huge numbers. According to Waldman, "It's estimated that eels once made up one-fourth of all the fish biomass in rivers of the Eastern Seaboard."[61] But they need unobstructed waters that empty into the Atlantic, and though astonishing in their ability to overcome natural obstructions such as waterfalls in their ascent up rivers and streams, they will be blocked by dams and landfills. Most of the decline seems to have occurred in the last century. Bean reported in 1902 that eels were trapped using thousands of eel pots that were fastened to stakes set in a straight line in the shallow bottom of the bay at Bellport, Long Island, and such practices were widespread along the South Shore. The pots were baited with morsels of horseshoe crab or other favored eel food. In the winter months, when they are torpid and usually burrow into the mud, they were speared. "Myriads" of eels inhabited Long Island's bays and streams in Bean's time. In 2015, the US Fish and Wildlife Service did not list the American eel as endangered, despite their "reduced numbers over the past century and habitat loss from dams and other obstructions." Just the year before, in 2014, the International Union for Conservation of Nature listed it as endangered, having declined at least 50 percent over its last three generations (about thirty-six years).

The organization cited a number of causes, including obstructions (dams, hydroelectric facilities), pollution, diseases, and climate change that may be altering ocean currents. And two years before this assessment, the Atlantic States Marine Fisheries Commission declared it depleted in US waters.[62]

What happened to bring about the declines in diadromous fish? Overfishing? Obstructions? Pollution? Perhaps a combination of all three. As John McPhee documented in *The Founding Fish*, the only river not dammed was the Delaware, where fishermen continued to harvest shad in the early twentieth century—but by the 1940s, those harvests had plummeted, then rebounded after passage of the Clean Water Act of 1972. Pollution seems to be the culprit here. Now, climate change is complicating their chances of survival.[63]

Certainly, dams have obstructed fish runs, a fact well documented by Waldman. Construction of water-powered milldams peaked between 1780 and 1860—sixty-five thousand by 1840 as counted in 872 counties in the eastern United States.[64] The period coincides with steep declines of anadromous fish like shad and alewives, declines that rippled through the marine food system. Waldman, in an eloquent essay in the *New York Times*, declares unequivocally that "no single action has caused as much injury as the construction of barriers along their migratory routes." He quotes Henry David Thoreau, whose journey on the Concord and Merrimack Rivers in 1849 yielded distressing sights and insights regarding the migratory fish who once ran up rivers in such multitudes in spring that the waters "ran silver." Dams blocked their passages, stymying their powerful instinctive urge to perpetuate their species as they had done for countless generations. "Who hears the fishes when they cry?" asked Thoreau. "Poor shad! Where is thy redress?" Waldman comments, "Now these same Atlantic rivers are fettered and tired, falling to the sea with the stilted tempo of the subjugated. Runs of the dozen or so river-sea migratory fish have, in many cases, been obliterated or reduced to fractions of their former plenitude. No longer ecologically relevant or societally important, they have become, in effect, 'ghost fishes.'"[65] For Waldman, nothing less than the dismantling of river dams will allow both rivers and migratory fishes to recover.

Recovering Alewives

At the first thaw in late winter, Joe and I set out for Big Fresh Pond in the town of Southampton, where one of the largest alewife runs on Long Island occurs. We drive along the Noyac Road, and just where it makes a T with North Sea Road, we pass a stand of phragmites marking the confluence of a freshwater creek and a saltwater inlet of Peconic Bay. This creek is the highway for alewives migrating to Fresh Pond. They swim into the Peconic Bay from the ocean, and wherever they can gain entry, they migrate upstream. At Noyac Road and again at North Sea Road they make their way through culverts. We pull into the parking lot of Emma Rose Elliston Park and follow the short trail to the creek. The spring thaw has encouraged the skunk cabbage to open its fetid flowers to attract pollinating flies, their leaves the brightest green in the wet woodland. The trail skirts the pond and takes us to a little bridge, where we can peer into the clear stream and watch for alewives. It's possible none will show up—it's early in the season yet—but there have been rains recently and the creek flows full, and lucky for us, a few alewives dart beneath the bridge into the lake. Not hundreds, not dozens, just a few. But they will spawn here and pass on their genes to another generation of alewives, who, when mature, will begin the cycle anew. We watch them pass beneath the bridge, their silvery iridescent bodies shimmying over the gravelly bottom. Waldman describes their passage as a "silvery mass of fragility and power."[66]

The alewife is the anadromous fish most likely to be seen in Long Island's fresh waters. Historically, they numbered in the millions on their spring runs, crowding into every river and stream that led them to a protected fresh pond. Now they number in the thousands, their migrations thwarted by dams and other obstructions. At sea, alewives range from Newfoundland to North Carolina and locally inhabit the coastal waters off Cape Cod and Long Island at depths below 150 feet. Between three and five years of age, they begin their spring spawning runs, when they may return to their natal fresh waters—if they are unobstructed. On Long Island, they begin arriving in March and head toward glacial ponds, as they have done from time

Figure 5.5. Alewife Creek in Southampton. During spring runs, alewives migrate from the salt waters of the ocean to the fresh waters of coastal ponds, where they will spawn. When mature, the young will return along the same little waterway to the ocean. Photo by author.

immemorial. Young of the year remain in their freshwater nurseries until early fall, then migrate back toward the sea. On both the spring and fall migrations, the waters must run high enough to enable them to swim; nothing should block their way, such as a new dam or clogged culvert. Alewives may live up to ten years and do not grow much larger than a foot. While a minor food source for human consumption, their greatest ecological importance is their role as prey for more esteemed food fish, such as tuna, cod, striped bass, and bluefish. Because of its importance in the food chain, the National Oceanic and Atmospheric Administration listed the alewife as a "Species of Special Concern" in 2006, and the Atlantic States Marine Fisheries Commission passed an amendment in 2012 ordering state river herring fisheries closed if they did not implement a sustainable fishery plan. As of 2017, alewives and other river herring remain depleted, but in the Hudson River, at least, they show signs of recovery, largely due to removal of obstructions. In 2021, the commission proposed a closure of fisheries for river herring in the streams of Long Island until their status could be further studied and a sustainability measure determined.[67]

Efforts to assist alewives in their spring runs have included building fish ladders over or around dams, and in some cases removing dams and other obstructions, or providing culverts for passage beneath roads. Beginning in the early 1800s, five dams were constructed along the Peconic. As early as 1995, under the auspices of the NYSDEC, alewives were physically lifted over the small dam at Grangebel Park in Riverhead. Over the years, Robert Conklin, a biology teacher and native Long Islander who grew up along the river, enlisted his students in a bucket brigade to lift and pass the fish over the dam to a pond on the other side—really the ponded portion of the Peconic created by dams on both ends. In 2000, the first experimental fish ladder, a thirty-foot aluminum chute—was installed at Grangebel. Apparently, it was successful in increasing the numbers of spawning alewives. In 2008, the first permanent fish ladder on Long Island was installed in the Carmans River at Hards Lake, followed by permanent ladders in the Peconic River at Grangebel Park Dam and in Massapequa Creek (the latter on the South Shore). Since 2006, surveys of Long Island alewife populations have been conducted by the Seatuck Environmental Association. Between 2006 and 2010, volunteers found alewives spawning in thirteen of twenty-eight tributaries surveyed, including the Carmans, Carlls, and Swan Rivers. Alewife Creek was the largest alewife spawning run, followed by the Peconic River, perhaps because it's the only unobstructed run. In 2017, the estimated total spawning run for all Long Island tributaries was about sixty thousand, compared with about forty thousand in 2010, which indicates the construction of fish ladders has had some success.[68] As laudable as these efforts are, their success has been limited and, according to Waldman, "have failed to reverse these declines" of river-sea migratory fish. In Waldman's view, only the removal of dams will allow the rivers to run silver again.[69]

CHAPTER 6

Grasslands at the Glacier's Edge

MOORS, DOWNS, AND A LOST PRAIRIE

It feels like old Long Island here, rural Long Island, a region mostly unchanged for decades, but it's deceptive. Old farms have disappeared, and industries come and gone. Now land lies vacant, acres and acres of it, tempting the commercial developer.

Joe and I have come to the Calverton Grasslands, close by the Calverton Ponds in the Central Pine Barrens, in search of the grasshopper sparrow, which has returned to breed here. It's a typical June day, warm and humid, but a light breeze ripples the grasses. We revel in the sense of space and solitude, the green expanse stretching to the horizon, the blue sky like a transparent dome. We listen for the sparrow's insect-like song, so high-pitched the breeze easily snatches it away. But there, we spy the tiny bird atop a cedar, its beak open and singing. It's not a beautiful song, nor is it a beautiful bird. It's a rather plain pale brown, with a streaked back and buffy breast. Its song is a high-pitched twitter, dry and chirpy like an insect's, but its song is not the reason for its name. The name refers to its diet of grasshoppers and other insects found in its grassland habitat, supplemented by seeds gleaned from the ground. Perhaps not a beautiful song, but to hear it, to pick it out like a thread of sound from the background sound of wind rustling through grasses, is a joy. And to see one alight in full view, open its bill wide and sing, is thrilling. We know we have a special bird here, special because it is declining with its habitat.

The grasshopper sparrow breeds in grasslands, particularly prairies, although it may choose pastures and old fields. Once a common breeder on

Figure 6.1. A grasshopper sparrow shows himself atop a wildflower stalk. This once-common grassland bird is declining because of loss of habitat. Photo by author.

Long Island, it is now fairly scarce. Another once-common grassland bird, the eastern meadowlark, has recently been confirmed as a breeder in this grassland—the only place known on Long Island. Other grassland birds that once bred on Long Island—savannah sparrow, bobolink, upland sandpiper, and short-eared owl—have all but disappeared. In the early 1900s, the owl was described as outnumbering all other owls; now we are lucky to observe one here in winter at dusk, flying low and silent over the fields hunting for small rodents.[1]

This 800-acre grassland is part of a 2,900-acre swath of undeveloped land known as EPCAL (Enterprise Park at Calverton), which includes portions of the core Long Island Pine Barrens, designated a special groundwater protection area, and the watersheds of the Peconic Estuary and Long Island Sound. Audubon New York recognizes the region as an Important Bird Area, and New York State lists the parcel in its open space plan.[2] This land was not always undeveloped—an old, cracked runway attests to its use in aviation. The core retains a ten-thousand-foot-long runway and a railroad spur. The US Navy owned the land, once the site of the Naval Weapons Industrial Reserve at Calverton, and leased it to Grumman Aircraft Corporation (now

Northrop-Grumman) to assemble and test its military aircraft. It was here, in the 1960s, that they made and tested the lunar landing module used by the Apollo astronauts. Grumman shut down its Long Island operations in 1994, and in 1998, the navy turned over EPCAL to the Town of Riverhead. For the past two decades, the land has been the focus of dispute over its future uses. Proposals have been put forward to build a resort, a waterpark, an industrial park, a housing development—developers' dreams and schemes colliding with the dreams of preservationists who see the value in our grasslands and seek to preserve and restore them as viable habitats.[3]

We do not know if Calverton Grasslands was always a grassland; it may have been cleared in centuries past for the use of cattle, whose grazing may have helped maintain it as grassland, just as its later use for aviation had done. But Long Island does possess original grasslands: the Hempstead Plains in the middle of the island, a dry prairie, and the maritime grasslands of the South Fork, known as the Montauk Downs and Moors.

A Lost Prairie

"Toward the middle of the island lyeth a plain sixteen miles long and four broad, upon which plain grows very fine grass, that makes exceeding good hay, and is very good pasture for sheep or other cattel; where you shall find neither stick nor stone to hinder the horse heels, or endanger them in their races, and once a year the best horses in the Island, are brought hither to try their swiftness, and the swiftness rewarded with a silver cup, two being annually procured for that purpose."[4] These lines were written by Daniel Denton in 1670, part of a promotional tract he published that year in London. Denton had moved with his clergyman father to New England in the 1640s, eventually settling in Hempstead, Long Island. Following in his father's footsteps, he became pastor of the Presbyterian church in the town of Jamaica, where he was also town clerk. After the English takeover of New York, he actively promoted settlement in the new colony, extolling its natural riches and proclaiming the easy availability of land to those denied such opportunities in England: "Here, anyone may furnish himself and live rent-free, yea, with such a quantity of land, that he may weary himself with

Figure 6.2. A map of western Long Island made by the British during their Long Island campaign in 1776 clearly shows the Hempstead Plains (Hamsted Plains). Courtesy of the Library of Congress. "Sketch of the Country Illustrating the Late Engagement in Long Island," London, 1776, https://www.loc.gov/item/gm71002206/.

walking over his fields of corn, and all sorts of grain." And for the cattle, "grass as high as a man's knees, nay, as high as his waist." Indeed, with the fervor of a preacher, he evoked biblical imagery to describe the land: "If there be any terrestrial Canaan, 'tis surely here, where the Land floweth with milk and honey."[5] His language anticipated the suburban boosters of the nineteenth century, and like them, he stood to gain as a land speculator.

Where Denton saw horses racing across the plains, Walt Whitman saw cattle ambling home. He described the plains of his boyhood as "quite prairie-like, open, uninhabited, rather sterile, cover'd with kill-calf and huckleberry bushes, yet plenty of fair pastures for the cattle mainly milch-cows, who fed there by the hundreds, even thousands, and at evening . . . might be seen taking their way home, branching regularly in the right places. I have often been out on the edges of these plains toward sundown, and can yet recall in fancy the interminable cow-processions, and hear the music of the tin or copper bells clanking far or near, and breathe the cool of the sweet and slightly aromatic evening air, and note the sunset."[6] Whitman's reminiscences of Long Island, his birthplace, are tinged with romantic longing for a lost childhood and fading sense of place. The land he tirelessly walked and explored and experienced was on the verge of disappearing. By the time he began setting down his reminiscences while on a short visit to his childhood home in 1881, developers had begun parceling off the plains, as we will see.

Another walker in the land was Reverend Timothy Dwight (1752–1817), a Congregationalist minister and the president of Yale, who perambulated Long Island before Whitman was born. His descriptions of the land lack the color and emotion of Whitman's, offering more of a natural history—cataloging its topography, geology, flora, and fauna—as well as notes on its institutions. He correctly recognized that Hempstead Plain was "a continuation of that vast level which extends from Canoe Place [Westhampton] to Jamaica, about eighty miles." Before it was understood that glaciers had shaped Long Island, he discerned what geologists now call the Outwash Plain, the flat expanse of Long Island's southern half, composed of pine barrens, scrublands, and grasslands.[7] His *Travels in New England and New York* was typical of natural histories and travelogues of the era. A similar endeavor was undertaken by Samuel Latham Mitchill, professor at Columbia College, a renowned physician and naturalist who founded the New York Academy of Sciences (then known as the Lyceum of Natural History). Born in 1764 at Plandome, his family house in North Hempstead, he may well have explored the plains as a boy, but we have no hint of that in his account. He described Hempstead Plain as a "prairie or savannah" twenty miles long and three miles wide. As far as he knew, it was treeless even when the Europeans arrived, a place of long grass and shrubbery, but because of its use as pasture by "vast herds of cattle and flocks of sheep," much of the original grassland had been reduced to "a land of barren appearance."[8] Nathaniel Prime, a clergyman who toured Long Island in 1845 documenting its churches, described the land he traveled through. Of the plains he wrote, "This whole tract appears as smooth and unbroken as the surface of the sea in a calm, though as you pass over it, you meet with slight undulations, and the views of the traveller over the whole expanse is unobstructed, by tree, or shrub or any other vegetable production. Within the memory of persons still living, there was scarcely an enclosure in this whole compass." People had tried unsuccessfully to cultivate it, and farms were encroaching on its northern edges, but even these had to be replenished "every year because of its gravelly substratum."[9]

This prairie, and the adjacent oak brush plains (another unique habitat), was also a favorite shooting ground in the fall, when shooters would camp out in dry hollows and erect grass blinds, setting out decoys to lure the plovers that were migrating through. Native Long Islander Daniel Tredwell recalled a plover shoot in the 1840s. Within three hours, he wrote in his diary, they took eighty-two birds from the blind, and another party on horseback took over a hundred. These were no doubt American golden plovers, which I myself have observed alighting in sod fields and ranchlands in Suffolk County during fall migration, though one is lucky to see more than one. Tredwell's description of their habit is memorable: "They spy the decoy at a great distance and they come sweeping down in their rough and tumble flight all in a heap before lighting; then is the time to fire." They challenge the amateur shooter, he explained, because of their peculiar habit of not flushing straight up but at an angle as they swerve toward the object of their alarm before veering off.[10] Golden plovers have never bred here, but are birds of the Arctic tundra, migrating southward in fall, alighting in grasslands and sod fields to feed on grasshoppers and other insects. Overhunting may have decimated them by the 1890s, but they have rebounded somewhat in the last seventy years. Perhaps they have adapted to human-altered habitats, feeding in golf courses and airports as well as unspoiled grasslands.

In the mid-1800s, department store magnate Alexander Turney Stewart purchased seven thousand acres of Hempstead Plains on Long Island to build a suburban community of homes, gardens, and parks intended for working-class renters, most of whom were his own employees. He called it Garden City. *Harper's Weekly* commented on the project in its April 7, 1869, issue: "With the improvements which Mr. Stewart's project will carry out; with a township of beautiful and healthy homes; with parks, gardens, and public buildings for educational purposes and for those of amusement, Hempstead Plains, hitherto a desert, will be made to blossom as the rose; it will be the most beautiful suburb in the vicinity of New York. God speed the undertaking."[11] Stewart's utopian working-class suburb never materialized, for there were simply not enough takers, perhaps due to the rental arrangement— after all, the dream was to become a homeowner, an ideal voiced by Whitman: "A man is not a whole and complete man unless he owns a house and the ground it stands on."[12] Whitman certainly revered his old family homestead in Huntington, but surely he would have been dismayed at the piece-by-piece carving up of the Hempstead Plain.

In 1907, Roland M. Harper conducted a survey of the Hempstead Plain for the American Geographical Society, which he published in 1911. There's "not another place exactly like it in the world," he wrote. He noted that the prairie was associated with many place-names indicative of its topography: Plainview, Plain Edge, Island Trees, East Meadow Brook. In previous excursions around the edges of the prairie, he found that development had erased the original flora; but when he ventured deeper into the plain in July 1907, going beyond the periphery to what botanists knew as a "collecting ground," he "was surprised to find that there are still thousands of acres on which the flora is practically all native." Why, he asked, was so much "still in a state of nature," after being settled for 250 years? He speculated it was the "toughness of the sod, the thinness of the soil, and especially the scarcity of water" that had discouraged agriculture. But with the decline of farming and the expansion of the New York metropolis, he glumly predicted that New York City was "bound to cover it all with houses sooner or later, and it behooves scientists to make an exhaustive study of the region before the opportunity is gone forever."[13] Harper was correct in his predictions. By the time he did his survey, 20 percent of the prairie had been lost; within decades, 99 percent would be consumed by development.[14]

Levittown, New York, is a prime example of the postwar suburb with its standardized, single-family, detached houses set back on patches of lawn. It's a historical irony that William Levitt bought and subdivided Alexander Stewart's estate, called Island Trees, in 1946. In contrast to Stewart's failed working-class utopia of Garden City, the Island Trees development—later called Levittown—would be spectacularly successful, meeting the postwar demand for affordable housing by working-class white people who aspired to a middle-class life. By 1960, the Levitt Brothers had built seventeen thousand houses, all owned and occupied by working-class families who were mostly employed in the aviation industry on Long Island—Grumman, Republic, and Sperry.[15]

As noted by the curator of the Cradle of Aviation Museum, Joshua Stoff, the Hempstead Plains made a "natural airfield." It has been the site of many historic flights, beginning with the Golden Flyer biplane of Glenn Curtiss in 1909 and extending into the "golden age" of aviation, highlighted by the transatlantic flight to Paris piloted by Charles Lindbergh in 1927. "By the early 1930s," Stoff informs us, "Roosevelt Field was the largest and busiest civilian airfield in America with over 150 aviation businesses and 450 planes based there."[16] Roosevelt Field was returned to commercial use after World War II, closed as an airfield in 1951, and sold to real estate developer William Zeckendorf. The developer built an open-air mall designed by I. M. Pei, which opened in 1956. One of the earliest shopping malls, Roosevelt Field Mall—just down the highway from Levittown—spanned 360 acres of the prairie. Dubbed "markets in the meadows" by *Architectural Forum* in 1956, shopping centers and malls with their huge parking lots came to define the suburban landscape.

I have often shopped at Roosevelt Field Mall, zipping along the Meadow-brook Parkway—the name a nod to the brook that once meandered through the prairie—and exiting on the ramp signed as "Shopping Mall," just past the Zeckendorf exit. All the signage is quite clear, pointing this way and that way to individual stores and their adjacent lots. Getting out of the giant out-door parking lots and back to the parkway is not so clear and easy. It's a flat expanse of concrete and tarmac, treeless as a prairie, and just as disorient-ing, as I have found myself going around in circles if not exiting on the wrong road. It always brings to mind the description of the prairie by Nathaniel Prime in 1845: "It was cut up with roads or wagon-paths, in almost every direction, so that the stranger, and even the experienced traveler in the night-time, or when the ground was covered with snow, was constantly liable to lose his way."[17]

The plains may once have been part of a continuous band of sand-prairie grassland that extended from New Jersey to Massachusetts. Like the mid-western prairies, it was a tallgrass prairie, dominated by big bluestem, little bluestem, Indian or nut grass, and switchgrass. Growing among these prai-rie grasses was an array of wildflowers, including wild indigo, butterfly weed, and several species of goldenrod.[18] These native grasses and wildflowers are still present today in what remains of the prairie, even in its degraded and fragmentary state. "Although no portion of virgin Hempstead Plains exists today," wrote Richard Stalter and Eric Lamont in 1987, "the Mitchell Field site is the least disturbed remnant of original Long Island prairie vegeta-tion."[19] Mitchell Field is another example of how its use for aviation may have saved or preserved at least a sliver of the prairie.

Mitchell Field got its start as the Hazelhurst Aviation Field #2 in 1917 (Roo-sevelt Field was #1) and was long used as an army training base. In 1940, Mitchell Field became the site of the US Army's Air Defense Command, and later as a US Air Force base. In 1960, the federal government turned over Mitchell Field to Nassau County, and it is now the site of the Nassau County Museum, Nassau Community College, Nassau Coliseum, and other large complexes. With the loss of the airfields and the gradual diminution of the aerospace industry that had been centered here, whatever was left of the Hempstead Plains was even more vulnerable to development.

Professor Betsy Gulotta of Nassau Community College was instrumental in saving a patch of the prairie. The Hempstead Plains Preserve was established on a nineteen-acre parcel of land at Nassau Community College. The Friends of Hempstead Plains organized themselves in 2001 under Gulotta's leadership and have worked tirelessly to protect their bit of prairie and restore it to its original state. That has entailed assiduous efforts in rooting and burning out nonnative and invasive plants, and reseeding or planting species native to the plains. They have protected the preserve from dumping and trashing and attempted to guide development along its fringes to be compatible with the preserve. They have also reached out to the community and promoted good stewardship, building an environmental education center to teach a new generation about the value of preserving endangered native ecosystems like the plains. On their website, they state, "It represents one of the most rapidly vanishing habitats in the world, along with scores of birds, butterflies, and other animals that are vanishing with it." Of the 250 plant species that grow in this habitat, a few are globally rare and a number are endangered.[20] These include bird's-foot violet, listed as "exploitably vulnerable" in New York.[21] Its delicate flowers once stained the grasslands purple in spring.

According to the New York Natural Heritage Program, the encroachment of invasive and woody species threatens the viability of this "globally rare community." Fire suppression is also implicated in the decline, allowing it to transition to successional shrublands. Out of an original 15,000 hectares (about 38,000 acres), "less than 15 hectares (37 acres) remain today, or one percent, and most of these are severely degraded."[22] Stalter and Lamont give an even higher figure for the original prairie—24,300 hectares—which concurs with historical records.[23] The New York Natural Heritage Program urges implementation of a regular fire regime and protection from further development.

In 2018, the New York Natural Heritage Program conducted a survey of the flora of the Hempstead Plains grassland with the goal of identifying the extant rare plants and documenting invasive plants. The surveyors mapped sixteen different natural or ecological communities, including "variants" of the Hempstead Plains grassland community. In other words, the grassland parcels had all undergone human alteration in the course of time. Out of an original grassland of fifty square miles, they estimated that a mere 24.17 acres remained—a lower estimate than that of Stalter and Lamont. Despite the severe fragmentation and degradation of the prairie, fourteen rare plant species are still extant.[24]

WILD MOORS AND ROLLING DOWNS

It's an alluring name, conjuring an ancient landscape—Shadmoor—and indeed the eastern shadbush does bloom in creamy profusion here in spring, but the grassland preserved in this state park is not a true moor. When English colonists first saw the maritime grasslands of Montauk Peninsula, they were reminded of English moors like the rolling heathery expanses of Yorkshire, but what grows here is more a mix of bunch-forming grasses, low heath shrubs, and reindeer moss. Shadmoor is composed of maritime grassland and shrubland, heathland, and freshwater wetland, a ninety-nine-acre tract just east of the village of Montauk between Montauk Highway and the ocean. The tract once belonged to the US Army and was used as a lookout station during World War II, its two concrete bunkers now picturesque ruins. Earlier still, in 1898, it was part of Camp Wikoff, where Theodore Roosevelt and his Rough Riders were quarantined with more than twenty-nine thousand soldiers at the end of the Spanish-American War. One of the trails is Roosevelt Run Trail.

On a June day I take the Shad Run Trail, which winds past one of the bunkers. It's edged by shadbush and black cherry, now setting fruit. A male eastern towhee whistles like a teakettle from atop a tree, his calico plumage bright in the sunlight, and a gray catbird mews from within a shrub. I emerge onto the top of the one-hundred-foot-high bluff, walking through a sunlit fragrant expanse of grasses and bayberries and an occasional stunted pitch pine. A song sparrow sings exuberantly. In the wildflowers along the edges, fat bumblebees drone. A tiger swallowtail drifts languidly, then alights in a tangle of wild grapes. The view is spectacular, offering vistas of the glittering ocean and miles of coastal bluffs extending east and west. Waves break below, seething around glacial boulders and soughing onto the sand.

Figure 6.3. Topographic map of Montauk Point, based on a 1954 aerial survey. Shadmoor State Park, not yet created when the map was made, is located between the village of Montauk and Ditch Plains. Montauk Downs, a vanished grassland, was on the site of Montauk Downs Golf Course, west of Lake Montauk. Big Reed Pond and Oyster Pond are to the east of Lake Montauk. Hither Hills is west of Fort Pond. Courtesy of United States Geological Survey, USGS Historical Quadrangle Scanning Project, 2023.

Bank swallows fly in and out from the bluff walls where they nest, darting overhead and twittering.

This coastal grassland is one of a few remaining on Long Island— Shadmoor, Montauk Downs, Big Reed, Oyster Pond, and Hither Hills—all concentrated on Montauk Peninsula. They are considered rare plant communities, their fragments scattered on Long Island, Block Island, Martha's Vineyard, Nantucket, and Cape Cod. It's believed these fragments once formed a continuous swath of grassland that took root after the last glacier receded. They may have been maintained as grasslands by wildfires and perhaps browsing by mammals such as white-tailed deer and, later, domestic cattle. Humans, who arrived after the retreat of the last glacier, may well have used fire to maintain the grassland habitat so ideal to their prey animals.[25]

As with the Montauk Moors, the Montauk Downs were likely given their name by an English colonist who noticed their superficial resemblance to the chalk Downs of England. Like the English Downs, they are a rolling treeless landscape, but unlike the Downs they're not underlain by chalk. The Montauk Peninsula is an artifact of the ice age, its hills and hollows testaments to the advances and retreats of glaciers. J. A. Ayres described the downs he observed in 1849: "Of these hills it is almost impossible to convey a correct idea. Rounded and rolling, but in many cases quite steep and abrupt, not arranged in ridges, but scattered apparently at random; with no level land among them, but deep, cup-shaped hollows seeming like reversed copies of the hills themselves; bare of trees and covered only with a smooth turf, as close as though it had been shorn, their appearance is sui generis."[26] Norman Taylor, curator of the Brooklyn Botanic Garden, conducted a survey of the downs' grassland flora in 1923. He noted that Ayres's impression of turf was just that, an impression; in fact, unlike the tall-grass prairie of Hempstead Plains, the dominant grass of the downs was little bluestem, growing with common hairgrass and poverty-grass—"all plants that grow in close, dense tufts, or clumps, and do not tend to make a real turf." Beneath these bunch grasses was reindeer lichen, "which often carpets the Downs and through which all the species are apt to force their way.[27] He estimated the downs to be about six thousand acres and posed the question, still unanswered, as to whether these grasslands were always there (that is, since the last glacier receded and a "modern" flora emerged), or whether they were products of human management. He noted that while the Montaukett Indians did not graze cattle, as the Europeans did, they did use fire to preserve the kind of landscape attractive to deer. He cited an agreement between Wyandanch, who represented the Montaukett in land deals with the English of East Hampton and other sites on Long Island, that specified the Indians not set fire to the grass "before the month of March, without consent of the town."[28] Taylor speculated that more than fire management, the ocean and maritime climate may have been the main influences shaping the windswept landscape. He noted the plants associated with the grasses possessed either narrow or flat, ground-hugging leaves adapted to wind. The associated herbs were plantain pussytoes (also known as ladies tobacco and everlasting), racemed milkwort, toothed white-topped aster, and sandplain gerardia, now called sandplain agalinis.

Taylor's description of the purple-stained hills of the Montauk Peninsula evokes a vanished landscape, where he could expect to find "untold millions of Agalinis acuta, with small purple flowers," blooming in late summer.[29] Sandplain agalinis is now an endangered plant, growing in small colonies in just four known places on Montauk. Historically, it has been confined to coastal grasslands in New York, Connecticut, Massachusetts, and Maryland—fifty-one documented populations, reduced to a mere dozen when it was placed on the endangered species list in 1988 (it remains endangered throughout its historical range). Why the demise of a once-common flower? As Marilyn Jordan, conservation scientist for the Nature Conservancy, wrote in 2003, sixty thousand acres of native coastal grassland in the Northeast had been reduced to two hundred acres: "Sandplain gerardia needs a prairie habitat dominated by native bunchgrasses, especially little bluestem. It is thought that a hemi-parasitic relationship exists between sandplain gerardia and bluestem, with the gerardia getting nutrients and moisture from the bluestem roots. This plant cannot be grown in your backyard; it needs high quality native grassland habitat. The best way to protect endangered species like the sandplain gerardia is to preserve and restore ecosystems in which they grow."[30] She noted that historically, fire and grazing maintained the grasslands as grasslands—what Taylor called "an arrested climax" community—but these forces were no longer (or rarely) at work, allowing shrubs and weeds to invade the grasslands.[31] She also noted that the nonnative cotton-tailed rabbit eats the gerardia plant before it sets seed, preventing its propagation. Jordan managed the Nature Conservancy's recovery program for the endangered plant. At the time she wrote, the population had increased from five hundred in 1990 to eighty thousand—seemingly a spectacular success story, the result of management efforts that included prescribed burns, mowing, and fencing to protect and maintain desired grassland habitat, combined with reseeding. But a drought in 2005, it's surmised, devastated the plant.

One grassland where this endangered flower blooms is at Sayville, on Long Island's South Shore, where 127 acres are overseen by the US Fish and Wildlife Service (FWS). It's not open to the public. The Sayville Grassland contains the largest naturally occurring population of this plant on Long Island. In an article written for the Long Island Botanical Society in 1993, Robert Laskowski described his first encounter with the Sayville Grasslands in the 1970s, when he was conducting a survey for the New York Breeding Bird Atlas. He found a high diversity of birds—thirty species—and also noted the diversity of native plants, an important correlation. His description recalls Taylor's of the downs, with bunch grasses interspersed with lichen. He noted that ten species of rare plants could be found here, including sandplain gerardia and New England blazing-star, which grew "in abundance."[32] What he meant by abundance is hard to gauge; the FWS offers statistics on the sandplain gerardia population: in 1985, the number of plants was three hundred, and in 1991, the number had plummeted to three. Due to FWS efforts, a decade later the population had rebounded to thirteen thousand. Starting in 1995, the FWS pursued an aggressive management strategy that involved annual controlled burns and reseeding. As recently as April 2016, it conducted a controlled burn on forty-one acres. By 2017, the plants had rebounded to over fifteen thousand at all sites on Long Island. Without a doubt, sandplain gerardia benefits from fire, growing more robustly in a burned-over landscape than one maintained by mowing.[33]

The fortunes of this little flower wax and wane with the weather. Droughts like those of 2005 and 2012 may devastate its population. But belying its delicate appearance, it rebounds in the right conditions. It likes bare soil, and fire clears the way for a colony to take root. It also thrives in disturbed ground, which may explain why these flowers grew well where the cattle roamed—and even why they can be found so close to a hiking trail in Montauk, which is where I came upon a tiny colony at Shadmoor State Park. It was easy to miss, easy to pass by as I followed the trail to the bluff, but knowing what I was looking for, keeping an eye out, I found the delicate pink flowers glowing on purplish wiry stems in the shadows amid ferns and a sparse covering of little bluestem. I gazed into their speckled pale throats and watched as a bee landed on the protruding white anther. The flower would live just a day, so this was the chance for pollination. Once the plant set seed and dropped its seed capsules, it would die—but the seeds of the next generation would be scattered in the soil, waiting for the right conditions. The seeds remain viable for just four years or so, and populations will disappear from a site if conditions do not favor them. Though I have checked the Shadmoor site every year since I first encountered the sandplain gerardia, I have not seen them. I counted myself lucky that day.[34]

The decline of coastal grasslands has also spelled the decline of pollinators. While grasses are pollinated by wind, most of the wildflowers that grow in grasslands depend on pollinating insects such as butterflies, bees, and beetles. With the loss of grasslands to croplands, and the increasing use by farmers and gardeners of pesticides and especially herbicides like Roundup, butterflies in particular have been hard-hit. The monarch, a migratory butterfly, is iconic of this decline.

Seven studies published by the *Annals of the Entomological Society of America* in 2015 offered a more complex picture than loss of milkweed (the host plant for the larvae) and nectaring plants to account for the decline of the eastern populations of the monarch butterfly.[35] Counts conducted by volunteers between 1993 and 2014 indicated that eastern monarchs were not declining significantly along their migration routes and in their breeding grounds—data at odds with the steep declines documented in their wintering grounds in Mexico, more than 80 percent during the same time span.[36] How to explain such a dramatic long-term decline? Scientists have speculated that the monarchs are experiencing high mortality along their *fall*

Figure 6.4. A migrating monarch nectars in wildflowers in late summer.
Photo by author.

migration routes, the result of a complex of factors, including habitat loss
and fragmentation, severe weather events such as drought, and insecticides
and herbicides.[37] In March 2016, the US Geological Survey predicted that the
eastern monarch population could collapse within two decades. "Restoration of their breeding habitat" was viewed as "the most effective way" to pull
back the population from the brink of extinction.[38] In July 2022, the International Union for Conservation of Nature's Red List recorded the western
population of our migratory monarch butterfly as a globally endangered species "threatened by habitat destruction and climate change."[39] As of 2023,
the eastern population is a "candidate" for being listed as threatened.[40]

Perhaps it is anecdotal, but I can only attest to the dramatic drop in numbers of monarchs observed along the Long Island coast in fall migration. I
recall decades ago—the 1980s—how they draped the coastal goldenrods so
thickly they turned the golden flowers orange and bent them down with their
combined weight. And this was not in a country field but in a Brooklyn
neighborhood, where goldenrods grew in an undeveloped patch along an

esplanade. Perhaps those flowers were like an oasis in an urban desert to them, and they became concentrated on this small stand of goldenrod. When a new house was built and the esplanade became privatized in the 1990s, the owners apparently decided—if they gave any thought to it at all—that gold-enrods were weeds and had to go. But no matter where I wander on Long Island, whether in an urban park or country field, I now feel lucky to see one, two, three in a season. A few years ago, organic farmer Scott Chaskey, then director of the community farm of Quail Hill in Amagansett, turned over an entire field to milkweed, but defying the adage that if you build it they will come, precious few have come and laid their eggs on them.[41]

The monarch is not the only beneficial insect that visits grassland wild-flowers. Healthy native grasslands support a diversity of insects, some that are pollinators and others that serve as beneficial predators of harmful insects; in turn, these beneficial insects support the grassland ecosystem, increasing the diversity of native plants and birds that feed on the fruits and seeds of the plants as well as on the insects. The milkweed planted at Quail Hill may not have drawn the numbers of monarchs hoped for, but it did attract an endangered beetle, and that was hopeful. The nine-spotted ladybug, a once-common ladybug named the New York State insect in 1989 for its valued role in suppressing insect pests, was thought to be locally extinct by 2006, when it was proposed in the state legislature the beetle be replaced as the state insect. But on a July day in 2011, a volunteer in Cornell University's Lost Ladybug Project was surveying Chaskey's field of milkweed. This little bug was clearly different from the larger red milk-weed beetles that often cover the leaves and pods and are considered a noxious pest by those who want healthy stands of milkweed. This one had four spots on each wing and a spot split in the middle: the object of the lost ladybug quest. That summer, twenty more were found on the farm. It was drawn to the milkweed not as a food source but as a host for aphids and other bugs that are the ladybug's food sources. A whole ecosystem in a flower.[42]

Healthy native grasslands support a diversity of native flowering plants. The more croplands replace grasslands and farmers eradicate weeds and insects with indiscriminate spraying of herbicides and insecticides, the more species are lost. The loss of a beetle is about more than its economic and utilitarian value as a natural controller of pests; the loss of a butterfly is about more than its aesthetic value as a thing of beauty; the loss of a grassland is about more than its environmental value as open space or even its ecological value as native habitat—all these losses, one by one in a cascade of losses, unravel the very fabric of nature and diminish us.

Figure 7.1. A prairie warbler perches in a pitch pine tree. Photo by author.

Figure 7.2. A stunted pitch pine tree grows like a bonsai in the wild. Photo by author.

CHAPTER 7

Falling Trees

OUR DIMINISHING FORESTS

A light ascending rill of notes streams through the blue air. It's the song of the prairie warbler. I swing my binoculars toward the sound and spot the bright yellow-and-black bird in the boughs of a stunted pitch pine, his beak wide open, his throat trembling with the notes. At my approach he ceases his song and flies off to another tree, not wanting me to get too close to his nest. He is a breeder here in the Dwarf Pine Barrens, his preferred habitat, having flown from his wintering grounds in the West Indies to mate and raise his brood until they all fly back south come fall.

TREES OF ICE AND FIRE

Though early June, it's hot in these woods, where the quartz gravel substrate reflects heat. Dry pine needles crunch under my shoes, releasing their fragrance, and the chunky bark of the pines gives off a resinous scent. These gnarled, bonsai-like pitch pines are rooted in a thick layer of glacial outwash on the south slope of the Ronkonkoma Moraine, thriving in nutrient-poor ground, weathering drought. Tough and enduring, they can withstand temperatures of up to 2,000 degrees Fahrenheit. In fact, they thrive on fire. Their small, tightly closed cones are serotinous, needing fire to open them and release their seeds. The trees have evolved in a habitat where brush fires were regular, seasonal occurrences.

This is the Dwarf Pine Barrens, an ecologically unique segment of the Central Pine Barrens of Long Island and one of three such barrens on the planet. (The other two dwarf pine barrens are in the New Jersey Pine-lands and the Shawangunk Ridge.) At one time, the Long Island Pine Bar-rens encompassed 250,000 acres, stretching as far west as Oyster Bay, where it transitioned into the Oak Brush Plains and the Hempstead Prairie, two other unique habitats on Long Island. In 1993, New York State designated 100,000 acres of the barrens a protected natural area, the "third largest for-est preserve in New York State," as stated in the Central Pine Barrens Man-agement Plan adopted in 1995.[1] Specifically, the Pine Barrens Protection Act restricted development in the Core Pine Barrens, a zone of 52,500 acres, and allowed planned development in the peripheral Compatible Growth Area of 47,500 acres. The Central Pine Barrens spans a swath of land in the island's midsection from Riverhead to Coram. It encompasses the Peconic River, which flows west to east for around twelve miles from its headwaters near Ridge to its mouth in Flanders Bay, and the upper Carmans River, which flows north to south from its headwaters at Middle Island and cuts through the Ronkonkoma Moraine. The pine barrens crests the moraine at Bald Hill, its highest point at around 295 feet, and cloaks the moraine's north and south slopes. On its south slope, rooted in glacial outwash, is the dwarf pine plains. Besides the dwarf pine barrens, the pine barrens complex includes forests of pitch pine and oak; pitch pine, oak, and heath; and oak and pine, as well as Atlantic white-cedar swamps like that of Cranberry Bog State Park and coastal plain ponds like those in the Calverton Ponds Reserve. Globally unique, the Long Island Pine Barrens holds high eco-logical value: in 1997, the US Fish and Wildlife Service designated the Long Island Pine Barrens a "Significant Habitat Complex" harboring 147 rare, endangered, or threatened species; and in the same decade, the Nature Conservancy named the Peconic Biosphere Reserve one of the "Last Great Places" on the planet, which encompasses not only the Central Pine Barrens but the peripheral barrens communities—the Edgewood Oak Brush Plains, Brentwood Oak Brush Plains, Pinelawn Cemetery, and Setauket Pine Barrens.[2]

In the Dwarf Pine Barrens, where I meet the prairie warbler, pitch pines and scrub or bear oak dominate the mesic woodland. Pitch pines are easily recognized by their deeply furrowed bark and bundles of three needles. Their

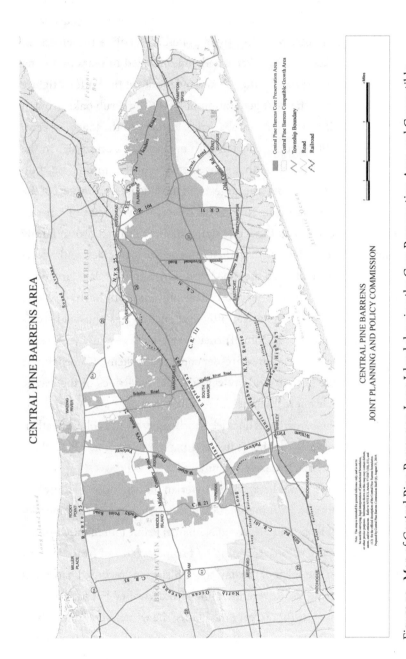

Figure 7.3. Map of Central Pine Barrens on Long Island showing the Core Preservation Area and Compatible Growth Area. Courtesy of New York State Central Pine Barrens Commission, 2018.

branches and cones are prickly. In late spring, the trees send up new shoots like pale candles, and yellow male cones emerge in protruding clusters at the base of the shoots, releasing their pollen to fertilize the emergent strawberry-pink female cones. Fertilized cones formed in years past cling to the branches, newer ones at the top and older ones at the bottom, tightly holding the seeds of the next generation of trees. The scrub oaks grow in thick stands, their small pointed-lobe leaves leathery to the touch, or crisp where they litter the ground. I search with my eyes for a caterpillar in the leaves, one with bristly spines that sting the hand of the unwary, but I do not find one. These oaks host "the largest and most dense population" of the coastal barrens buckmoth in New York, where it is a species of "special concern."[3] Hunters named these day-flying moths of the silkworm family buckmoths because the time of their emergence coincides with deer-hunting season in October. At the time I visit, early summer, their larvae can be found feeding on the oak leaves. In late July they will burrow several inches into the soil beneath the leaf litter and pupate. This unusual habit is explained by local naturalist John Turner as the moth's evolutionary strategy to protect itself from fire in a fire-dependent ecosystem.[4] Come fall, the moths will emerge to mate and lay eggs on the undersides of the leaves, beginning the cycle anew. The pitch pines and scrub oaks are underlain by heath: lowbush blueberry, black huckleberry, bearberry, and golden heather. When I visit, the golden heather is just coming into bloom, its yellow flowers as bright as the prairie warbler's plumage.[5]

In the early 1840s, a middle-aged Presbyterian minister whose family had lived for generations in Huntington, Long Island, set out to write an ecclesiastical history of the island. Reverend Nathaniel Prime toured the churches and met with congregations, traveling by turnpike and rail from the west end to the east. In the spirit of the day, when historians recorded natural as well as cultural features, Reverend Prime also described the varied landscapes he encountered. The "Great Pine Plains," he wrote, were "one unbroken forest": "In traveling these forests, you will occasionally fall upon a small oasis, which cheers the stranger's eye, as it well may the heart of the solitary occupant, but in many places, even at the present day, you may pass through five, six and even seven miles of unbroken forest, without discerning a human habitation, or the least trace of the hand of man except the stumps of felled trees."[6] Though barren as a human habitat in Prime's day, the pinelands were commercially valuable, as he duly noted. The stumps told the story: the timber of pitch pine was processed into railroad ties, boxes, pallets, mill wheels and cogs, and the like, and the sap of the pines was processed into turpentine or pitch (hence the name). To tap the pitch, it was necessary to cut into the tree a foot above the base, a practice that eventually killed the tree.[7] As described by Prime, whole stands of pines from the barrens as well as tracts of oaks and hickories from the upland forests were clear-cut for fuel. Before anthracite coal came into widespread use as fuel, thousands of cords of combustible wood were transported by rail and boat from Long Island forests to New York City markets in the nineteenth century. Tracts were "cut entirely smooth," wrote Prime, who found it remarkable how quickly the forests regenerated: in the upland oak-hickory forests, "the same ground has often been cut over in twenty or twenty-five years, and every successive growth is equally productive," while the "pines from the sandy lands" take somewhat longer to regrow, but even these grow back "with astonishing rapidity."[8] Prime disputed the myth that Long Island lacked forests; on the contrary, he asserted, it was more forested than the lands of the Hudson Valley, where he had spent many years. Despite the clear-cutting, Long Island had extensive forests, a fact he attributed to the landowners who saw it in their interest to preserve and replenish commercially valuable woods. Today, the pine barrens is Long Island's most extensive preserved forest thanks to concerted preservation efforts since the mid-1900s, but Prime's "unbroken forest" was hardly untrammeled.[9]

Little more than a century after Reverend Prime traveled through the barrens, suburban tract houses would replace unbroken tracts of forests. With the completion of the Long Island Expressway, postwar suburban development nearly quadrupled the population from 1960 to 1990, from 12,500 to 57,000.[10] Before the ecoregion was completely erased, it became imperative to put in place a land use plan. This took on urgency once it was recognized that preserving the pine barrens was vital to protecting the sole source of pure fresh water for most of Long Island, the Magothy Aquifer, which lies beneath the two-hundred-foot-deep substrate of sand and gravel. The pine barrens is the recharge region for the aquifer, and maintaining water quality is critical (see chapter 5, "Copious Waters and Multitudes of Fish"). The Long Island Pine Barrens Protection Act was passed into law in 1993 and the Central Pine Barrens Land Use Plan in 1995.[11]

One of the critical components of pine barrens preservation recognized by the 1993 act is fire. The barrens is a "disturbance based ecosystem" that evolved in a landscape of seasonal fires.[12] In the recent past (since heavy settlement), fire suppression has encouraged prolific undergrowth and accumulation of deadwood—literally fuel for a catastrophic fire. In the hot, dry summer of 1995, what became known as the Rocky Point and Sunrise Fires devastated the pine barrens, burning over 4,500 acres, including over 3,000 acres of the Dwarf Pine Barrens.[13] In the aftermath of the burn, a comprehensive fire management plan for the pine barrens was put into place, one that recognized the need for modifying aggressive fire suppression strategies (allowing controlled and contained burns in unpopulated wild areas, for example), while at the same time keeping fire suppression as a central goal in what has become a heavily populated area (outside the core region). In the fire management plan published in 1999 by the Central Pine Barrens Joint Planning and Policy Commission, the authors note "that the threat to human lives and property justifies the suppression and control of these wildfires and, further, that aggressive fire suppression must remain a cornerstone for response to wildfires in the Central Pine Barrens, given the development and condition in the surrounding Compatible Growth Area." However, they distinguish "aggressive fire suppression" to protect lives and property, and "total fire suppression" that "would result in continued, unchecked fuel build-up, which increases the risk of catastrophic fires outside the natural variability of this fire regime. Experience elsewhere in the country has shown there is a point of negative return from total suppression."[14] Periodic fires clear out undergrowth and deadwood in any forest. But in the pine barrens, which evolved in a wildfire environment, periodic fires are essential to the generation and propagation of the pitch pines. In 2021, the commission published a *Prescribed Fire Management Plan* that forcefully argues for the necessity of prescribed fires in the barrens. Put simply, "lack of wildfire disturbance" increases "wildfire risk." On its website, it also notes that climate change is increasing that risk by lengthening the wildfire season. Prescribed fire "is a primary and justified management tool," it declares.[15] The Central Pine Barrens is a complex, fire-dependent ecosystem that encompasses not only pitch pine forests but coastal plain ponds and grasslands, as well as the native species associated with these eco-communities. Without a prescribed burn regimen, the Central Pine Barrens—a "globally rare ecosystem which supports some of the rarest species found in New York State"—may collapse.[16]

I often drive through the Central Pine Barrens region on Sunrise Highway, skirting the southern edge of the Ronkonkoma Moraine. Stretching on both sides of the highway are the Dwarf Pine Barrens, including the Dwarf Pines Plains Preserve just south of exit 31. It was in this region that the Sunrise Fire, a towering inferno that jumped Sunrise Highway, burned for four days and torched 3,200 acres before it was contained. Over the years I have noted the fresh green growth of new pitch pine trees in the burned-out area. In the immediate aftermath of a fire, we see a blackened landscape and charred stumps—a disheartening specter—but it takes a long time and a long view, a generation as measured by our lifetimes, to see their regeneration. Look closely, and you will see bright green shoots emerging from the charred stumps. The serotinous cones scattered on the ground have released their seeds; in time, they will germinate, sending up delicate saplings that in twenty years will grow into beautiful stands of dwarf pitch pines. Leave it alone, give it a chance, let nature take its course, and the forest will renew itself.

As my car crests a hill and continues east, I see an undulating sea of deep green stretching down to the blue horizon. These are the taller pitch pines of the Core Pine Barrens rising on both sides of the highway. Approaching Riverhead, where the North and South Forks split, I notice large swaths of pines with brown needles and denuded trees with blackened trunks—dying and dead trees devastated by the southern pine beetle. This little beetle—the size of a grain of rice—is not an alien invasive; on the contrary, it's native to the Southeast, an inhabitant of—and consumer of—pine forests. Historically, the insect has played a role in pine forest ecology. It prefers weakened, stressed, overcrowded trees, in effect culling forests. But when their numbers explode, they ravage thousands of acres of pine forests. Each beetle tunnels into the inner bark (the cambium layer) to lay its eggs, and both adults and larvae feed on the living tissue under the bark. This kills the trees in two to four months, though the trees put up a valiant defense, secreting pitch to enclose and immobilize them. But the beleaguered trees are overwhelmed by numbers—thousands of beetles on a single tree, producing two to four broods a year. As our winters have become warmer and milder, the beetle has migrated north and spread like wildfire. It was first discovered in New Jersey in 2001, where it has devastated fifty thousand acres of pine barrens. It invaded Long Island's Central Pine Barrens in 2014, and by 2020 spread to Long Island's South Fork, killing hundreds of thousands of trees, mostly pitch pines.

One reason for the beetle's rapid spread might be fire suppression, allowing pines to grow too densely and weakening them as they compete with oaks and shrubs. Once here, the beetle cannot be eradicated, only controlled. In 2016, the strategy of control in New York was to cut and thin stands—culling eight thousand trees in the Core Preservation Area, for example. In June 2017, New York State foresters began implementing a more aggressive plan that includes periodic burns. However, prescribed burns are not feasible in densely populated areas like the Hamptons, so thinning has been the prime strategy. The Central Pine Barrens has become a central battleground with the beetle, since preserving the trees is part and parcel of preserving the water quality of the aquifer. Yet just as valuable as the barrens' critical role in protecting Long Island's aquifer is its vital ecological role as a globally rare habitat complex harboring rare or threatened plants and animals. If the southern pine beetle spreads unchecked, it could destroy the pine barrens forever, and with this reduce Long Island's—and the planet's—biodiversity.[17]

I've observed whole forests fall to this scourge. The beetle reached Long Island's South Fork by 2020. Where sunlight once filtered through pine needles it now shines in clearing after clearing littered with fallen trees. I have driven along Sunrise Highway in Napeague and in a single season seen the pitch pines dying, mile after mile, their needles browning, bark sloughing off, forming large stands of deadwood. Napeague's unique green-and-gold landscape of pitch pines and dunes is vanishing before my eyes. It feels like watching someone you love rapidly succumb to a fatal disease. In Napeague State Park, the state has been culling not only beetle-infested trees but also surrounding healthy trees to create a buffer zone, since these beetles do not travel far as they move from tree to tree. It's radical surgery and heart-wrenching to watch. I see the pitch pine–dune community transforming before my eyes into something else. But hope may reside in the little seeds that lie within the cones scattered amid the debris, in pitch pine seedlings that will grow and in time reach their gnarled branches toward the sky. It's nature's way of regeneration.[18]

On a crisp, bright winter day, I set out in search of a grove of old-growth white pines known as Wilson's Grove, all that's left of a five-thousand-acre pine forest that once cloaked the morainal uplands of Northwest Woods in East Hampton. While native to the Northeast, the white pine is uncommon on Long Island, growing in a slender south-to-north swath from East Hampton to Greenport.[19] As such, the pines would have been greatly valued as timber, their straight tall trunks especially desirable for ship masts. Northwest Landing was the first shipping port in East Hampton before being supplanted by Sag Harbor in the early 1800s. Since the late 1700s, farming and lumbering have cleared the woods here, and more recently upscale housing developments have made their inroads. Wilson's Grove was preserved because of the stewardship of the landowner, Marillyn Wilson. She first donated a conservation easement of 22.7 acres to the Peconic Land Trust in 2002, allowing the East Hampton Trails Preservation Society to construct a section of the Paumanok Path through it; in 2007, she donated the entire grove of 45 acres.[20]

Following the Paumanok Path as it climbs the Amagansett Moraine through second-growth pine woods and gently descends into a hollow, I enter the grove, treading a thick carpet of fallen needles, listening to the soughing wind and chatter of chickadees. I look up through a lacework of intersecting branches and appreciate how sunlight falls in shafts onto the woodland floor. Nature's cathedral. A few fallen trees bear silent testimony to hurricane-force winds, but also to nature's resilience: young white pines are springing up in the clearings. They will grow as long as they have sunlight and are not crowded by oaks that may shade them out.

Pines are pioneer species that colonize cleared land. After the last glacier receded from the region, tundra-like conditions prevailed, but as the climate warmed, spruce forests gradually replaced tundra in a patchwork pattern. Pine barrens composed of jack pine—a species of pine that favors a cold climate—took root in sandy outwash. A patchwork landscape of spruce swamps, pine barrens, cranberry bogs, and grasslands would persist from around nineteen thousand years ago to twelve thousand years ago. The barrens, bogs, and grasslands have remained to this day, but the species of pines that inhabit the barrens have changed. Jack pine migrated northward, replaced by pitch pine. Spruce forests were replaced by pine forests dominated by white pine. By nine thousand years ago, a pine forest extended from New York to Wisconsin, bordered on the south by a deciduous forest dominated by oaks. The oak forest migrated northward, rooting in glacial till. Over the ensuing millennia, an oak-hickory-chestnut forest evolved with a complex understory of berry-laden shrubs and trees such as hollies and viburnums.[21]

Unlike the pitch pine, which with its deep root system favors warm and dry, even droughty, conditions, the white pine thrives in cool and moist conditions. According to Long Island naturalist Larry Penny, the white pines on Long Island grow where the water table is close to the surface, as it is along Northwest Creek. He postulates that they stay cool because they are drawing up water that is cool—50 to 60 degrees Fahrenheit during the summer—and because they are maintaining a microclimate through the evaporation of water from their needles.[22] Writing in 1997, he speculated about what a warming climate might mean, whether pitch pines would take over or, given the white pines' remarkable staying power, "it may never happen"—but that was before the rapid rate of warming became so manifest. In 2013, after inspecting damage to white pines by Hurricane Sandy (minimal except in Northwest Woods), Penny put more emphasis on the impact of climate change: "Global warming will gradually do in the white pines here, just as it did in the hemlocks, spruces, and other cold climate conifers that used to call Long Island their home a few hundred years ago."[23] Pitch pine, as well as being a fire-climax species, is much more tolerant of heat and drought, indeed thrives in warm conditions.

FORESTS OF FALLING LEAVES

Long Island is pocketed with a variety of deciduous woodlands, ranging from oak-hickory forests of the uplands to red maple swamps of the lowlands. On the high hills of Long Island's North Shore, tulip trees predominate in the oak forests. One of the oldest, the Alley Pond Giant, hangs on at Alley Pond Park in Queens, protected by a chain-link fence. Thought to be the oldest living tree on Long Island, it rises 133.8 feet as measured in 2000, with a girth of 18.6 feet. This venerable tree may be 350 years old, perhaps as old as 425 years.[24] Most of Long Island's trees are younger than the Revolutionary War, when British soldiers cut them down for fuel. Those trees spared the ax grew in inaccessible places such as boggy woods and swamps. In one such swamp, a boggy tract in Blydenburgh State Park, an ancient black tupelo grows, its stooped posture and deeply furrowed bark showing its age. In 2008, Daniel Karpen, then sixty years old, discovered it in his forest rambles. An engineer by profession, a student of forestry by vocation, and a tracker of old-growth trees on Long Island, Karpen estimated it to be seven hundred years old, a claim that experts think is exaggerated. However, Fred Breglia, director of Landis Arboretum and self-described "Old Tree Hunter," allowed for the possibility, given the nutrient-poor conditions of the swamp habitat that may have slowed its growth and prolonged its life. But whether the age is overestimated or not, what matters is the preservation of our forests, whether strictly "old growth" (more than 250 years old, or prerevolutionary) or the secondary old growth that characterizes most of Long Island's old forests.[25]

Most of our northeastern forests were cut and otherwise exploited after humans settled the region, going back thousands of years. The Algonquians cleared woodlands by slash-and-burn and girdling techniques to create cropland, although they did not grub the stumps and allowed their corn, squash, and bean plants to grow among the stumps. They cut trees for building materials, tools, and firewood. Moreover, they practiced forest management through prescribed burns. They annually burned the woods, if nature did not, both to maintain desired edge and grassland habitats and to create parkland-type forest cleared of underbrush that was more accessible for the hunter and trekker.[26]

Once Europeans colonized the country in the 1600s, the scale of harvesting ratcheted up. Trees now became marketable commodities, particularly valuable to seafaring nations whose forests had been depleted: tall pines supplied ship masts and century-old oaks supplied ship timbers—several thousand were felled to furnish a single British warship, for example. Forests were harvested for domestic purposes: Atlantic white cedar swamps were quickly depleted of trees, felled for their rot-resistant wood to shingle houses, as noted disapprovingly by Swedish naturalist Pehr Kalm in the mid-1700s. Kalm, who toured New York and Pennsylvania in the mid-1700s to catalog and collect specimens of plants for his sponsor, Carl Linnaeus, was appalled at the wasteful clear-cutting he observed. Forests provided fuel for industrial and domestic uses. Once bog iron was discovered in the early1700s, whole tracts of pine were cut and burned into charcoal to feed voracious iron blast furnaces, which were located in the woods that fueled them. Oak and pine cordwood kept home fires burning in New York City and fired the steam engines that powered ships, factories, and trains in the 1800s before coal came into widespread use.[27]

A mosaic of grasslands and parkland-type forests with pockets of bogs and swamps, a landscape long managed by humans, may once have characterized all Long Island. It's best represented on the Montauk Peninsula (see chapter 6, "Grasslands at the Glacier's Edge"). Hither Woods and Point Woods, now encompassed by Montauk Point State Park and Hither Hills State Park, have existed at least since colonial times and may be fragments of once-vaster tracts. J. A. Ayres wrote in 1849, "There are two tracts of woodlands, known as 'the Hither Woods' and 'the Point Woods.' Solitary and decaying trunks all over the country show that not many years since it was covered much more extensively and perhaps wholly with forest."[28] The peninsula was never wholly forested but rather a mix of grassland, heath, and forest; as noted by Norman Taylor in 1923, historical records indicate "there

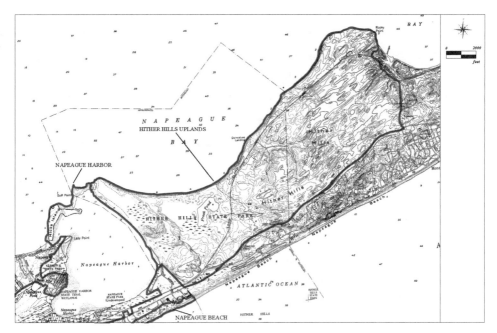

Figure 7.4. Map of Hither Hills Uplands, including Hither Woods Preserve on the eastern edge and Napeague Harbor to the west. "Significant Coastal Fish and Wildlife Habitats," New York Department of State, Division of Coastal Resources, 2002.

has always been, within historic times at least, a distinct separation of grassland and woodland."[29] But Ayres's observation of deforestation nonetheless
holds true. East Hampton town records dating back to the late 1600s and
early 1700s testify to an alarming decrease of timber, necessitating regulations governing its cutting. A court of sessions in 1676 ordered "that no person not having an allotment and thereby a right in the commons should cut
timber in Easthampton."[30] The April 7, 1713, record of the Town of East
Hampton proclaimed,

> Also in regard of the scarcity for timber at Montauk for the enclosures
> and for the prevention of its being destroyed or improved to wrong uses,
> it is ordered by the said Trustees that whosoever shall presume to fell or
> cut down tree or trees standing on any part of Montauk or carry or any
> way bring off from Montauk any part of its growth by land or water except
> such as have authority so to do by virtue of some former deed or contract
> or by permission from the Trustees for the time being, he or they for so
> offending shall forfeit to the use of said Trustees for each and every tree
> cut down aforesaid the sum of ten shillings and for each and every load
> of timber any way carried off as aforesaid the sum of forty shillings.[31]

In 1923, when Taylor conducted his study of the Montauk Peninsula
flora, he visited Hither Woods and Point Woods. In Hither Woods, he
found a forest of black, white, and a few red oaks with an understory of
holly, mountain laurel, shadbush, black huckleberry, low-bush and high-
bush blueberry, and two vines, Virginia creeper and catbrier. He found the
oaks "of great age," judged not so much by height but by their thick festoons
of lichens, standing "clad in the misty grayness of antiquity."[32] Another
indication of "long occupancy" by the oaks was the number of fallen trees,
rotting where they had toppled over, undisturbed. Sassafras was rare—only
saplings. All of these trees, shrubs, and vines are found in the woods today.
The lichens, too, though not in "thick festoons." Many of the wildflowers he
listed are also familiar, among them asters, goldenrods, and golden-asters.
He described Point Woods as richer in species than Hither Woods, primarily because of its diverse habitats, which include ponds, bogs, and swamps.

One of the spring wildflowers he encountered in profusion was dragon's mouth or swamp pink (*Arethusa bulbosa*): "In the boggy places, about the end of May, this part of the peninsula is aflame with *Arethusa bulbosa*." This orchid is now threatened in New York State and globally imperiled. I've explored many of the trails in Montauk Point State Park, but I have never seen this rare flower, although as late as 2019 a small colony was discovered on a private estate.[33] Thankfully, the mountain laurels Taylor described still light up the June woods with their splashy white blossoms. The mountain laurel (*Kalmia latifolia*) was named after Swedish botanist Pehr Kalm, who described its pollen dispersal mechanism: "A single open flower, closely examined, will show ten stamens bowed like umbrella ribs. The tip of each stamen is a pollen pouch (anther) that fits into a small pocket which holds the stamen in the bowed shape. When the blossom edge is touched, the stamens act as catapults to release the pollen. Usually, foraging bees are the targets."[34]

Figure 7.5. Mountain laurel flowers brighten the Hither Woods in June. Photo by author.

Forest Dwellers

The woods of Hither Hills ring with the songs of neotropical birds in June. More species of warblers breed in this state park preserve than at any other place on Long Island: pine warbler, black-and-white warbler, prairie warbler, blue-winged warbler, redstart, ovenbird, yellow warbler, common yellow-throat, and in some years the northern parula.

Joe and I first discovered the northern parula breeding in Hither Woods in the early 2000s. The parula needs usnea, or beard moss, to make its nest—that's the lichen Taylor most likely found festooning the oaks here, although we were hard put to find much of the stuff. Lichen is highly sensitive to pollution. We have heard and often observed the parula high up in the canopy during spring migration, heading to more northerly grounds to breed. But on our June walk in search of breeding warblers, we made the happy discovery of a parula nesting in the vicinity of Fresh Pond, occupying a delicate, improbable cup nest made of hanging strands of beard moss. The female usually constructs the nest, often placing it high in the tree, but in this case the nest was low enough for us to spot. The parula is a beautiful bird with a blue-gray hood and wings, olive-tinged back, dark gray collar, and orange-tinged yellow throat, the orange coloring especially prominent in males; though not melodious, his song is distinctive, an ascending series of high notes ending in a "ping." Almost impossible to see in spring when he forages in the high canopy gleaning insects from the oak flowers like many other warblers, here he was flitting to and from the nest on a low-hanging branch, bringing food for his offspring. We returned the following year and found the breeding pair again, nesting in the same vicinity, but in subsequent years we could not locate them. It would be ten years before we found another pair breeding in these woods, and now we have found several locales on the South Fork where the parula breeds. One can only speculate as to reasons why the parula is no longer a common breeder on Long Island. The dwindling supply of usnea? Fragmented forests? Disturbances in his wintering grounds in Mexico or the West Indies? Yet we always observe the warbler on Long Island in migration. He is not uncommon and will breed up and down the coast from Canada to Florida and into Texas, and recently even as far west as Northern California, wherever he can find beard moss (or, in the American South, Spanish moss). He once bred on eastern Long Island but was extirpated by the 1950s, breeding only in the Adirondacks.[35] Scarcity of usnea seems a likely explanation, an example of how one species depends on the viability of another in an intact habitat. In this case, however, the habitat is intact—Hither Woods is preserved—but pollution is far reaching, carried by wind. Usnea cannot thrive in polluted air, and parulas use the material to build their nests—yet they can be adaptable as necessity demands. They have been observed using other materials if epiphytes are absent, or even nesting inside river debris caught in high branches during a flood.[36] Perhaps it's a combination of factors: the loss of usnea and fragmentation of forests. Parulas prefer not only epiphytic mosses for their nests but also mature forests near water. Our parula located his nest right by Fresh Pond.

Wood warblers are forest dwellers, as their common name suggests. With few exceptions, they need mature forests, which have the complex layers they need, with most nesting on the ground, and some at midlevel. They need the cover of the woods—its protective understory and its shady density, and the provisions of the woods, such as nesting materials and insects (they are insectivorous). Many, like the parula, are highly adapted to the forest habitat, needing specific species of trees—pines for the pine warbler, for example—or plants like usnea in the parula's case.

A threat to both forests and forest-dwelling birds are white-tailed deer, particularly on eastern Long Island, where their populations have exploded. These herbivores are hardly predators, but they are stripping forest understories, changing their composition and fragmenting them. A patch of woods cleared of low-bush blueberry and other heaths is a testimony to the depredation of deer. As they consume the woodland understory and groundcover, both herbal and woody, they are destroying the protective cover needed by low- or ground-nesting birds such as the black-and-white warbler, ovenbird, eastern towhee, and several species of thrush, to name a few. Moreover, fruit-eating birds are deprived of berry-laden shrubs. The habitat disturbance caused by the deer has changed the composition of the forests. In deciduous woods, catbrier has taken over, shunned by deer because of its thorniness. Native wildflowers have mostly disappeared, and woods have become invaded by weedy plants. Since the 1950s, foresters have known that white-tailed deer, when their numbers become unsustainable, can negatively affect forest regeneration, consuming seedlings and saplings before the young trees can establish themselves. For example, Richard S. Mitchell described the effects of overbrowsing by deer in the Hudson Valley in 1997: "After personally exploring hundreds of miles, seeking every habitat in Harriman State Park and surrounding areas, I can tell you first-hand that the vegetation there has been devastated by deer. Nearly every green thing has been nipped, often to the ground. Orchids and other rare herbs have shown a steep decline since the 1940s, and serious forage damage is evident throughout, from dry ridge-tops to trampled wetlands."[37]

The denuding of the forest understory by browsing deer has had a direct impact on forest-breeding birds throughout the Northeast. In 2005, the New Jersey Audubon Society came out as an advocate of hunting deer to reduce their numbers and restore the forests that are so vital to birds. Its report cited the facts: fourteen bird species alone had disappeared from their forest sanctuaries and some thirty species of native wildflowers had been extirpated, including wood anemone, dwarf ginseng, and trout lily. Emile DeVito, a conservation ecologist who is the manager of science and stewardship for the New Jersey Conservation Foundation, published an opinion piece in the *New York Times* in 2008 in which he argued in no uncertain terms that drastic reduction in the deer population—down to five deer per square mile in winter (from two hundred per square mile in parts of New Jersey)—was a necessity. Deer, he asserted, had become "superabundant" and were having a "catastrophic impact" on tree regeneration and forest biodiversity in metropolitan New York. "This uncontrolled population explosion of deer has led to the conversion of our forests to a collection of alien weeds and vines in the understory, in which there is absolutely no reproduction of native woody trees and shrubs or herbaceous wildflowers. Our native forests and associated biodiversity will melt away, as can already be seen in many places, if we continue to ignore these threats."[38]

Another group of species severely affected by deer is the lepidoptera, the butterflies and moths that pupate in forest leaf litter or nectar in woodland wildflowers. Multiple regional studies undertaken since the 1940s have documented the direct effects of increasing white-tailed deer density on woodland understories. Unquestionably, high deer density has drastically reduced the diversity of the herbal understory, extirpating native flowering plants such as trillium and increasing the growth of grasses, sedges, and ferns, resulting in a simpler (as opposed to more complex and diverse) forest ecosystem. The indirect effects of browsing by high numbers of deer include declining insect diversity, particularly specialist pollinators. Grasses, sedges, and ferns provide no pollen or nectar. "Because insects and vascular plants represent two of the most diverse taxonomic groups known and 70 percent of all described species," wrote Thomas Rooney and Donald Waller in 2003, "high deer densities appear to represent a clear and present threat to biological diversity."[39]

Deer, when their populations are unchecked, are changing forest ecology. Deer-resistant species of plants increase and deer-consumed species disappear; thus, for example, grasses, sedges, and ferns take over, reducing biodiversity. "Ecologists have a term for this phenomenon," writes forester Thomas Rawinski, "retrogressive succession. The term describes temporal changes in ecological communities that lead to simpler states of those communities, with less biomass, diminished structural complexity, and fewer species over time."[40] Rawinski argues that it's possible for deer and forests to coexist "in healthy balance" and defines what such a balance is, quoting the Pennsylvania Department of Conservation and Natural Resources: "It's about reading the forest. When we find a wide variety and abundance of young trees, shrubs, and wildflowers—a healthy understory—and the forest exhibits the ability to replace itself, then we know we are close to finding that critical balance between deer and the forest."[41] What tips that balance? "Concerns arise when deer, at high population densities, deplete palatable forage and resort to desperate measures. They will strip and eat bark from witch hazel and hemlock and dig into the ground—like wild hogs—in search of Indian cucumber roots. They can degrade nearly every square foot of understory vegetation. Suffering the consequences of their own overbrowsing, whitetails become undernourished, undersized, and more susceptible to winter die-off."[42] Rawinski concludes with a quote from Aldo Leopold to illuminate what a healthy ecological balance means: "Conservation is a state of health in the land. The land consists of soil, water, plants, and animals, but health is more than a sufficiency of these components. It is a state of vigorous self-renewal in each of them, and in all collectively. Such collective functioning of interdependent parts for the maintenance of the whole is characteristic of an organism. In this sense, land is an organism, and conservation deals with its functional integrity, or health."[43]

———

On a cool, sunny day in early May, I seek the spring ephemerals. These are the woodland wildflowers that, like their name suggests, appear briefly and then disappear until the following spring. They are becoming scarce as deer consume the understory, so whatever I find is all the more precious. At Big Reed Pond on the Montauk Peninsula, I follow a narrow, overgrown trail through tangled stands of sumac and bayberry that grow in a sunny clearing into a shady woodland of oak, pignut hickory, beech, and red maple. The oak and hickory, trees that favor uplands, remind me that I am traversing a moraine. Their drooping catkins attract insects that attract migrating warblers. I hear the sweet strains of a yellow warbler and the loud staccato notes of the ovenbird, both common breeders in our woods. The white five-petaled flowers of wild strawberry and yellow flowers of common cinquefoil brighten the trail edges. The ground grows spongy as I descend to a boggy depression. The woods are deeply shaded now, the understory a thicket of budding shrubs. A colony of wood anemone spangles the forest floor with hundreds of starry white flowers. Red maple, also called swamp maple, grows in the boggy edges of a stream oxbow; one of the first trees to bloom in spring, the maple has already flowered and is now leafing out and dangling its characteristic winged seeds, also a rosy red. I gingerly tread a rickety boardwalk across the bog and over the stream. A toppled tree rests in the still, dark water. I stop a moment to look into the clear, slow-moving stream, its waters stained by tannins in the oak leaves that have fallen into it. Along its moss-bright banks, skunk cabbages thrust fat green leaves through the mud. Lady ferns carpet the ground, and wild geraniums add their amethyst counterpoint to the lacy green tapestry. I am a little late in the season to see the trout-lily flowering, though I remember observing them here a decade before, their yellow flowers dancing on wiry stalks above purple-mottled green leaves that reminded one botanist of speckled trout. I find none. I look for the colonies of jack-in-the-pulpit that I know to grow here and spot a few scattered flowers at the base of an oak tree as I make my way up the trail. I recognize the characteristic leaflets and hooded spathes enclosing their flowers. The female plants are larger than the male plants and are fertilized when pollinating flies visit the flowers. I do not expect to find lady's slippers, not because it is too early—for I would recognize the leaves—but because it is increasingly rare to find a colony at all, anywhere.

As I make my way back through the red maple swamp, I imagine a woman like me in spring, heading to the stream edges where the American ground-nut grows. She would dig in the mud for its nutritious tuberous "potatoes"—it's hard work, bending over, mud under the nails, her feet in the muck, but well worth the effort in stocking a pantry. I imagine she knew the forest well, not just for its utilitarian purposes but for its beauty, its aesthetic value. I am sure she appreciated the sounds and motions of birds—perhaps she even called back, imitating their calls. I am sure she appreciated the ephemeral beauty of woodland wildflowers. I feel she walks with me, savoring the musical quiet of the forest.

She was a Montaukett, the original people of Montauk. Big Reed was the site of a village with extensive corn fields, expansive marshes, fields and woods, ponds and streams. It was both a wild and managed landscape, and they were the original stewards of the land, clearing and cultivating fields, maintaining grasslands and woodlands with fire, harvesting without depleting. They lived like this for thousands of years. In their way of thinking, there was no distinction between nature and culture, between the natural and human environments, between the wild and not-wild. There was no concept of wild at all. There was just the land and they were dwellers in it.

I think about this as I leave the forest. We have become disconnected from the nature that has sustained humans for tens of millennia. We have become wanderers in an alien land; we have lost our way. This preserve is hardly an untouched-by-humans place, but it has been cared for by land stewards who understand on some level the need for restoring a healthy balance, to get back to a state of self-renewal both for our forests and for ourselves. Over a century and a half ago, Henry David Thoreau perambulated his local woods in

Concord, Massachusetts, where he traversed a red maple swamp. He was not trekking in a remote wilderness, but out on a ramble through the woods close to town, in a landscape of woodlots and fenced pastures and cultivated fields. As a surveyor he knew it well. He did not seek a wilderness experience, just a state of wildness, to recover what his mentor Ralph Waldo Emerson called the "aboriginal self." And he found it close to home: "When I would recreate myself, I seek the darkest wood, the thickest and most interminable and, to the citizen, most dismal, swamp. I enter a swamp as a sacred place, a sanctum sanctorum. There is the strength, the marrow, of Nature. The wildwood covers the virgin mould, and the same soil is good for men and trees."[44]

Appendix

Alewife (*Alosa pseudoharengus*)

American beachgrass (*Ammophila breviligulata*)

American eel (*Anguilla rostrata*)

American golden-plover (*Pluvialis dominica*)

American groundnut (*Apios americana*, also called Indian potato)

American robin (*Turdus migratorius*)

Atlantic bay scallop (*Argopecten irradians*)

Atlantic bluefin tuna (*Thunnus thynnus*)

Atlantic cod (*Gadus morhua*)

Atlantic horseshoe crab (*Limulus polyphemus*)

Atlantic mackerel (*Scomber scombrus*)

Atlantic silverside (*Menidia menidia*)

Atlantic white-cedar (*Chamaecyparis thyoides*)

Banded sunfish (*Enneacanthus obesus*)

Bank swallow (*Riparia riparia*)

Bayberry (*Morella pensylvanica*, also called *Myrica pensylvanica*)

Beach plum (*Prunus maritima*)

Bearberry (*Arctostaphylos uva-ursi*)

Bear oak (*Quercus ilicifolia*)

Beluga (*Delphinapterus leucas*)

Big bluestem (*Andropogon gerardi*)

Bird's-foot violet (*Viola pedata*)

Black-and-white warbler (*Mniotilta varia*)

Black-bellied plover (*Pluvialis squatarola*)

Black cherry (*Prunus serotina*)

Black-crowned night heron (*Nycticorax nycticorax*)

Black duck (*Anas rubripes*)

Black huckleberry (*Gaylussacia baccata*)

Black tupelo (*Nyssa sylvatica*)

Blue crab (*Callinectes sapidus*)

Bluefish (*Pomatomus saltatrix*)

Blue mussel (*Mytilus edulis*)

Blue-winged warbler (*Vermivora cyanoptera*)

Bobolink (*Dolichonyx oryzivorus*)

Brook trout (*Salvelinus fontinalis*)

Bufflehead (*Bucephala albiola*)

Bushy frostweed (*Crocanthemum dumosum*)

Butterfly weed (*Asclepias tuberosa*)

Canada cinquefoil (*Potentilla canadensis*)

Catbrier (*Smilax rotundifolia*)

Chain pickerel (*Esox niger*)

Channeled whelk (*Busycotypus canaliculatus*)

Chenille weed (*Dasya baillouviana*)

Clapper rail (*Rallus crepitans*)

Coastal barrens buckmoth (*Hemileuca maia subspecies*)

Common hairgrass (*Avenella flexuosa*)

Common periwinkle (*Littorina littorea*)

Common strawberry (*Fragaria virginiana*)

Common tern (*Sterna hirundo*)

Common yellowthroat (*Geothlypis trichas*)

Cordgrass (*Sporobolus alterniflorus*)

Cranberry (*Vaccinium macrocarpon*)

Diamondback terrapin (*Malaclemys terrapin*)

Dog whelk (*Nucella lapillus*)

Dragon's mouth or swamp pink (*Arethusa bulbosa*)

Dulse (*Palmaria palmata*)

Dunlin (*Calidris alpina*)

Dwarf ginseng (*Panax trifolius*)

Early goldenrod (*Solidago juncea*)

Eastern mudminnow (*Umbra pygmaea*)

Eastern mud snail (*Ilyanassa obsoleta*)

Eastern oyster (*Crassostrea virginica*)

Eastern towhee (*Pipilo erythrophthalmus*)

Eelgrass (*Zostera marina*)

Few-flowered nut sedge (*Scleria pauciflora*)

Five-angled dodder (*Cuscuta pentagona*)

Fragrant waterlily (*Nymphaea odorata*)

Glossy ibis (*Plegadis falcinellus*)

Golden heather (*Hudsonia ericoides*)

Grass pink (*Calopogon tuberosus*)

Grasshopper sparrow (*Ammodramus savannarum*)

Gray catbird (*Dumetella carolinensis*)

Gray goldenrod (*Solidago nemoralis*)

Great blue heron (*Ardea herodius*)

Great cormorant (*Phalacrocorax carbo*)

Great egret (*Ardea alba*)

Greater yellowlegs (*Tringa melanoleuca*)

Green frog (*Lithobates clamitans*)

Green heron (*Butorides virescens*)

Green milkweed (*Asclepias viridiflora*)

Hairy small-leaved tick-trefoil (*Desmodium ciliare*)

Hairy woodpecker (*Dryobates villosus*)

Hemlock (*Tsuga canadensis*)

Herring gull (*Larus argentatus*)

High-bush blueberry (*Vaccinium corymbosum*)

Holly (*Ilex opaca* var. *opaca*)

Humpback whale (*Megaptera novaeangliae*)

Hyssop-leaved boneset (*Eupatorium hyssopifolium*)

Indian or nut grass (*Sorghastrum nutans*)

Irish moss (*Chondrus crispus*)

Jack-in-the-pulpit (*Arisaema triphyllum*)

Kelp (*Laminaria* species)

Killifish (*Fundulus* species)

King rail (*Rallus elegans*)

Knobbed whelk (*Busycon carica*)

Lady fern (*Athyrium angustum*)

Lady's slipper (*Cypripedium acaule*)

Laughing gull (*Leucophaeus atricilla*)

Little bluestem (*Schizachyrium scoparium*)

Low-bush blueberry (*Vaccinium angustifolium*)

Low frostweed (*Crocanthemum propinquum*)

Marsh elder (*Iva frutescens*)

Meadowlark (*Sturnella magna*)

Menhaden (*Brevoortia tyrannus*)

Midland sedge (*Carex mesochorea*)

Minke whale (*Balaenoptera acutorostrata*)

Monarch (*Danaus plexippus plexippus*)

Mountain laurel (*Kalmia latifolia*)

Mummichog (*Fundulus heteroclitus*)

Narrow-leaved bush-clover (*Lespedeza angustifolia*)

Narrow-leaved white-topped aster (*Sericocarpus linifolius*)

New England blazing-star (*Liatris scariosa* var. *nova-angliae*)

Nine-spotted ladybug (*Coccinella novemnotata*)

North Atlantic right whale (*Eubalaena glacialis*)

Northern dewberry (*Rubus flagellaris*)

Northern parula (*Setophaga americana*)

Northern rock barnacle (*Semibalanus balanoides*)

Nuttall's milkwort (*Polygala nuttallii*)

Osprey (*Pandion haliaetus*)

Ovenbird (*Seiurus aurocapilla*)

Painted turtle (*Chrysemys picta picta*)

Peregrine falcon (*Falco peregrinus*)

Pine warbler (*Setophaga pinus*)

Piping plover (*Charadrius melodus*)

Pitch pine (*Pinus rigida*)

Poverty-grass (*Danthonia spicata*)

Prairie warbler (*Setophaga discolor*)

Pumpkinseed (*Lepomis gibbosus*)

Pussytoes (*Antennaria plantaginifolia*, also known as ladies tobacco and everlasting)

Pygmy sperm whale (*Kogia breviceps*)

Quahog (*Mercenaria mercenaria*)

Racemed milkwort (*Polygala polygama*)

Red-breasted merganser (*Mergus serrator*)

Redfin pickerel (*Esox americanus americanus*)

Red-headed woodpecker (*Melanerpes erythrocephalus*)

Red knot (*Calidris canutus* ssp. *rufa*)

Red maple (*Acer rubrum*, also called swamp maple)

Redstart (*Setophaga ruticilla*)

Red-winged blackbird (*Agelaius phoeniceus*)

Reindeer lichen (*Cladonia rangiferina*)

Ribbed mussel (*Geukensia demissa*)

Rockweed (*Fucus distichus*)

Roseate tern (*Sterna dougallii*)

Rose pogonia (*Pogonia ophioglossoides*)

Rose tickseed (*Coreopsis rosea*)

Rough hedge nettle (*Stachys hyssopifolia* var. *hyssopifolia*, also called hyssop hedge nettle)

Ruby-crowned kinglet (*Corthylio calendula*)

Ruddy turnstone (*Arenaria interpres*)

Salt-marsh cordgrass (*Sporobolus alterniflorus*, also called *Spartina alterniflora*)

Salt marsh snail (*Melampus bidentatus*)

Saltmarsh sparrow (*Ammospiza caudacuta*)

Salt meadow hay (*Sporobolus pumilus*, also called *Spartina patens*)

Salt spray rose (*Rosa rugosa*)

Sand fiddler crab (*Leptuca pugilator*)

Sandplain agalinis (*Agalinis decemloba*, also called sandplain gerardia)

Savannah sparrow (*Passerculus sandwichensis*)

Scaup (*Aythya affinis* and *Aythya marila*)

Seabeach amaranth (*Amaranthus pumilus*)

Seaside sparrow (*Ammospiza maritima*)

Shad (*Alosa sapidissima*)

Shadbush (*Amelanchier canadensis* and *Amelanchier nantucketensis*)

Sheepshead minnow (*Cyprinodon variegatus*)

Short-eared owl (*Asio flammeus*)

Skate (*Leucoraja erinaceus*)

Skunk cabbage (*Symplocarpus foetidus*)

Slender blue flag (*Iris prismatica*)

Slipper shell (*Crepidula fornicata*)

Snowy egret (*Egretta thula*)

Song sparrow (*Melospiza melodia*)

Southern pine beetle (*Dendroctonus frontalis*)

Spotted sandpiper (*Actitis macularius*)

Spotted turtle (*Clemmys gutatta*)

Stargrass (*Aletris farinosa*, also called white colic-root)

Stiff-leaved aster (*Ionactis linariifolia*)

Striped bass (*Morone saxatilis*)

Swamp darter (*Etheostoma fusiforme*)

Switchgrass (*Panicum virgatum*)

Tiger salamander (*Ambystoma tigrinum*)

Tiger swallowtail (*Papilio glaucus*)

Toothed white-topped aster (*Sericocarpus asteroides*)

Trout lily (*Erythronium americanum*)

Tulip tree (*Liriodendron tulipifera*)

Upland sandpiper (*Bartramia longicauda*)

Virginia creeper (*Parthenocissus quinquefolia*)

Whip-poor-will (*Antrostomus vociferus*)

White pine (*Pinus strobus*)

White-tailed deer (*Odocoileus virginianus*)

Wild geranium (*Geranium maculatum*)

Wild indigo (*Baptisia tinctoria*)

Willet (*Tringa semipalmata*)

Wood anemone (*Anemone quinquefolia* var. *quinquefolia*)

Yellow-crowned night-heron (*Nyctanassa violacea*)

Yellowfin tuna (*Thunnus albacares*)

Yellow warbler (*Setophaga petechia*)

Acknowledgments

This book is the culmination of ten years of research and field exploration. From its inception to its realization, people have helped me along the way.

I thank my first readers, John Waldman and Kenneth Able, who both enthusiastically endorsed the project. I am grateful for John's encouragement over the years and in particular for his support of this book from the outset, when I first shared the idea with him. As a reader of the manuscript, he offered illuminating comments and helpful suggestions, as well as a few specific corrections reflecting his expertise. Kenneth offered many invaluable suggestions for revision, based on his close reading of the entire manuscript. In their evaluations, both readers helped me see that ten years spent on researching and writing this book were years well spent.

I also wish to thank Bret Bennington, chair of the Department of Geology, Environment, and Sustainability at Hofstra University, who critiqued my chapter on Long Island's geology. He generously shared his knowledge with me, readily responding to my questions and offering suggestions that helped me update the geological story to reflect current thinking. Working closely with me, he produced a very fine illustration for the geology chapter. The other illustration was generously provided by his colleague Charles Merguerian, who gave me critical feedback on the geology material in my first book, *City at the Water's Edge: A Natural History of New York*.

I wish to thank my editor at Rutgers University Press, Peter Mickulas, for his belief in the book. His enthusiastic support for the project gave me much-needed motivation to keep moving forward. Whenever I needed feedback on a particular chapter I was revising, he was immediately responsive. He also guided me through the arduous process of getting the manuscript to print.

Finally, I thank my life partner and husband, Joe Giunta, for his unwavering belief in me as a writer. He has always been there for me, encouraging me to keep going when I found myself discouraged. Writing can be a lonely endeavor, but Joe's companionship and support have made it less so. And his infectious love of nature—particularly of bird life—has never failed to rally my spirits. He has been my companion on many of the field walks described in this book.

Notes

CHAPTER 1 — WALKING THE GLACIER'S EDGE

1. Sarah Wilford, "Mammoth Fossil Found in Baisley Park," *Long Island Daily Press*, September 7, 1935, https://fultonhistory.com/Newspaper%2014/Jamaica%20 NY%20Long%20Island%20Daily%20Press/Jamaica%20NY%20Long%20Island %20Daily%20Press%201935/Jamaica%20NY%20Long%20Island%20Daily%20 Press%201935%20-%205057.pdf. My thanks to geologist Bret Bennington for sharing this article.

2. John A. Black and R. S. Welch, "The Montauk Peninsula: Data and Preliminary Interpretations of the Ditch Plains Area," paper presented at Geology of Long Island and Metropolitan New York, April 19, 1997, State University of New York at Stony Brook, in *Long Island Geologists Program with Abstracts* (Stony Brook: State University of New York, 1997), https://www.stonybrook.edu/commcms/geosciences /about/_LIG-Past-Conference-abstract-pdfs/Assorted-Abstracts/black-97.pdf.

3. Les Sirkin, *Eastern Long Island Geology: History, Processes, and Field Trips* (Watch Hill, RI: Book and Tackle Shop, 1995).

4. Sirkin. Sirkin assigned a so-called Woodfordian age to both the Harbor Hill and Ronkonkoma Moraines, "Woodfordian" being a geological term designating the last advance of the Laurentide ice sheet during the last stage of the Wisconsinan ice age. The early, middle, and late Wisconsinan stages together spanned two million years.

5. John E. Sanders and Charles Merguerian, "Evidence for Pre-Woodfordian Ages of Long Island's Terminal Moraines," paper presented at Geology of Long Island and Metropolitan New York, April 22, 1995, State University of New York at Stony Brook, in *Long Island Geologists Program with Abstracts* (Stony Brook: State University of New York, 1995), 91–106, https://dspace.sunyconnect.suny.edu /bitstream/handle/1951/48207/SANDER00-95.PDF?sequence=1&isAllowed=y; John E. Sanders et al., "Pleistocene Multi-glacier Hypothesis Supported by Newly Exposed Glacial Sediments, South Twin Island, the Bronx, New York," paper

presented at Geology of Long Island and Metropolitan New York, April 19, 1997, State University of New York at Stony Brook, in *Long Island Geologists Program with Abstracts* (Stony Brook: State University of New York at Stony Brook, 1997), 111–122, https://dspace.sunyconnect.suny.edu/bitstream/handle/1951/48069/SANDER 00-97.pdf?sequence=1&isAllowed=y.

6. Bret J. Bennington, "New Observations for the Glacial Geomorphology of Long Island from a Digital Elevation Model (DEM)," paper presented at Geology of Long Island and Metropolitan New York, April 12, 2003, State University of New York at Stony Brook, https://dspace.sunyconnect.suny.edu/bitstream/handle/1951 /48205/index-Bennington.pdf?sequence=1.

7. In his 2003 paper, Bennington did not assign any dates to these glacial advances and retreats, and in a personal communication to me he indicated that without firmly supported dates, the timeline for glacial advances and retreats on Long Island remains speculative. However, a recent method of dating the minerals in glacial erratics exposed at the surface, known as cosmogenic dating, may provide some hard evidence. Dating of glacial erratics in both moraines so far suggests that the deposition of the Harbor Hill and Ronkonkoma moraines may not be as far apart in time as believed, perhaps merely a thousand years apart, which appears to support a single-glacier hypothesis. Bret Bennington, personal communication, April 2, 2023.

8. Charles Merguerian credits Bret Bennington (2003) for presenting "convincing geomorphologic evidence that the Harbor Hill Moraine truncates the older Ronkonkoma Moraine near Roslyn Heights." Charles Merguerian, "The Narrows Flood—Post-Woodfordian Meltwater Breach of the Narrows Channel, NYC," paper presented at Geology of Long Island and Metropolitan New York, April 12, 2003, State University of New York at Stony Brook, https://dspace.sunyconnect.suny.edu /bitstream/handle/1951/47860/merguerian-03.pdf?sequence=1.

9. Les Sirkin, *Western Long Island Geology: History, Processes, and Field Trips* (Watch Hill, RI: Book and Tackle Shop, 1995), 8.

10. Merguerian, "Narrows Flood," 10.

11. Sirkin, *Western Long Island Geology*.

12. Sirkin, 134.

13. Sirkin, 14, 17.

14. Sirkin, 134; "Geology of Garvies Point," Garvies Point Museum and Preserve, accessed October 9, 2023, https://www.garviespointmuseum.com/geology-of-garvies -point.php; "Garvies Point Preserve—Late 'Age of Dinosaurs' Rock on Long Island," New York State Geological Survey, New York State Museum, accessed October 9, 2023, http://www.nysm.nysed.gov/research-collections/geology/resources/garvies -point-preserve.

15. See the website of Michael Klimetz for lovely photos of late Cretaceous fossils imprinted in micaceous siltstone found at Caumsett State Park (not far from Garvies Point), predominantly sassafras and *Cinnamomum*, a subtropical tree with fra-

grant leathery leaves in the laurel family. Michael Klimetz, Regents Earth Science Regents Physics and AP Physics 1 and AP Physics 2 Online Resource, last updated June 6, 2023, http://earthphysicsteaching.homestead.com.

16. Charles Arthur Hollick, *The Cretaceous Flora of Southern New York and New England*, United States Geological Survey, Monograph 50 (Washington, DC: Government Printing Office, 1906).

17. An exciting discovery was recently made by William Hart and Bret Bennington of Hofstra University, who have been excavating the Cretaceous outcrops of the North Shore. At Makamah Beach, they collected samples of sandy and clay layers, which they processed in their lab to search for animal fossils. Peering through their compound light microscope, they found a fish vertebra, possibly that of a ray-finned fish, in a sandy layer, and a vertebrate bone pebble, or chip, of an unidentified animal in a silty clay layer, the first such Cretaceous vertebrate fossils found on Long Island. Hart and Bennington are confident that the outcrops will yield more vertebrate fossils, "including the remains of Cretaceous dinosaurs, birds, and mammals." William Jude Hart and J. Bret Bennington, "First Vertebrate Fossils Reported from Cretaceous Strata on Long Island with New Sedimentological Data and Observations," paper presented at Thirtieth Conference on the Geology of Long Island and Metropolitan New York, April 2023, courtesy of Bret Bennington.

18. William B. Gallagher, *When Dinosaurs Roamed New Jersey* (New Brunswick, NJ: Rutgers University Press, 1997), 74.

19. Gallagher, 76–80.

20. Gallagher, 82–88.

21. Gallagher, 110.

22. Gallagher, 114–115.

CHAPTER 2 — SHIFTING SANDS AND WALKING DUNES

1. Benjamin Franklin Thompson, *History of Long Island, Containing an Account of the Discovery and Settlement; with Other Important and Interesting Matters to the Present Time* (1839; repr., Forgotten Books Classic Reprint Series, 2012), 445.

2. Thompson, 21.

3. Jay Tanski, *Long Island's Dynamic South Shore: A Primer on the Forces and Trends Shaping Our Coast*, rev. ed. (New York Sea Grant, 2012), 11–12, https://nyseagrant.org/cprocesses/pdfs/LIDynamicSouthShore.pdf.

4. Cheryl J. Hapke et al., *National Assessment of Shoreline Change; Historical Shoreline Change along the New England and Mid-Atlantic Coasts*, Open-File Report 2010-1118 (Reston, VA: US Geological Survey, 2011), https://pubs.usgs.gov/of/2010/1118.

5. John R. Gillis, *The Human Shore: Seacoasts in History* (Chicago: University of Chicago Press, 2012), 19.

6. Thompson, *History of Long Island*, 34–35.

7. Daniel M. Tredwell, *Personal Reminiscences of Men and Things on Long Island*, pt. 1 (New York: Charles Andrew Ditmas, 1912), 144, Google Books, https://play .google.com/books/reader?id=7A8zAQAAIAAJ.

8. Tredwell, 144.

9. Les Sirkin, *Eastern Long Island Geology: History, Processes, and Field Trips* (Watch Hill, RI: Book and Tackle Shop, 1995), 81.

10. The piping plover has been listed by the US Fish and Wildlife Service (FWS) as threatened in the northeast region and endangered in the Midwest region since 1985; the roseate tern has been listed as endangered in the northeast region and threatened in the southeast region since 1987; and the seabeach amaranth has been listed as threatened "wherever found" since 1993. "Piping Plover (*Charadrius melodus*)," FWS Environmental Conservation Online System, accessed October 30, 2023, https://ecos.fws.gov/ecp/species/6039; "Roseate Tern (*Sterna dougallii dougallii*)," FWS Environmental Conservation Online System, accessed October 30, 2023, https://ecos.fws.gov/ecp/species/2083; "Seabeach Amaranth (*Amaranthus pumilus*)," FWS Environmental Conservation Online System, accessed October 30, 2023, https://ecos.fws.gov/ecp/species/8549.

11. Christopher Walsh, "Town Loses Napeague Beach Access Battle," *East Hampton Star*, September 15, 2021.

12. Wampum, tubular beads of quahog and whelk shell woven into belts and headbands, had long been considered sacred objects by the Algonquians. After Europeans colonized the region, they became the currency of exchange. Wampum manufacture became a lucrative enterprise among coastal Algonquians. One of the wampum mints was Fort Massapeag, at Sunset Park in Massapequa, excavated by Ralph Solecki in 1938. It's now a National Historic Landmark. See Anne-Marie Cantwell and Diana diZerega Wall, *Unearthing Gotham: The Archaeology of New York City* (New Haven, CT: Yale University Press, 2001), 132–142.

13. Carl Safina, *The View from Lazy Point: A Natural Year in an Unnatural World* (New York: Picador/Henry Holt, 2011), 132–136.

14. James Gorman, "A Decrease in Horseshoe Crabs Raises Concern," *New York Times*, May 27, 2002.

15. Deborah Cramer, *The Narrow Edge: A Tiny Bird, an Ancient Crab, and an Epic Journey* (New Haven, CT: Yale University Press, 2015), 84.

16. Atlantic States Marine Fisheries Commission, *2013 Horseshoe Crab Stock Assessment Update*, prepared by Atlantic States Marine Fisheries Commission Horseshoe Crab Stock Assessment Subcommittee, August 2013, 16, http://www .asmfc.org/uploads/file/52a88db82013HSC_StockAssessmentUpdate.pdf.

17. Cramer, *Narrow Edge*, 58.

18. Alexander Wilson, *Wilson's American Ornithology*, ed. T. M. Brewer (Boston: Otis, Broaders, 1840), 481, quoted in Cramer, *Narrow Edge*, 62.

19. Horseshoe crab blood is blue because it contains copper. It also contains coagulogen, which is used in biomedical labs to screen any solution for bacteria that may come into contact with blood. The horseshoes are collected and bled, then returned to the sea. It was thought to be a fairly benign practice with low mortality, but recent studies indicate it may affect breeding success, since females may be weakened by the bloodletting. See Alexis C. Madrigal, "The Blood Harvest," *Atlantic*, February 26, 2014, https://www.theatlantic.com/technology/archive/2014/02/the-blood-harvest/284078.

20. Statistic from "Service Protects Red Knot as Threatened under the Endangered Species Act," press release, US Fish and Wildlife Service, December 9, 2014, https://www.fws.gov/press-release/2014-12/service-protects-red-knot-threatened-under-endangered-species-act. The most recent status report was published in September 2020: *Species Status Assessment Report for the Rufa Red Knot (Calidris canutus rufa)*, version 1.1, North Atlantic-Appalachian Region (Interior Region 1), New Jersey Field Office (Galloway, NJ: 2020), https://ecos.fws.gov/ServCat/DownloadFile/187781.

21. "Red Knot Shorebird Listed as Threatened by the Fish and Wildlife Service," press release, American Bird Conservancy, December 9, 2014, https://abcbirds.org/article/red-knot-shorebird-listed-as-threatened-by-u-s-fish-and-wildlife-service. See also Deborah Cramer, "Red Knots Are Battling Climate Change—on Both Ends of the Earth," *Audubon Magazine*, May–June 2016, https://www.audubon.org/magazine/may-june-2016/red-knots-are-battling-climate-change-both-ends. Cramer highlights the threats to red knots and other shorebirds posed by climate change, including rising sea levels that inundate shorelines and barrier beaches, and acidification of the oceans by carbon dioxide. The acidification is thinning the shells of mollusks on which they feed.

22. John R. Gillis, "Why Sand Is Disappearing," *New York Times*, November 4, 2014.

23. Tanski, *Dynamic South Shore*, 22.

24. Orrin H. Pilkey and J. Andrew G. Cooper, *The Last Beach* (Durham, NC: Duke University Press, 2014).

25. Pilkey and Cooper, 83.

26. Pilkey and Cooper, xi, xiv.

27. Tanski, *Dynamic South Shore*, 19–20. For more technical information on the Westhampton groin project, see Gilbert K. Nersesian, Nicholas C. Kraus, and Fulton C. Carson, "Functioning of Groins at Westhampton Beach, Long Island, New York," *Coastal Engineering Proceedings* 1, no. 23 (January 1992): 3357–3370, https://icce-ojs-tamu.tdl.org/icce/index.php/icce/article/view/4935.

28. Mireya Navarro and Rachel Nuwer, "Resisted for Blocking the View, Dunes Prove They Blunt Storms," *New York Times*, December 3, 2012.

29. Beth Young, "Army Corps Awards Bid for Montauk Project; Defend H2O Sues over Shoreline Hardening," *East End Beacon*, March 23, 2015, https://www .eastendbeacon.com/army-corps-awards-bid-for-montauk-project-defend-h2o -sues-over-shoreline-hardening/.

30. Bottini quoted in Ashton Goggans, "Montauk Fighting to Save Dunes," *Surfer Magazine*, November 10, 2015, https://www.surfer.com/features/montauk-fighting-to -save-dunes.

31. Sue McCormack quoted in Michael Wright, "Sandbags to Be Fixed Soon," *East Hampton Press*, October 5, 2016.

32. US Army Corps of Engineers, New York District, *Evaluation of a Stabilization Plan for Coastal Storm Risk Management in Response to Hurricane Sandy and Public Law 113-2* (June 2014), 1, https://www.nan.usace.army.mil/Portals/37/docs /civilworks/projects/ny/coast/fimp/FIMI_Docs/HSLRR/A-FINAL_FIMI_HSLRR _Report.pdf.

33. US Army Corps of Engineers, 1.

34. Alison Branco and Fred Thiele quoted in Polly Mosendz and Eric Roston, "Unlimited Sand and Money Still Won't Save the Hamptons," *Bloomberg*, October 29, 2021, https://www.bloomberg.com/graphics/2021-hamptons-real-estate-beach -climate-proofing/.

35. New York City Panel on Climate Change, *Climate Risk Information 2013: Observations, Climate Change Projections, and Maps*, ed. C. Rosenzweig and W. Solecki, prepared for the City of New York Special Initiative on Rebuilding and Resiliency, New York, New York, June 11, 2013, https://seagrant.sunysb.edu/media/sandy12/A -NYPanelOnClimateChange-June2013.pdf; Vivien Gornitz et al., "Sea Level Rise," in *New York City Panel on Climate Change Report 2019*, published in *Annals of the New York Academy of Sciences* 1439, no. 1 (March 2019): 71–94, https://doi.org/10.1111 /nyas.14006. On historical sea level rise, see Radley Horton et al., "Climate Risk Information," in "Climate Change Adaptation in New York City," special issue, *Annals of the New York Academy of Sciences* 1196, no. 1 (May 2010): 147–228, https:// doi.org/10.1111/j.1749-6632.2010.05323.x.

36. Mosendz and Roston, "Unlimited Sand and Money." They cite statistics from Climate Central (https://www.climatecentral.org).

37. Walt Whitman, "Paumanok, and My Life on It as Child and Young Man," in *Complete Prose Works* (Philadelphia: David McKay, 1892), https://whitmanarchive .org/published/other/CompleteProse.html.

38. Jaspar Dankers and Peter Sluyter, *Journal of a Voyage to New York and a Tour in Several of the American Colonies in 1679–80*, ed. Henry C. Murphy, vol. 1 of *Memoirs of the Long Island Historical Society* (Brooklyn: published by the society, 1867), 118, 279, Google Books, https://www.google.com/books/edition/Journal_of_a _Voyage_to_New_York/XThi4cOyFZUC?gbpv=1.

CHAPTER 3 — THE BLUE SURROUND

1. Scott W. Shumway, *Atlantic Seashore: Beach Ecology from the Gulf of Maine to Cape Hatteras* (Guilford, CT: Falcon Guides / Globe Pequot, 2008), 29.

2. Deborah Cramer, *Great Waters: An Atlantic Passage* (New York: W. W. Norton, 2001), 28.

3. Cramer, 50.

4. Shumway, *Atlantic Seashore*, 2.

5. The Lenapes, also known as the Munsees (distinguished by the Algonquian dialect they spoke), lived in the region of the Hudson and Delaware Rivers from western Long Island across New Jersey to eastern Pennsylvania; the spelling of their name for the Hudson, really a transliteration of a spoken word, varies.

6. "Proposed Designation of Hudson Canyon National Marine Sanctuary," National Oceanic and Atmospheric Administration (NOAA), accessed October 10, 2023, https://sanctuaries.noaa.gov/hudson-canyon/.

7. K. O. Emery and R. Edwards, "Archaeological Potential of the Atlantic Continental Shelf," *American Antiquity* 31 (1966): 733–737, cited in Daria E. Merwin, "Paleolandforms and Prehistoric Site Potential on the Mid-Atlantic OCS" (PowerPoint presentation, Department of Archaeology, Stony Brook University, 2003), https://www.boem.gov/sites/default/files/uploadedFiles/BOEM/BOEM_Newsroom/Library/Publications/2012/PowerPoint_Source_Files/2D_0135_Merwin_PPT.pdf. See also Daria E. Merwin, "Submerged Evidence of Early Human Occupation in the New York Bight" (PhD diss., Stony Brook University, 2010).

8. Merwin, "Paleolandforms."

9. Diana diZerega Wall and Anne-Marie Cantwell, *Touring Gotham's Archaeological Past: 8 Self-Guided Walking Tours through New York City* (New Haven, CT: Yale University Press, 2004), 176.

10. Raymond McFarland, *A History of the New England Fisheries, with Maps* (New York: D. Appleton, 1911), 21, https://archive.org/details/historyofnewengloomcfarich/mode/2up.

11. Mark Kurlansky, *Cod: A Biography of the Fish That Changed the World* (New York: Penguin, 1998), 22–23, 43; Brian Fagan, *The Little Ice Age: How Climate Made History, 1300–1850* (New York: Basic Books, 2000), 69–70.

12. McFarland, *New England Fisheries*, 25–30.

13. John Brereton, "Briefe and True Relation of the Discoverie of the North Part of Virginia in 1602," in *Early English and French Voyages, Chiefly from Hakluyt, 1534–1608*, ed. Henry S. Burrage (New York: Charles Scribner's Sons, 1906), 331, https://www.americanjourneys.org/aj-039/.

14. Gosnold cited in Kurlansky, *Cod*, 64–65. See also Fagan, *Little Ice Age*, 78; and Bill Lawrence, *The Early American Wilderness as the Explorers Saw It* (New York: Paragon House, 1991), 103.

15. Russell Shorto, *The Island at the Center of the World: The Epic Story of Dutch Manhattan and the Forgotten Colony That Shaped America* (2004; New York: Vintage, 2005), 31.

16. Hessel Gerritsz, cartographer, "Novum Anglia Novum Belgium et Virginia," map, 1630, in Johannes de Laet, *Niewwe Wereld, Beschrijvinghe van West-indien* (Leiden, 1630), New Netherland Institute online exhibit, "Charting New Netherland: 1597–1682," https://www.newnetherlandinstitute.org/history-and-heritage/digital -exhibitions/charting-new-netherland-1600/the-maps/nova-anglia-novum -belgium-et-virginia-1630/. According to the New Netherland Institute, the map was "the first accurate depiction of the East Coast," depicting both Manhattan and Long Island as islands, and "the first printed map of New Netherland."

17. Adriaen van der Donck, *A Description of New Netherland*, ed. Charles T. Gehring and William A. Starna, trans. Diederik Willem Goedhuys (Lincoln: University of Nebraska Press, 2008), 58. See the editors' note regarding the spelling: these are not the actual Dutch words for the numbers but a play on words.

18. Van der Donck, 58.

19. "Bluefish," NOAA Fisheries, last updated May 10, 2023, https://fisheries.noaa .gov/species/bluefish/.

20. Gobler quoted in Denise Civiletti, "Marine Research Scientist: 'Mahogany Tide' Algal Bloom Caused Fish Kill in Peconic Estuary," *Riverhead Local*, May 30, 2015, https://riverheadlocal.com/2015/05/30/marine-research-scientist-mahogany -tide-algal-bloom-caused-fish-kill-in-peconic-estuary/.

21. Kirk Semple, "Long Island Sees a Crisis as It Floats to the Surface," *New York Times*, June 5, 2015. Semple cites the water resources study conducted by Suffolk County in 2015 in which it identified nitrogen overload as the primary culprit in triggering toxic algal blooms, decimating fisheries, and degrading wetlands. See the introduction to *Suffolk County Comprehensive Water Resources Management Plan*, March 2015, https://www.suffolkcountyny.gov/Portals/0/FormsDocs /Health/EnvironmentalQuality/ComprehensiveWaterResourceManagementPlan /Comprehensive_Water_Resource_Management_Plan.pdf.

22. "Bluefish Management Plan," NOAA Fisheries, last updated April 26, 2022, https://fisheries.noaa.gov/management-plan/bluefish-management-plan/; "Bluefish Allocation and Rebuilding Amendment, Amendment 7 to the Bluefish Management Plan," Mid-Atlantic Fishery Management Council, January 1, 2022, https://www .mafmc.org/actions/bluefish-allocation-amendment/.

23. Robert H. Boyle, *The Hudson River: A Natural and Unnatural History*, expanded ed. (1969; New York: W. W. Norton, 1979), 268.

24. The statistic comes from John Andre, "Bluefin Tuna Records," On the Water, April 8, 2021, https://www.onthewater.com/bluefin-tuna-records.

25. Carl Safina, *Song for the Blue Ocean: Encounters along the World's Coasts and beneath the Seas* (New York: John Macrae Books / Henry Holt, 1997), xiii.

26. Safina, 8–9.

27. Safina, 33.

28. See Kim Aarestrup et al., "First Tagging Data on Large Atlantic Bluefin Tuna Returning to Nordic Waters Suggest Repeated Behavior and Skipped Spawning," *Scientific Reports* 12, 11772 (2022), https://doi.org/10.1038/s41598-022-15819-x.

29. Paul Greenberg, *Four Fish: The Future of the Last Wild Food* (New York: Penguin Books, 2010), 200.

30. Greenberg, 216.

31. Greenberg, 217.

32. "Endangered Species Act Status Review of the Atlantic Bluefin Tuna (Thunnus thynnus)," NOAA Fisheries, May 20, 2011, https://www.fisheries.noaa.gov /resource/document/endangered-species-act-status-review-atlantic-bluefin-tuna -thunnus-thynnus.

33. "ICCAT Ignores Science and Increases Quota for Atlantic Bluefin Tuna," Pew Charitable Trusts, Global Tuna Conservation project, November 20, 2014, https:// www.pewtrusts.org/en/research-and-analysis/articles/2014/11/20/iccat-ignores -science-and-increases-quota-for-atlantic-bluefin-tuna. See also "Status Review of the Atlantic Bluefin Tuna."

34. "Recommendation by ICCAT Amending Recommendation 17-06 for an Interim Conservation and Management Plan for Western Atlantic Bluefin Tuna," International Commission for the Conservation of Atlantic Tunas, accessed October 10, 2023, https://www.iccat.int/Documents/Recs/compendiopdf-e/2021-07 -e.pdf.

35. Carl Safina, "Fisheries Management and Maximum Sustainable Yield; Part 2," carlsafina.org (blog), February 8, 2012 (post no longer exists).

36. Carl Safina, "Fisheries Management and Maximum Sustainable Yield; Part 2." See also Carl Safina and Elizabeth Brown, "Protected No Longer? Desperate Fisheries Managers Want to Open Closed Areas," carlsafina.org (blog), December 9, 2014, https://www.carlsafina.org/blog/protected-no-longer- desperate-fisheries-managers-want-to-open-closed-areas/. In a number of blog posts on his website between 2012 and 2017, Safina argued for rebuilding the populations of Atlantic menhaden (a species of herring considered the "most important food fish" for bluefin, whales, dolphins, bluefish, striped bass, and other western Atlantic marine species), which he asserted was overfished to serve the fish oil industry. See Carl Safina, "Menhaden, the Little Fish That Could—Won't," carlsafina.org (blog), November 16, 2017, https://www.carlsafina .org/blog/menhaden-the-little-fish-that-couldwont/. See also Callum M. Roberts, Julie P. Hawkins, and Fiona R. Gell, "The Role of Marine Reserves in Achieving Sustainable Fisheries," *Philosophical Transactions of the Royal Society* 360, no. 1453 (January 29, 2005): 123–132, http://rstb.royalsocietypublishing.org /content/royptb/360/1453/123.full.pdf/.

37. Desiree D'iorio, "'Extremely Rare' Humpback Whale Sightings in Long Island," *Long Island Press*, September 26, 2015, https://www.longislandpress.com/2015/09/26/extremely-rare-humpback-whale-sightings-in-long-island-sound-video/.

38. In its "final rule" regarding the status of the humpback whale, issued in September 2016, NOAA divided the global population into fourteen distinct population segments, evaluating the listing status of each. The West Indian population—where our humpbacks breed—was delisted as endangered and instead relisted as "NW"—not warranted for inclusion as either endangered or threatened, thus removing them from the protection of the Endangered Species Act. "Endangered and Threatened Species; Identification of 14 Distinct Population Segments of the Humpback Whale (Megaptera novaeangliae) and Revision of Species-Wide Listing," *Federal Register*, September 8, 2016, https://www.federalregister.gov/documents/2016/09/08/2016-21276/endangered-and-threatened-species-identification-of-14-distinct-population-segments-of-the-humpback/. See also "Final Recovery Plan for the Humpback Whale (Megaptera novaeangliae)," NOAA Fisheries, November 1991, https://www.fisheries.noaa.gov/resource/document/final-recovery-plan-humpback-whale-megaptera-novaeangliae. A Rutgers University study of the humpbacks in the New York Bight apex conducted in the years 2012–2018 found over half the whales in the New York–New Jersey Estuary were spotted more than once, indicating site fidelity. See Danielle M. Brown et al., "Site Fidelity, Population Identity and Demographic Characteristics of Humpback Whales in the New York Bight Apex," *Journal of the Marine Biological Association of the United Kingdom* 102, no. 1–2 (2022): 157–165, https://doi.org/10.1017/S0025315422000388.

39. Larry Penny, "Nature Notes: More Whales Lost," *East Hampton Star*, June 1, 2016.

40. "2016–2023 Humpback Whale Unusual Mortality Event along the Atlantic Coast," NOAA Fisheries, last updated September 26, 2023, https://www.fisheries.noaa.gov/national/marine-life-distress/2016-2023-humpback-whale-unusual-mortality-event-along-atlantic-coast.

41. John A. Strong, *The Montaukett Indians of Eastern Long Island* (2001; Syracuse, NY: Syracuse University Press, 2006), 26, 48.

42. Strong, 48.

43. Kathleen Bragdon, *Native Peoples of Southern New England, 1500–1650* (1996; Norman: University of Oklahoma Press, 2009).

44. David Gardiner, *Chronicles of the Town of Easthampton, County of Suffolk, New York* (1871; repr., Sag Harbor, NY: I. G. Mairs, 1973), 5, quoted in John Strong, "Shinnecock and Montauk Whalemen," *Long Island Historical Journal* 2, no. 1 (Fall 1989): 29. Gardiner was drawing from a 1631 account by Mohegan missionary Samson Occom.

45. In 2005, the Shinnecock Nation had to make a formal request to the town for the baleen, fins, and tail of a beached finback whale to display in their museum,

despite their ancient rights. Russell Drumm, "Finback Whale Drifts Ashore at South-ampton: 'History Repeats Itself' on the Ocean Beach," *East Hampton Star*, April 7, 2005. For a detailed account of the transactions between the English and Indians of Long Island in the 1600s, particularly as the deeds affected their rights to beached whales, see John A. Strong, *America's Early Whalemen: Indian Shore Whalers on Long Island, 1650–1750* (Tucson: University of Arizona Press, 2018), chaps. 2, 3. According to Strong, Wyandanch was appointed by the English as "Grand Sachem" to represent all sachems of the region, trading away their rights not only to beached whales but to traditional hunting territories. He made many enemies among his people, possibly resulting in his death by poisoning.

46. Eric Jay Dolin, *Leviathan: The History of Whaling in America* (2007; New York: W. W. Norton, 2008), Kindle, chap. 1. Two other species of right whale exist, the Southern and the North Pacific right whale.

47. "North Atlantic Right Whale," NOAA Fisheries, last updated October 4, 2023, https://www.fisheries.noaa.gov/species/north-atlantic-right-whale.

48. Dolin, *Leviathan*, chap. 1.

49. Alex Aguilar, "A Review of Old Basque Whaling and Its Effect on the Right Whales (Eubalaena glacialis) of the North Atlantic," *Report of the International Whaling Commission* special issue 10 (January 1986): 191–199, https://www.researchgate.net/publication/235407504; Dolin, *Leviathan*, chap. 1.

50. James Rosier, *Prosperous Voyage*, March of America Facsimile Series 17 (1605; Ann Arbor: University Microfilms, 1966), quoted in Dolin, *Leviathan*, chap. 1.

51. Strong, *Montaukett Indians*, 50–52; Strong, *America's Early Whalemen*, 58–61; Dolin, *Leviathan*, chap. 3. Dolin suggests that the Indians were hired not so much for their unique skills as for their cheap labor.

52. Strong, *America's Early Whalemen*, 26–27.

53. William "Tangier" Smith cited in Strong, *Montaukett Indians*, 53. See also Strong, *America's Early Whalemen*, chap. 6.

54. Dolin, *Leviathan*, chap. 4; Alexander Starbuck, *History of the American Whale Fishery from Its Earliest Inception to the Year 1876* (Waltham, MA, 1878).

55. Quoted in Dolin, *Leviathan*, chap. 3.

56. Obed Macy, *The History of Nantucket* (1835; repr., Clifton, NJ: Augustus M. Kelley, 1972), 27–30, cited in Dolin, *Leviathan*, chap. 4. Long Island would once again become a major whaling center, with Sag Harbor as its main port, when sperm whales—mythologized by Herman Melville in his great novel *Moby Dick*, became the prime catch, prized for their superior oil and spermaceti. But the pursuit of the sperm whale, which inhabited deep waters, involved extended journeys into inter-national waters, outside the purview of this book. On the decline of shore whaling, see also Strong, *America's Early Whalemen*, chap. 8.

57. Randall R. Reeves and Edward Mitchell, "The Long Island, New York, Right Whale Fishery: 1650–1924," *Report of the International Whaling Commission*

special issue 10 (1986): 201–220, https://archive.iwc.int/pages/search.php?search =%21collection34&k=.

58. NOAA Fisheries, *North Atlantic Right Whale (*Eubalaena glacialis*) 5-Year Review: Summary and Evaluation* (Gloucester, MA: NOAA Fisheries, August 2012), https://repository.library.noaa.gov/view/noaa/17038. On the unusual mortality event, see "2017–2023 North Atlantic Right Whale Unusual Mortality Event," NOAA Fisheries, last updated October 4, 2023, https://www.fisheries.noaa.gov/national/marine -life-distress/2017-2023-north-atlantic-right-whale-unusual-mortality-event.

59. Deborah Cramer, *Ocean: Our Water, Our World* (New York: Smithsonian Books / HarperCollins, 2008), 178.

60. Cramer, 178.

61. Jaspar Dankers and Peter Sluyter, *Journal of a Voyage to New York and a Tour in Several of the American Colonies in 1679–80*, ed. Henry C. Murphy, vol. 1 of Memoirs of the Long Island Historical Society (Brooklyn: published by the society, 1867), 123, Google Books. By Dankers's time, oysters had become a considerable industry, as indicated in a town ordinance: "To prevent the destruction of oysters in South Bay, by the unlimited number of vessels employed in the same, it is ordered that but ten vessels shall be allowed, and that each half-barrel tub shall be paid for at the rate of 2d., according to the town act of Brookhaven." Ernest Ingersoll, *The Oyster Industry: Tenth Census of the United States* (Washington, DC: Government Printing Office, 1881), 99.

62. Peter [Pehr] Kalm, *Peter Kalm's Travels in North America: The English Version of 1770*, ed. Adolph B. Benson (1937; repr., New York: Dover, 1964), 1:122–126.

63. Timothy Dwight, *Travels in New England and New York*, ed. Barbara Miller Solomon (Cambridge, MA: Harvard University Press, 1969), 3:214.

64. Samuel Latham Mitchill, *The Picture of New-York, or The Traveler's Guide through the Commercial Metropolis of the United States* [. . .] (New York, 1807), 11–12, 14–18, 175–178, excerpted in *Journeys on Old Long Island: Travelers' Accounts, Contemporary Descriptions, and Residents' Reminiscences, 1744–1893*, ed. Natalie Naylor (Interlaken, NY: Empire State Books, 2002), 117.

65. Ingersoll, *Oyster Industry*, 100.

66. Ingersoll, 101–102.

67. Ingersoll, 88, 94.

68. Ingersoll, 92.

69. Ingersoll, 118.

70. *New York Times*, May 27, 1877, quoted in Betsy McCully, *City at the Water's Edge: A Natural History of New York* (New Brunswick, NJ: Rivergate/Rutgers, 2007), 84.

71. George Rafter and M. N. Baker, *Sewage Disposal in the United States* (New York: Van Nostrand, 1900), 71–72; New York State Committee on Regional Plan of New York and Its Environs, *Regional Survey of New York and Its Environs:*

Physical Conditions and Public Services, comp. Harold Maclean Lewis, vol. 8 (New York: Regional Plan of New York and Its Environs, 1929). For a detailed account of the pollution of New York Harbor and its remediation, see McCully, *City at the Water's Edge*, 84–93. See also John Waldman, *Heartbeats in the Muck: The History, Sea Life, and Environment of New York Harbor*, rev. ed. (New York: Fordham University Press / Empire State Editions, 2013), chap. 3.

72. New York City Department of Environmental Protection (NYCDEP), *Jamaica Bay Watershed Protection Plan* (New York: NYCDEP, October 1, 2014), 6. See also NYCDEP, *Jamaica Bay Watershed Protection Plan Update 2018* (New York: NYCDEP, 2018), https://www1.nyc.gov/assets/dep/downloads/pdf/water/nyc-waterways/jamaica -bay/jamaica-bay-watershed-protection-plan-update-2018.pdf.

73. NOAA Fisheries, "Status Review of the Eastern Oyster (Crassostrea virginica)," February 16, 2007, NOAA Technical Memorandum, NMFS F/SPO-88, cited in Chester B. Zarnoch and Martin P. Schreibman, "Growth and Reproduction of Eastern Oysters, *Crassostrea Virginica*, in a New York City Estuary: Implications for Restoration," *Urban Habitats* 7, no. 1 (March 2012), https://www.urbanhabitats .org/v07n01/easternoysters_full.html.

74. "Hudson-Raritan Estuary Oyster Reintroduction," Center for Urban Environmental Sustainability, Rutgers University, accessed October 10, 2023, https://cues .rutgers.edu/oyster-restoration/.

75. US Army Corps of Engineers and Port Authority of New York and New Jersey, *Hudson-Raritan Estuary Comprehensive Restoration Plan*, draft, vol. 1 (US Army Corps of Engineers and Port Authority of New York and New Jersey, March 2009), 53.

76. It had already been determined that growing oysters in Jamaica Bay would be successful. See Zarnoch and Schreibman, "Growth and Reproduction," based on their 2003 study.

77. Raymond Grizzle et al., *Oyster Restoration Research Project, Final Technical Report* (January 31, 2012), 4, http://www.oyster-restoration.org/wp-content/uploads /2012/06/ORRP-FINAL-REPORT_2013-02-20.pdf. Launched in 2014, the Billion Oyster Project aims to plant one billion oysters in New York waters by 2035. See Billion Oyster Project, homepage, accessed October 10, 2023, https://www .billionoysterproject.org. Under the aegis of the US Army Corps of Engineers, the *Hudson-Raritan Estuary Comprehensive Restoration Plan* published in 2014 set a goal of two thousand acres of oyster reefs in New York City waters by 2050. See US Army Corps of Engineers, *Hudson-Raritan Estuary Comprehensive Restoration Plan: Executive Summary* (US Army Corps of Engineers, September 2014), https://www.nan .usace.army.mil/Portals/37/docs/harbor/CRP%20Planning%20Regions/Exec_Sum _2014_Aug.pdf.

78. NYCDEP, *Jamaica Bay Watershed Protection Plan* (2014), 4, 43–46; NYCDEP, *Jamaica Bay Watershed Protection Plan Update 2018*, 22.

79. "Fishing," Long Island Traditions, accessed October 10, 2023, https://longislandtraditions.org/fishing/.

80. Susan M. Novick, "Flourishing, Oysters Go from Long Island Sounds' Floor to the Holiday Table," *New York Times*, December 20, 2014; Christopher Brooks, "As Lobsters Dwindle in Long Island Sound, Oysters Thrive," *New York Times*, September 10, 2015; Long Island Sound Study, homepage, accessed October 10, 2023, https://longislandsoundstudy.net. In 2017, the Long Island Shellfish Restoration Project was launched by New York State, with the goal of seeding oyster and clam beds at five sites in Suffolk and Nassau Counties; the Cornell Cooperative Extension Marine Program is involved in transplanting tens of millions of shellfish in these designated "sanctuary sites." See Long Island Shellfish Restoration Project, homepage, accessed October 10, 2023, https://lishellfishrestorationproject.org.

81. "Scallop Program: Overview and Results," Suffolk County Scallop Program, Cornell Cooperative Extension, last updated February 11, 2021, https://ccesuffolk.org/marine/aquaculture/scallop-program/scallop-program-overview-and-results.

82. Thomas J. Knudson, "Long Island Gambles on a Scallop Transplant," *New York Times*, September 16, 1986.

83. "Scallop Program." Christopher F. Smith is now listed as "Senior Educator, Natural Resources" at the Cornell Cooperative Extension Marine Program of Suffolk County. He coauthored an article with Stephen T. Tettelbach of Long Island University: "Bay Scallop Restoration in New York," *Ecological Restoration* 27, no. 1 (March 2009): 20–22.

84. Cornell Cooperative Extension, Eelgrass Program, homepage, accessed October 10, 2023, http://www.seagrassli.org/.

85. Robert D. Brumbaugh et al., *A Practitioners Guide to the Design and Monitoring of Shellfish Restoration Projects, an Ecosystems Services Approach* (Arlington, VA: Nature Conservancy, 2006), 6, https://repository.library.noaa.gov/view/noaa/42053.

CHAPTER 4 — SEAS OF GRASS

1. Daniel M. Tredwell, *Reminiscences of Men and Things on Long Island*, pt. 1 (New York: Charles Andrew Ditmas, 1912), 142, Google Books, https://play.google.com/books/reader?id=7A8zAQAAIAAJ.

2. Tredwell, 135–139.

3. Tredwell, 148.

4. J. P. Giraud, *Birds of Long Island* (New York: Wiley and Putnam, 1844), 228, Google Books, https://play.google.com/books/reader?id=yfkOAAAAYAAJ.

5. Giraud, 252.

6. John M. Levinson and Somers G. Headley, *Shorebirds: The Birds, the Hunters, the Decoys* (Centreville, MD: Tidewater, 1991), 40.

7. "Salt Water Marsh Hen," John J. Audubon's Birds of America, accessed October 11, 2023, https://www.audubon.org/birds-of-america/salt-water-marsh-hen.

8. Michael A. Farina, "A Tale of Two Rails," *Kingbird* 56, no. 4 (December 2006): 311–315.

9. Giraud, *Birds of Long Island*, 207.

10. South Shore Estuary Reserve Council and New York Department of State, *Long Island South Shore Estuary Reserve Comprehensive Management Plan, 2022*, 2, https://dos.ny.gov/system/files/documents/2022/09/2022-sser-cmp.pdf.

11. I have consulted two excellent books for my description of salt marsh ecology: Judith S. Weis and Carol A. Butler, *Salt Marshes: A Natural and Unnatural History* (New Brunswick, NJ: Rutgers University Press, 2009); and Scott W. Shumway, *Atlantic Seashore: Beach Ecology from the Gulf of Maine to Cape Hatteras* (Guilford, CT: Falcon Guides / Globe Pequot, 2008).

12. Weis and Butler, *Salt Marshes*, 62–63, 68; Shumway, *Atlantic Seashore*, 152.

13. Weis and Butler, *Salt Marshes*, 71–73; Katie Morosky, "'Massive' Die-Off of Turtles: Dozens of Dead Diamondback Terrapins Wash Up along Flanders Bay Beaches," *Riverhead Local*, May 13, 2015, https://riverheadlocal.com/2015/05/13/massive-die-off-of-turtles-dozens-of-dead-diamondback-terrapins-wash-up-along-flanders-bay-beaches/. Kevin McAllister is the founder and president of Defend H2O, an organization founded in 2014 to protect the waters, wetlands, and beaches of Long Island. See also the chapter "Diamondback Terrapins" in John Turner's book *Exploring the Other Island: A Seasonal Guide to Nature on Long Island*, 2nd ed. (New York: Harbor Electronic, 2011), 157–163.

14. Alexandra K. Kanonik and Russell L. Burke, "Demographic Analysis of the Jamaica Bay Diamondback Terrapin Population: Implications for Survival in an Urban Habitat," in *Final Reports of the Tibor T. Polgar Fellowship Program*, ed. D. J. Yozzo, S. H. Fernald, and H. Andreyko (Hudson River Foundation, 2009), V-5, http://hudsonriver.org/wp-content/uploads/library/Polgar_Kanonik_TP_05_09_final.pdf.

15. Nate Schweber, "Studying What Lures Turtles to a Tarmac at Kennedy Airport," *New York Times*, July 3, 2014.

16. Kanonik and Burke, "Demographic Analysis," V-21.

17. Weis and Butler, *Salt Marshes*, 8.

18. Benjamin Franklin Thompson, *History of Long Island, Containing an Account of the Discovery and Settlement; with Other Important and Interesting Matters to the Present Time* (1839; repr., Forgotten Books Classic Reprint Series, 2012), 34.

19. Ralph W. Tiner, Kevin McGuckin, and Matthew Fields, *Changes in Long Island Wetlands, New York: Circa 1900 to 2004* (Hadley, MA: National Wetlands Inventory Program, Northeast Region, US Fish and Wildlife Service, April 2012), https://www.nawm.org/wetlandsonestop/changes_in_long_island_wetlands.pdf.

20. New York City, *New York City Wetlands Strategy, Draft for Public Comment*, 2012, 17, https://www.nyc.gov/html/planyc2030/downloads/pdf/wetlands_strategy.pdf.

21. Daniel M. Hendrick, *Jamaica Bay*, Images of America (Charleston, SC: Arcadia, 2006), 53–64.

22. Robert Moses, *Public Works: A Dangerous Trade* (New York: McGraw-Hill, 1970), 188.

23. Hendrick, *Jamaica Bay*, 76, 79.

24. Robert A. Caro, *The Power Broker: Robert Moses and the Fall of New York* (New York: Vintage Books / Random House, 1975), 641, 476; Hendrick, *Jamaica Bay*, 65–80, 93.

25. This figure comes from John B. O'Dowd, "Gerritsen Creek Ecosystem Restoration, Section 1135," US Army Corps of Engineers (USACE), October 2003.

26. "Tidal Wetlands Trends," New York State Department of Environmental Conservation, accessed October 11, 2023, https://www.dec.ny.gov/lands/5113.html.

27. "Jamaica Bay Marsh Islands," USACE, New York District, accessed October 11, 2023, https://www.nan.usace.army.mil/Missions/Environmental/Environmental -Restoration/Elders-Point-Jamaica-Bay-Salt-Marsh-Islands/.

28. Ellen K. Hartig et al., "Anthropogenic and Climate Change Impacts on Salt Marshes of Jamaica Bay," *Wetlands* 22, no. 1 (March 2002): 71–89, https://www.dec .ny.gov/docs/fish_marine_pdf/accismjamnyc.pdf.

29. USACE, New York District, *Draft Integrated Feasibility Report and Environmental Assessment*, appendix E-2, *Alternatives Development, Jamaica Bay and Marsh Islands* (USACE, New York District, February 2017), https://www.nan.usace .army.mil/Portals/37/docs/Environmental/Appendix%20E2.pdf?ver=2017-03-02 -113002-417.

30. Ron Rozsa, "Human Impacts on Tidal Wetlands: History and Regulations," in *Tidal Marshes of Long Island Sound: Ecology, History and Restoration*, Bulletin No. 34, ed. Glenn D. Dreyer and William A. Niering (New London, CT: Connecticut College Arboretum, December 1995), 44–50, https://marchmania.conncoll.edu /media/website-media/green/arbo/greenlivingdocs/Human_Impacts_on_Tidal _Wetlands-History_and_Regulations.pdf.

31. Weis and Butler, *Salt Marshes*, 104–105. See also Nancy L. Niedowski, *Salt Marsh Restoration and Monitoring Guidelines* (Albany: New York State Division of Coastal Resources, December 15, 2000), 28–29.

32. Weis and Butler, *Salt Marshes*, 127.

33. Ecology and Environment, *Nassau County Mosquito Control Plan*, prepared for Nassau County Department of Public Works (New York: Ecology and Environment, October 2009), sec. 7.1.3.1, https://www.nassaucountyny.gov/DocumentCenter /View/1290/NassauCountyMosquito-Control-Plan.

34. Ecology and Environment, sec. D-3.

35. New York City Department of Health and Mental Hygiene, "Health Department to Spray Pesticide to Reduce the Number of Mosquitoes and the Risk of West

Nile Virus in Selected Parts of Queens and Brooklyn," press release, September 18, 2015. Spraying of Anvil 10 + 10 to control West Nile virus is done throughout New York City. See "Twenty-Three Years On, NYC to Spray Toxic Pesticides over All of Central Park, Upper West Side, Manhattan, Brooklyn, Queens, Bronx This Week," No Spray Coalition, September 13, 2022, https://nospray.org/2022/09/13/23-years-nyc -toxic-pesticide-spraying-central-park-more/.

36. "West Nile Virus: Historic Data (1999–2022)," Centers for Disease Control and Prevention, last reviewed June 13, 2023, https://www.cdc.gov/westnile/statsmaps /cumMapsData.html#six.

37. Julian Horwitz, "West Nile Virus: Just How Bad Is It?," *NYU Langone Online Journal of Medicine*, March 5, 2014, https://www.clinicalcorrelations.org/2014/03/05 /west-nile-virus-just-how-bad-is-it/.

38. "Estrogenic and Antiprogestagenic Activities of Pyrethroid Insecticides," *Biochemical and Biophysical Research Communications* 251, no. 3 (October 1998): 855–859, cited in Abby Stahl, "The Health Effects of Pesticides Used for Mosquito Control," Citizens Campaign for the Environment and Citizens Environmental Research Institute, August 2002, https://www.pesticidefreelawns.org/assets/media/documents /mosquito/documents/citizensHealthEffectsMosqP.pdf. See also "Information Sheet: Anvil and Mosquito Control," Publication 2738, New York State Department of Health, April 2009, rev. October 2019, https://www.health.ny.gov/publications/2738/.

39. Weis and Butler, *Salt Marshes*, 129; K. Wick et al., "Methoprene General Fact Sheet," National Pesticide Information Center, Oregon State University Extension Services, July 2012, http://npic.orst.edu/factsheets/methogen.html. See also "Methoprene Fact Sheet," US Environmental Protection Agency, June 2001, https:// www3.epa.gov/pesticides/chem_search/reg_actions/reregistration/fs_PC-105401 _1-Jun-01.pdf. For a scientific overview of methoprene and its toxicity, see Sharon P. Lawlor, "Environmental Safety Review of Methoprene and Bacterially-Derived Pesticides Commonly Used for Sustained Mosquito Control," *Ecotoxicology and Environmental Safety* 139 (2017): 335–343, https://doi.org/10.1016/j.ecoenv.2016.12.038.

40. Rachel Carson, *Silent Spring* (Boston: Mariner Books / Houghton Mifflin, 2002), 7–8.

41. Diana diZerega Wall and Anne-Marie Cantwell, *Touring Gotham's Archaeological Past: 8 Self-Guided Walking Tours through New York City* (New Haven, CT: Yale University Press, 2004), 174–180.

42. Wall and Cantwell, 174–180.

43. "Marine Park," NYC Parks, accessed October 11, 2023, https://www .nycgovparks.org/parks/marine-park/history; "Major Habitat Restoration and Trail Development Project Gets Underway This Fall in Marine Park," NYC Parks, December 15, 2015, https://www.nycgovparks.org/parks/marine-park/dailyplant/23521.

44. O'Dowd, "Gerritsen Creek Ecosystem Restoration."

45. New York City Department of Environmental Protection (NYCDEP), *Jamaica Bay Watershed Protection Plan: Interim Report* (New York: NYCDEP, September 1, 2006).

46. PlaNYC, *New York City Wetlands Strategy, May 2012* (New York: Mayor's Office of Long-Term Planning and Sustainability, May 2012), 3, https://www.nyc.gov /html/planyc2030/downloads/pdf/nyc_wetlands_strategy.pdf.

47. PlaNYC, 28.

48. PlaNYC, 9.

49. PlaNYC, 7.

50. Long Island Sound Study (LISS), *Long Island Sound Comprehensive Conservation and Management Plan 2015: Returning the Urban Sea to Abundance* (Stamford, CT: US Environmental Protection Agency, Long Island Sound National Program Office, September 2015), 28, https://longislandsoundstudy.net/2015/09/2015-com prehensive-conservation-and-management-plan/.

51. LISS, *Returning the Urban Sea to Abundance: A Five-Year Review of the 2015 Comprehensive Conservation and Management Plan* (Stamford, CT: US Environmental Protection Agency, Long Island Sound National Program Office, December 2020), 10, https://longislandsoundstudy.net/2021/06/five-year-progress-report -for-the-comprehensive-conservation-and-management-plan-2015-2019/.

52. LISS, *National Estuary Program Summary Work Plan for Federal Fiscal Year 2022 Funding for Comprehensive Conservation and Management Plan* (Stamford, CT: US Environmental Protection Agency, Long Island Sound National Program Office, July 2022), 35, https://longislandsoundstudy.net/2022/07/2022-work-plan/.

53. "DEP Completes Alley Creek Combined Sewer Overflow Facility," press release, NYCDEP, May 25, 2011, https://www.nyc.gov/html/dep/html/press_releases/11-40pr .shtml?translate=off#.ZBB2OS-B1pR; "Restoration of Tidal Wetlands Help to Improve the Health of Alley Creek and Little Neck Bay," press release, NYCDEP, April 22, 2019, https://www1.nyc.gov/html/dep/html/press_releases/19-027pr.shtml#.Y9_Ohy-B1pS.

54. LISS, *Comprehensive Conservation and Management Plan 2015*, 7.

CHAPTER 5 — COPIOUS WATERS AND MULTITUDES OF FISH

1. US Fish and Wildlife Service (FWS), Southern New England–New York Bight Coastal Ecosystems Program, "Long Pond Greenbelt, Complex #10," in *Significant Habitats and Habitat Complexes of the New York Bight* (Charlestown, RI: FWS, 1997).

2. A full list of rare species inhabiting the coastal plain pond complex can be found in "Coastal Plain Pond Shore Guide," New York Natural Heritage Program (NYNHP), last updated April 7, 2021, https://guides.nynhp.org/coastal-plain-pond-shore/.

3. "Slender Blue Flag," NYNHP, last updated November 17, 2011, https://guides .nynhp.org/slender-blue-flag/; "Banded Sunfish," NYNHP, last updated July 1, 2019, https://guides.nynhp.org/banded-sunfish/; "Swamp Darter," NYNHP, last updated April 19, 2019, https://guides.nynhp.org/swamp-darter/.

4. "Tiger Salamander," NYNHP, last updated April 18, 2019, https://guides.nynhp .org/tiger-salamander/.

5. Gregory J. Edinger et al., eds., *Ecological Communities of New York State: A Revised and Expanded Edition of Carol Reschke's Ecological Communities of New York State*, 2nd ed. (Albany: New York Natural Heritage Program, New York State Department of Environmental Conservation [NYSDEC], March 2014), 51–52, https:// www.nynhp.org/documents/39/ecocomm2014.pdf; "Eastern Tiger Salamander Fact Sheet," NYSDEC, accessed October 11, 2023, https://www.dec.ny.gov/animals/7143 .html; "Spotted Turtle Fact Sheet," NYSDEC, accessed October 11, 2023, https://www .dec.ny.gov/animals/7150.html.

6. New York Environmental Conservation Law Section 15-1528, last modified September 22, 2014, https://newyork.public.law/laws/n.y._environmental_conservation _law_section_15-1528.

7. New York Water Science Center, "State of the Aquifer System, Long Island, New York," US Geological Survey, May 30, 2017, https://www.usgs.gov/centers/new -york-water-science-center/science/long-island-hydrogeologic-units?qt-science _center_objects=0#qt-science_center_objects; "Our Long Island Aquifers: The Basics," Nassau Suffolk Water Commissioners' Association, accessed October 11, 2023, http://www.nswcawater.org/water_facts/our-long-island-aquifers-the-basics/.

8. New York Water Science Center, "State of the Aquifer System"; NYSDEC, *Water Quality Monitoring Data for Pesticides on Long Island, NY* (NYSDEC, July 11, 2014), https://www.dec.ny.gov/docs/materials_minerals_pdf/suffolkdata.pdf.

9. "History of Ronkonkoma: Settlers and Early Residents," Ronkonkoma Chamber of Commerce, accessed November 1, 2023, https://www.ronkonkomachamber .com/settlers-early-residents/; "Lake Ronkonkoma," NYSDEC, accessed October 11, 2023, https://www.dec.ny.gov/outdoor/24173.html.

10. Les Sirkin, *Western Long Island Geology: History, Processes, and Field Trips* (Watch Hill, RI: Book and Tackle Shop, 1995), 117, 122.

11. "Red-Headed Woodpecker Life History," All about Birds, Cornell Lab of Ornithology, accessed October 11, 2023, https://www.allaboutbirds.org/guide/Red -headed_Woodpecker/lifehistory.

12. "History," Friends of Caleb Smith Preserve, accessed October 11, 2023, https:// www.friendsofcalebsmith.org/history.php/. See also Nick Karas, *Brook Trout: A Thorough Look at North America's Great Native Trout—Its History, Biology, and Angling Possibilities* (1997; New York: Skyhorse, 2002), Kindle, chap. 12.

13. Karas, chap. 12.

14. The Long Island Greenbelt Trail connects the South Shore to the North Shore with a thirty-two-mile trail system that essentially follows the courses of the Connetquot and Nissequogue Rivers, albeit broken here and there by roads and residential neighborhoods. See Lee McAllister, *Hiking Long Island: A Comprehensive Guide to Parks and Trails* (Mahwah, NJ: New York–New Jersey Trail Conference, 2001), 94–97.

15. Geologist Gilbert Hanson of Hofstra University proposed that the Connetquot, Carmans, and Nissequogue Rivers may have originated as tunnel valleys, which are subglacial streams draining a glacier. He noted that the Carmans cuts right through the Ronkonkoma Moraine, as revealed on a digital elevation map. As for the Peconic, he theorized that it occupies so-called dry valleys that were etched into permafrost by glacial meltwater. They are called dry valleys because the groundwater was still low; when the sea level rose, groundwater levels also rose and began to fill lower portions of the dry valleys. Gilbert N. Hanson, "Geological Setting of Tidal Marshes on Long Island," *Memoirs of the Torrey Botanical Society* 26 (2010): 6–13, http://www .jstor.org/stable/43391918. Geologist Bret Bennington of Hofstra University disputes the tunnel valley hypothesis, proposing that both the Nissequogue and Peconic eroded their own drainage channels. The Carmans and Connetquot, he suggests, were formed when a glacial lake impounded by the Ronkonkoma Moraine breeched the moraine at two points and carved two wide outwash channels. The Connetquot occupies one and the Carmans the other, both flowing north to south and emptying into the Atlantic. Bret Bennington, professor and chair, Department of Geology, Environment and Sustainability, Hofstra University, personal communication, March 29, 2023.

16. Edinger et al., *Ecological Communities*, 25; Dean Bouton and Eileen C. Stegemann, "Endangered and Threatened Fishes of New York," updated by Doug Carlson, NYSDEC, accessed October 11, 2023, https://www.dec.ny.gov/animals /7008.html.

17. "Peconic River," Coastal Fish and Wildlife Habitat Assessment Form, New York State Department of State, revised May 15, 2002, https://dos.ny.gov/system/files /documents/2020/03/peconic_river.pdf; FWS, Southern New England–New York Bight Coastal Ecosystems Program, "Long Island Pine Barrens-Peconic River Complex, Complex #8," in *Significant Habitats*.

18. NYSDEC, "In the Matter of the Proposed 'Community' Designations for Two Locations within the Recreational Segment of the Peconic River Corridor in Suffolk County, New York, Town of Riverhead Proposal and Suffolk County Proposal," January 12, 2010.

19. James M. Swank, *History of the Manufacture of Iron in All Ages, and Particularly in the United States from Colonial Times to 1891* (Philadelphia: American Iron and Steel Association, 1892), 142.

20. Peter Ross, *The History of Long Island, from Its Earliest Settlement to Its Present Time* (New York: Lewis, 1902), http://dunhamwilcox.net/ny/riverhead_hist.htm.

21. Karas, *Brook Trout*, chap. 12.

22. "Grasshopper Sparrow," All about Birds, Cornell Lab of Ornithology, accessed October 11, 2023, https://www.allaboutbirds.org/guide/Grasshopper_Sparrow; "Short-Eared Owl," All about Birds, Cornell Lab of Ornithology, accessed October 11, 2023, https://www.allaboutbirds.org/guide/Short-eared_Owl/.

23. NYSDEC, *Unit Management Plan for the Peconic Headwaters Natural Resources Management Area*, January 2006, p. 2, https://www.dec.ny.gov/docs/lands_forests _pdf/peconicump.pdf. The Peconic and Flanders Bays, as well as the Long Island Pine Barrens where the Calverton Ponds region is located, are designated as Important Bird Areas. See New York Audubon, Important Bird Areas, https://ny.audubon.org /conservation/long-island-important-bird-areas.

24. Henry William Herbert, *Frank Forester's Fish and Fishing of the United States and British Provinces of North America, Illustrated from Nature by Henry William Herbert*, rev. ed. (New York: W. A. Townsend, 1859), 266.

25. Herbert, 260.

26. Quoted in Karas, *Brook Trout*, chap. 12.

27. Herbert, *Frank Forester's Fish and Fishing*, 262.

28. The hatchery, after experiencing an outbreak of infectious pancreatic necrosis in the early 2000s, was closed. In 2015, it was restored with the help of monies raised by the Friends of Connetquot and Idle Hour Fishing Club, although as of 2023 they still need donors to fund the operation. Their plan, according to Joseph Albanese, is to produce thirty thousand trout annually to stock not only the Connetquot but other Long Island river preserves. The river is stocked yearly with rainbow, brown, and brook trout. Joseph Albanese, "Then and Now: Connetquot River State Park Preserve," Fisherman, April 2020, https://www.thefisherman.com/article/then -now-connetquot-river-state-park-preserve/. See also Joseph Albanese, "Fishing the Connetquot River for Trout," On the Water, May 24, 2021, https://www.onthewater .com/fishing-the-connetquot-river-for-trout/.

29. Karas, *Brook Trout*, chap. 12.

30. Herbert, *Frank Forester's Fish and Fishing*, 267. Herbert was not exaggerating. The pond was made famous by Daniel Webster, an avid trout fisherman, who reportedly caught a brook trout of fourteen and a half pounds in Sam Carman's pond in 1827. Karas, *Brook Trout*, chap. 12.

31. Herbert, *Frank Forester's Fish and Fishing*, 264.

32. Quoted in Karas, *Brook Trout*, chap. 4.

33. Tarleton H. Bean, *Catalogue of the Fishes of Long Island*, reprinted from the Sixth Annual Report of the Forest, Fish and Game Commission of the State of New York ([Albany, NY]: [Forest, Fish and Game Commission, 1902]), 401.

34. Karas, *Brook Trout*, chap. 6.

35. John Waldman, *Running Silver: Restoring Atlantic Rivers and Their Great Fish Migrations* (Guilford, CT: Lyons, 2013), 43–44.

36. Sam Carman would die in 1869, leaving his house to his son Henry and his mill to his son Robert; the house would stand until 1936, when it was bought by Charles E. Johnson for a duck farm; the mill operated until 1910, and all buildings— tavern, mill, and store—were torn down when Sunrise Highway was extended. Karas, *Brook Trout*, chap. 12.

37. Karas, chap. 12.

38. Town of Brookhaven, Long Island, *The Carmans River Conservation and Management Plan*, October 15, 2013, p. 25, https://www.brookhavenny.gov/Document Center/View/733/2013-Carmans-River-Conservation-and-Management-Plan-PDF.

39. Town of Brookhaven, 161.

40. Trout Unlimited, Long Island Chapter, homepage, accessed October 11, 2023, http://www.longislandtu.org.

41. Town of Brookhaven, *Carmans River*, 163.

42. Sabrina Garone and J. D. Allen, "A Fish Ladder Project Will Help Rejuvenate One of Long Island's Largest Rivers," NPR, February 8, 2023, https://www.wshu.org /long-island-news/2023-02-08/a-fish-ladder-project-will-help-rejuvenate-one-of -long-islands-largest-rivers.

43. Kevin McAllister, WSHU-NPR podcast *Higher Ground* (2021), quoted in Garone and Allen, "Fish Ladder Project."

44. Martin Van Lith, "Of Time and the River," *Pine Barrens Today* 28, no. 1 (Winter 2009): 2.

45. Town of Brookhaven, *Carmans River*, 112, 142.

46. Thomas Morton, *New English Canaan, or New Canaan, Containing an Abstract of New England* (Amsterdam, 1637), quoted in Waldman, *Running Silver*, 2.

47. William Wood, *New England's Prospect: A True, Lively, and Experimental Description of that Part of America Called New England* (London, 1634), Kindle, chap. 9.

48. James E. De Kay, *Catalogue of the Fishes Inhabiting the State of New-York*, n.d., quoted in Bean, *Fishes of Long Island*, 436. De Kay's catalog was apparently published as an appendix after publication of his tome *The Zoology of New York, or, The New York Fauna*, a five-volume work published between 1842 and 1844.

49. Waldman, *Running Silver*, 26. On the Chesapeake spawning ground, see John Waldman, personal communication, October 2022.

50. Bean, *Fishes of Long Island*, 436.

51. Waldman, *Running Silver*, 25.

52. Peter Matthiessen, *Men's Lives: The Surfmen and Baymen of the South Fork* (New York: Random House, 1986), quoted in Waldman, *Running Silver*, 28.

53. Samuel Hopkins Emery, *History of Taunton, Massachusetts: From Its Settlement to the Present Time* (Syracuse, NY: D. Mason, 1893), quoted in Waldman, *Running Silver*, 87 (brackets Waldman's).

54. Wood, *New England's Prospect*, chap. 9.

55. John Hay, *The Run* (Garden City, NY: Doubleday, 1959), quoted in Waldman, *Running Silver*, 21.

56. Bean, *Fishes of Long Island*, 395.

57. Paul Greenberg, *Four Fish: The Future of the Last Wild Food* (New York: Penguin Books, 2010), 248.

58. *New York Journal*, April 26, 1770, quoted in John McPhee, *The Founding Fish* (New York: Farrar, Straus and Giroux, 2002), 95.

59. McPhee, *Founding Fish*, 182.

60. Waldman, *Running Silver*, 80; "American Eel," Atlantic States Marine Fisheries Commission (ASMFC), accessed October 12, 2023, http://www.asmfc.org/species /american-eel; Kari H. Fenske et al., "An Age- and Sex-Structured Assessment Model for American Eels (Anguilla rostrata) in the Potomac River, Maryland," *Canadian Journal of Fisheries and Aquatic Science* 68, no. 6 (June 2011): 1024–1037, https://www .researchgate.net/publication/237175999_An_age-_and_sex-structured_assessment _model_for_American_eels_Anguilla_rostrata_in_the_Potomac_River_Maryland.

61. Waldman, *Running Silver*, 41.

62. Bean, *Fishes of Long Island*, 390; "American Eel," FWS, accessed November 1, 2023, https://www.fws.gov/species/american-eel-anguilla-rostrata; "American Eel, Anguilla rostrata," Red List of Threatened Species, International Union for Conservation of Nature, accessed October 12, 2023, http://www.iucnredlist.org/details /191108/0/; "American Eel," ASMFC; Carol Hoffman, "American Eels in New York," presentation at Second Annual Long Island Natural History Conference, 2012. Hoffman of NYSDEC has been studying glass eels in the Carmans since 2000. See the Seatuck website for its video library of lectures presented at the Long Island Natural History Conference from 2012 to 2019, including Hoffman's: https://seatuck.org /li-natural-history-conference/.

63. McPhee, *Founding Fish*, 212–214. McPhee cites the work of Boyd Kynard, who recorded the diminution in size and age of shad at spawning, which he explained as "a compensatory response to mortality," with the species threatened by loss of food sources related to climate change and increased predation by striped bass (215–217).

64. Waldman, *Running Silver*, 55. His statistics come from an analysis by R. C. Walter and D. J. Merritts, "Natural Streams and the Legacy of Water-Powered Mills," *Science* 319 (2008): 299–304. Waldman also cites a study by Stony Brook University on the historical declines of fish due to dams constructed between 1776 and 1824 (182).

65. John Waldman, "Thoreau's Distressing Canoe Trip," *New York Times*, July 12, 2017.

66. Waldman, *Running Silver*, 22.

67. "Species of Concern: River Herring (Alewife and Blueback herring)," NOAA National Marine Fisheries Service, November 2, 2007, https://www.nrc.gov/docs /ML1004/ML100481337.pdf; "Shad and River Herring," ASMFC, accessed October 12, 2023, http://www.asmfc.org/species/shad-river-herring. On their recent recovery, see "Stock Assessment Update Indicates River Herring Remain Depleted on a Coastwide Basis Though Improvements Have Occurred in Several River Systems," news release, ASMFC, August 3, 2017, http://www.asmfc.org/uploads/file/59

839543pr35RiverHerringStockAssmtUpdate.pdf. On the proposal to close Long Island river herring fisheries, see William W. Eakin, Gregg H. Kenney, and Carol Hoffman, *Sustainable Fishery Management Plan for New York River Herring Stocks* (ASMFC, February 2022), http://www.asmfc.org/files/RiverHerringSFMPs/NY _River_Herring_SFMP_2022_Final.pdf.

68. John Rather, "Detour (This One Useful) Aids in Spawning," *New York Times*, March 12, 2000; Brian Kelder, "Alewife Spawning Runs on Long Island: Report on 2010 Volunteer Monitoring Survey Efforts," Seatuck Environmental Association, April 2011. As noted by Byron Young of the NYSDEC in his summary report on the Long Island alewife restoration project, these numbers are "crude estimates" only, based on variable viewing conditions and imperfect measuring methods. Byron Young, *Long Island Alewife Restoration Efforts with Emphasis on the Peconic River— 2017* (February 15, 2018), https://www.peconicestuary.org/wp-content/uploads/2018 /03/2017-Alewife-Spawning-Report.pdf.

69. Waldman, "Thoreau's Distressing Canoe Trip."

CHAPTER 6 — GRASSLANDS AT THE GLACIER'S EDGE

1. "Short-Eared Owl," New York Natural Heritage Program (NYNHP), last updated June 29, 2020, https://guides.nynhp.org/short-eared-owl/. They cite E. H. Eaton, *Birds of New York* (New York: State University of New York, 1914).

2. New York State Department of Environmental Conservation, *2016 New York State Open Space Conservation Plan*, 81, https://www.dec.ny.gov/docs/lands_forests _pdf/osp2016final1.pdf; "Long Island Important Bird Areas," Audubon New York, accessed October 12, 2023, https://ny.audubon.org/conservation/long-island -important-bird-areas.

3. Tim Gannon, "Tarmacs in Calverton Could Get Turned into Grasslands," *Riverhead News-Review*, January 10, 2013, https://riverheadnewsreview.timesreview.com /2013/01/42513/town-tarmacs-in-calverton-could-get-turned-into-grasslands/. In May 2022, 1,643 acres were sold by the Town of Riverhead to Calverton Aviation and Technology, "representing the largest Long Island land sale in modern history," while 1,900 acres were preserved "as open space and to protect the region's environmental health." David Wenzelberg, "$40 Million EPCAL Sale Advances with IDA Transfer," *Long Island Business News*, March 24, 2022, https://libn.com/2022/03/24/40m -epcal-sale-advances-with-ida-transfer/.

4. Daniel Denton, *A Brief Description of New-York, Formerly Called New-Netherlands* (1670), ed. Paul Royster, Faculty Publications, UNL Libraries, Paper 22 (Digital Commons, University of Nebraska–Lincoln, 2009), 11, https://digital commons.unl.edu/libraryscience/22.

5. Denton, *Brief Description*, 23. See also Paul Royster, "Daniel Denton (c. 1626– 1703)," Faculty Publications, UNL Libraries, Paper 3 (Digital Commons, University of Nebraska–Lincoln, 1984), https://digitalcommons.unl.edu/libraryscience/3.

6. Excerpt from Walt Whitman, "Paumanok, and My Life on It as Child and Young Man," in *Complete Prose Works* (Philadelphia: David McKay, 1892), 17, https://whitmanarchive.org/published/other/CompleteProse.html.

7. Timothy Dwight, *Travels in New England and New York*, 4 vols. (1821–1822), ed. Barbara Miller Solomon (Cambridge, MA: Belknap Press of Harvard University Press, 1969), 3:269–320, excerpted in *Journeys on Old Long Island: Travelers' Accounts, Contemporary Descriptions, and Residents' Reminiscences, 1744–1893*, ed. Natalie A. Naylor (Interlaken, NY: Empire State Books, 2002), 96–97.

8. Samuel Latham Mitchill, *The Picture of New-York, or The Traveler's Guide through the Commercial Metropolis of the United States* [. . .] (New York, 1807), 158–166, excerpted in Naylor, *Journeys on Old Long Island*, 116.

9. Nathaniel S. Prime, *A History of Long Island from Its First Settlement by Europeans to the Year 1845* (New York, 1845), 16–21, excerpted in Naylor, *Journeys on Old Long Island*, 207.

10. Daniel M. Tredwell, *Personal Reminiscences of Men and Things on Long Island*, pt. 1 (New York: Charles Andrew Ditmas, 1912), 164–165, Google Books, https://play.google.com/books/reader?id=7A8zAQAAIAAJ.

11. Quoted in Barbara M. Kelly, *Expanding the American Dream: Building and Rebuilding Levittown*, SUNY Series in New Cultural History (Albany: State University of New York Press, 1993), 27.

12. Walt Whitman, *I Sit and Look Out* (New York: Columbia University Press, 1932), 145, quoted in Kenneth T. Jackson, *Crabgrass Frontier: The Suburbanization of the United States* (New York: Oxford University Press, 1985), 50.

13. Roland M. Harper, "The Hempstead Plains: A Natural Prairie on Long Island," *Bulletin of the American Geographical Society* 43, no. 5 (1911): 351–360, https://doi.org/10.2307/199103.

14. "Hempstead Plains Grassland," NYNHP, last updated June 22, 2021, https://guides.nynhp.org/hempstead-plains-grassland/.

15. Kelly, *Expanding the American Dream*, 12–27.

16. Joshua Stoff, "The Aviation Heritage of Long Island," Cradle of Aviation Museum, accessed October 12, 2023, https://www.cradleofaviation.org/history/history.

17. Prime, *History of Long Island*, excerpted in Naylor, *Journeys on Old Long Island*, 207.

18. For a complete list of flora, common and rare, see "Hempstead Plains Grassland," NYNHP.

19. Richard Stalter and Eric E. Lamont, "Vegetation of Hempstead Plains, Mitchell Field, Long Island, New York," *Bulletin of the Torrey Botanical Club* 114, no. 3 (July–September 1987): 330, https://doi.org/10.2307/2996472.

20. "About the Hempstead Plains," Friends of Hempstead Plains, last updated 2021, http://friendsofhp.org/site/index.php?id=3.

21. New York Codes and Regulations, Official Compilation of Codes, Rules and Regulations of the State of New York, Title 6, Department of Environmental Conservation, Chapter II, Lands and Forests, Part 193, Trees and Plants, Thomson Reuters Westlaw, last updated October 15, 2021, https://govt.westlaw.com/nycrr/Document/I21efe775c22211ddb7c8fb397c5bd26b?contextData=%28sc.Default%29&transitionType=Default.

22. "Hempstead Plains Grassland," NYNHP.

23. Stalter and Lamont, "Vegetation of Hempstead Plains." Daniel Tredwell, for example, wrote in a diary entry in 1839 that it comprised sixty-four square miles (40,960 acres): *Personal Reminiscences,* 86.

24. Gregory J. Edinger and Stephen M. Young, *Hempstead Plains: Ecological Community Mapping and Rare Plant Survey* (Albany: New York Natural Heritage Program, March 2018), http://www.friendsofhp.org/site/assets/files/Botanical%20Survey_March_2018.pdf. The rare plants are sandplain agalinis, stargrass, green milkweed, midland sedge, bushy frostweed, low frostweed, five-angled dodder, hairy small-leaved tick-trefoil, narrow-leaved bush-clover, Nuttall's milkwort, few-flowered nut sedge, narrow-leaved white-topped aster, rough hedge nettle, and bird's-foot violet.

25. US Fish and Wildlife Service (FWS), Southern New England–New York Bight Coastal Ecosystems Program, "Long Island Grasslands, Complex #9," in *Significant Habitats and Habitat Complexes of the New York Bight Watershed* (Charlestown, RI: FWS, November 1997), https://catalog.data.gov/dataset/significant-habitats-and-habitat-complexes-of-the-new-york-bight-watershed-from-1971-to-1996-nc.

26. Ayres quoted in Norman Taylor, *The Vegetation of Montauk: A Study of Grassland and Forest,* pt. 1 of *The Vegetation of Long Island,* vol. 2 of *Brooklyn Botanic Garden Memoirs* (New York: Brooklyn Botanic Garden, June 11, 1923), 7, https://archive.org/details/vegetationootayl/page/n5/mode/2up. Apparently, the treeless rolling landscape attracted a developer to create a golf course in 1927, still in operation today. The golf course and surrounding housing developments have obliterated most of the ancient grassland.

27. Taylor, 18–19.

28. Taylor, 10.

29. Taylor, 16.

30. Marilyn Jordan, "Sandplain Gerardia—a Success Story on Long Island, September 2003," *New York Flora Association Newsletter* 15, no. 2 (Summer 2004): 1–2, https://nyflora.org/wp-content/uploads/2020/02/NYFA_Newsletter_Vol_15_2_2004.pdf. See also Marilyn Jordan, *Agalinis acuta (Sandplain Gerardia) in New York: Population Monitoring, Habitat Management and Recovery Efforts in 2003–2004* (June 10, 2004), https://ecos.fws.gov/ServCat/DownloadFile/54246?Reference=53757.

31. Taylor, *Vegetation of Montauk,* 24.

32. Robert Laskowski, "The Sayville Grasslands on Long Island, *Long Island Botanical Society Newsletter* 3, no. 5 (September–October 1993), http://www .libotanical.org/newsletters/0305.pdf.

33. Mark W. Clough, "Intra-service Section 7 Consultation for Sandplain Gerardia," memorandum to refuge manager Mark Maghini, Long Island National Wildlife Refuge Complex, April 8, 2002, https://ecos.fws.gov/ServCat/DownloadFile /54023?Reference=53546/. See also "Sandplain Agalinis," NYNHP, last updated February 28, 2020, https://guides.nynhp.org/sandplain-agalinis/. Sandplain agalinis also grows in the Hempstead Plains Preserve. A survey conducted there in 2022 found 3,700 plants in flower, an increase over the previous two years. See Friends of Hempstead Plains, homepage, accessed October 12, 2023, http://www.friendsofhp .org/site/.

34. In 2019, the FWS released its five-year status review of sandplain gerardia. Citing the DNA studies conducted in 2006–2008 by M. C. Neel and J. B. Pettengill of the University of Maryland (published in 2011), it recommended delisting sandplain gerardia (Agalinis acuta) as endangered since it was no longer considered a species distinct from *A. decemloba* but synonymous with it. FWS, Region 5, New York Field Office, Cortland, New York, *Sandplain Gerardia: 5-Year Review: Summary and Evaluation*, May, 2019, 6, 10, https://ecos.fws.gov/docs/five_year_review/doc6037.pdf. In the Southeast, *A. decemloba* is known as ten-lobed false foxglove. Its range is larger than that of the former *A. acuta*, appearing in Pennsylvania, Maryland, DC, Virginia, the Carolinas, Kentucky, Alabama, and Tennessee, as well as in New York, Connecticut, Rhode Island, and Massachusetts. It is still rare and in New York State it is critically imperiled. The *Flora of North America*, the definitive taxonomic resource, declares that *A. decemloba* "is threatened and deserves protection." See "Agalinis decemloba (Greene) Pennell," *Flora of North America* 17 (2020): 450, http://floranorthamerica.org/Agalinis_decemloba.

35. Andrew K. Davis and Lee A. Dyer, "Long-Term Trends in Eastern North American Monarch Butterflies: A Collection of Studies Focusing on Spring, Summer, and Fall Dynamics," *Annals of the Entomological Society of America* 108, no. 5 (September 2015): 661–663, https://doi.org/10.1093/aesa/sav070. See also the summary of the studies offered by Emily DeMarco, "Monarchs Pose a Puzzle," *Science* 349, no. 6248 (August 7, 2015): 570–571, https://doi.org/10.1126/science.aac8968.

36. Specifically, see Leslie Ries, Douglas J. Taron, and Eduardo Rendon-Salinas, "The Disconnect between Summer and Winter Monarch Trends for the Eastern Migratory Population: Possible Links to Differing Drivers," *Annals of the Entomological Society of America* 108, no. 5 (September 2015): 691–699; and Brice X. Semmens et al., "Quasi-extinction Risk and Population Targets for the Eastern, Migratory Population of Monarch Butterflies (*Danaus plexippus*)," *Scientific Reports* 6 (March 21, 2016): article 23265, https://nature.com/articles/srep23265.

37. See Hidotashi Inamine et al., "Linking the Continental Migratory Cycle of the Monarch Butterfly to Understand Its Population," *OIKOS* 125, no. 8 (April 27, 2016): 1081–1091, https://doi.org/10.1111/oik.03196.

38. The US Geological Survey and Scripps Institute of Oceanography conducted a joint study of the wintering population of the eastern migratory monarch, which declined 84 percent from the winter of 1993–1994 to 2014–2015. Based on this information, they concluded, "There is a substantial chance—11 to 57 percent—of quasi-extinction over the next twenty years," meaning the population would no longer be viable and "as a whole will inevitably go extinct." Their study was published in Semmens et al., "Quasi-extinction Risk."

39. "Migratory Monarch Now Endangered—IUCN Red List," press release, International Union for Conservation of Nature, July 21, 2022, https://www.iucn.org/press-release/202207/migratory-monarch-butterfly-now-endangered-iucn-red-list.

40. "Monarch Butterfly (*Danaus plexippus*)," Environmental Conservation Online System, FWS, accessed October 12, 2023, https://ecos.fws.gov/ecp/species/9743.

41. Quail Hill is a Community Supported Agriculture (CSA) farm, part of the Peconic Land Trust, in Amagansett, Long Island. See "Quail Hill Farm," Peconic Land Trust, https://peconiclandtrust.org/our-work/projects/quail-hill-farm.

42. Susan S. Lang, "After 29 Years, Nine-Spotted Ladybugs Found on Long Island," *Cornell Chronicle*, October 3, 2011, https://news.cornell.edu/stories/2011/10/found-new-york-long-last-nine-spotted-ladybugs; "Nine-Spotted Ladybeetle," NYNHP, last updated March 30, 2015, https://guides.nynhp.org/nine-spotted-lady-beetle/. See also John E. Losey et al., "Ladybeetles in New York: Insidious Invasions, Erstwhile Extirpations, and Recent Rediscoveries," *Northeastern Naturalist* 21, no. 2 (June 1, 2014): 271–284. The Lost Ladybug Project at Quail Hill farm was overseen by Leslie Allee of Cornell University. In 2019, on a scouting visit to the farm, she found one nine-spotted ladybug. Scott Chaskey, personal communication, April 26, 2023.

CHAPTER 7 — FALLING TREES

1. Central Pine Barrens Joint Planning and Policy Commission (CPBC), *Central Pine Barrens Comprehensive Land Use Plan*, 2 vols. (Westhampton Beach, NY: CPBC, 1996, 2012), 1:31, https://pb.state.ny.us/public-information/comprehensive-land-use-plan/.

2. US Fish and Wildlife Service, Southern New England–New York Bight Coastal Eco-Systems Program, "Long Island Pine Barrens-Peconic River Complex, Complex #8," in *Significant Habitats and Habitat Complexes of the New York Bight Watershed* (Charlestown, RI: US Fish and Wildlife Service, 1997), accessed on US Fish and Wildlife Service website, March 23, 2017 (web page no longer exists); "The Peconic Estuary," The Nature Conservancy, https://www.nature.org/en-us/get-involved/how-to-help/places-we-protect/long-island-peconic-estuary/.

3. Gregory J. Edinger et al., eds., *Ecological Communities of New York State: A Revised and Expanded Edition of Carol Reschke's Ecological Communities of New York State*, 2nd ed. (Albany: New York Natural Heritage Program, New York State Department of Environmental Conservation, March 2014), 99, https://www.nynhp.org/documents/39/ecocomm2014.pdf.

4. John Turner, *The Other Island: A Seasonal Guide to Nature on Long Island* (Sag Harbor, NY: Harbor Electronic, 2011), 188.

5. Edinger et al., *Ecological Communities*, 98, 100–101.

6. Nathaniel S. Prime, *A History of Long Island from Its First Settlement by Europeans to the Year 1845* (New York, 1845), excerpted in *Journeys on Old Long Island: Travelers' Accounts, Contemporary Descriptions, and Residents' Reminiscences, 1744–1893*, ed. Natalie A. Naylor (Interlaken, NY: Empire State Books, 2002), 209–210.

7. Tom Casey, *A Sampler of Walks in the Long Island Pine Barrens*, map and brochure (Riverhead, NY: Long Island Pine Barrens Society, n.d.).

8. Prime, *History of Long Island*, excerpted in Naylor, *Journeys on Old Long Island*, 211. On industrial exploitation of the pinelands, see "History," CPBC, accessed October 13, 2023, https://pb.state.ny.us/central-pine-barrens/history/.

9. On nineteenth-century industrial exploitation in the barrens, see CPBC, *Central Pine Barrens Management Plan*, 2:28–29.

10. CPBC, *Central Pine Barrens Management Plan*, 2:30.

11. New York State, New York Environmental Conservation Law Article 57, 1993, last amended 2019, https://pb.state.ny.us/assets/1/6/LIPB_Maritime-Protection_Act1-websiterev.pdf. The land use plan and its subsequent amendments are in CPBC, *Central Pine Barrens Management Plan*.

12. CPBC, *Central Pine Barrens Comprehensive Prescribed Fire Management Plan* (Westhampton Beach, NY: CPBC, January 2021), 1, https://pb.state.ny.us/assets/1/6/CPMFMP_FINAL_210312.pdf.

13. CPBC, 37.

14. CPBC, *Central Pine Barrens Fire Management Plan* (Westhampton Beach, NY: CPBC, April 1999), 7, 14, https://pb.state.ny.us/file.aspx?DocumentId=1146.

15. CPBC, *Prescribed Fire Management Plan*, vii.

16. CPBC, 23. On climate change and increased wildfire risk, see "Overview," CPBC, accessed October 13, 2023, https://pb.state.ny.us/our-work/wildfire-management-and-prevention/program-overview/.

17. Stephen R. Clarke and J. T. Nowak, *Southern Pine Beetle*, Forest Insect and Disease Leaflet 49, US Forest Service, April 2009; New York State Department of Environmental Conservation (NYSDEC), *Southern Pine Beetle*, fact sheet (Albany, NY: NYSDEC, updated February 29, 2016), https://www.dec.ny.gov/docs/lands_forests_pdf/spbactsheet.pdf; Molly Hassett, Robert Cole, and Kevin Dodds, *New York State Southern Pine Beetle Management Plan* (NYSDEC, October 2018), https://www.dec

.ny.gov/docs/lands_forests_pdf/spb18mgtplan.pdf; "DEC Announces First Pre-scribed Fire of Demonstration Forest at Rocky Point Pine Barrens State Forest," press release, NYSDEC, March 29, 2021, https://www.dec.ny.gov/press/122628.html.

18. NYSDEC, *New York State Southern Pine Beetle Response, 2020 Annual Report*, https://www.dec.ny.gov/docs/lands_forests_pdf/spbannreport2020.pdf.

19. Larry Penny, "The Native White Pine Forest on Long Island's South Fork," *Long Island Botanical Society Newsletter* 7, no. 4 (July–August 1997), http://www.libotanical.org/newsletters/0704.pdf.

20. "Rare White Pine Forest in Northwest Woods Protected Forever," *Peconic Land Trust Newsletter* 14, no. 2 (Fall 2002); "Donor Profile: Marillyn Wilson and Wilson's Grove," *Peconic Land Trust Newsletter* 19, no. 2 (2007).

21. Les Sirkin, *Western Long Island Geology: History, Processes, and Field Trips* (Watch Hill, RI: Book and Tackle Shop, 1995), 50. See also Betsy McCully, *City at the Water's Edge: A Natural History of New York* (New Brunswick, NJ: Rivergate / Rutgers University Press, 2007), 38–39.

22. Penny, "Native White Pine Forest."

23. Larry Penny, "Nature Notes: White Pines Gone Brown," *East Hampton Star*, April 10, 2013.

24. "The Alley Pond Giant," New York City Parks and Recreation, Historical Signs Project, accessed October 13, 2023, https://www.nycgovparks.org/parks/alley-pond-park/highlights/19645/. The New York Old Growth Forest Association, now defunct, conducted surveys of old-growth forests throughout the state, including in Long Island and New York City. They defined old-growth trees as being above 250 years old, and old-growth forests as exhibiting certain characteristics such as complexity (varying ages and heights of trees, with a few very old trees), evidence of old fallen trees, and the presence of mosses and lichens. Surprisingly, there are several old-growth pockets on Long Island, including Alley Pond and the Whitney Estate, both in Queens.

25. Cory Kilgannon, "In the Swamp, on the Hunt for Trees, Old and Invisible," *New York Times*, March 16, 2008. The Old Growth Forest Network, founded by Joan Malouf, does not restrict the definition of old-growth forests to prerevolutionary but opens up the category to second-growth forests, which includes most of the remaining forests today, with rare exceptions. Malouf also acknowledges that the definition of "old growth" is a matter of dispute. Joan Malouf, *Nature's Temples: The Complex World of Old-Growth Forests* (Portland, OR: Timber, 2016), 15; Old-Growth Forest Network, homepage, accessed October 13, 2023, https://www.oldgrowthforest.net.

26. For a more detailed discussion of Algonquian land use and management, see McCully, *City at the Water's Edge*, 53–60, 120–121.

27. McCully, 116–123.

28. J. A. Ayres, *The Legends of Montauk* (New York: Putnam, 1849), https://archive.org/details/legendsofmontauk00ayre/page/106/mode/2up, quoted in Norman Tay-

lor, *The Vegetation of Montauk: A Study of Grassland and Forest*, pt. 1 of *The Vegetation of Long Island*, vol. 2 of *Brooklyn Botanic Garden Memoirs* (New York: Brooklyn Botanic Garden, June 11, 1923), 44, https://archive.org/details/vegetationootayl /page/44/mode/2up. Point Woods lies within Montauk Point State Park east of Oyster Pond, and Hither Woods straddles Montauk Point State Park and Hither Hills State Park west of Fort Pond Bay.

29. Taylor, *Vegetation of Montauk*, 9.

30. David Gardiner, *Chronicles of the Town of Easthampton, County of Suffolk, New York* (New York, 1871; repr., Sag Harbor, NY: I. G. Mairs, 1973), 62, quoted in Taylor, *Vegetation of Montauk*, 11–12.

31. *Records of the Town of East-Hampton*, 5 vols. (Sag Harbor, NY: J. H. Hunt, 1887), 3:294, https://archive.org/details/recordsoftownofe03east_0/page/294/mode/2up, quoted in Taylor, *Vegetation of Montauk*, 11.

32. Taylor, *Vegetation of Montauk*, 44.

33. Taylor, *Vegetation of Montauk*, 54; Jim Ash, personal communication, May 10, 2023. Ash, former director of the South Fork Natural History Museum, tells me he encountered a large colony on Montauk in the early 1970s at an abandoned construction site where the land was found too boggy to build on. Apparently, bulldozing had cleared the thickets and allowed the dormant, shade-intolerant arethusa to emerge.

34. Pehr Kalm quoted in Albert Hostek, *Native and Near-Native Plants: An Introduction to Long Island Plants* (Smithtown, NY: Environmental Centers of Setauket-Smithtown, 1976).

35. Emanuel Levine, ed., *Bull's Breeding Birds of New York State* (Ithaca, NY: Cornell University Press, 1997), 458.

36. "Northern Parula," All about Birds, Cornell Lab of Ornithology, accessed October 13, 2023, https://www.allaboutbirds.org/guide/Northern_Parula/lifehistory. For a more detailed account, see also Ralph R. Moldenhauer and Daniel J. Regelski, "Northern Parula (Setophaga americana)," Birds of the World, Cornell Lab of Ornithology, February 29, 2012, https://birdsoftheworld.org/bow/species/norpar/cur /introduction.

37. R. S. Mitchell, "White-Tailed Deer: An Editorial Comment," *New York Flora Association Newsletter* 8, no. 2 (June 1997): 3, https://nyflora.org/wp-content/uploads /2020/02/NYFA_Newsletter_Vol_08_2_1997.pdf, quoted in Thomas J. Rawinski, *Impacts of White-Tailed Deer Overabundance in Forest Ecosystems: An Overview* (Newtown Square, PA: US Department of Agriculture [USDA], Northeastern Area State and Private Forestry Service, June 2008), 4.

38. Emile DeVito, "Drastic Deer Damage Requires Drastic Deer Reduction," *New York Times*, April 21, 2008. See also David Kocieniewski, "Audubon Group Advocates Deer Hunting," *New York Times*, March 15, 2005. In 2012, the Natural Resources Conservation Service of New Jersey, a division of the USDA, reported in its fact sheet,

jointly produced with New Jersey Audubon, that the density of deer in New Jersey was as high as 114 per square mile as of 2010, down slightly from 1998 numbers. In the same fact sheet, it suggested that a density of "10–20 deer per square mile" was a reasonable goal, and that to reduce deer to these manageable numbers, hunting is "a very effective tool to control the white-tailed deer population." New Jersey Audubon Society and Natural Resources Conservation Service / USDA, "NJ Biology Technical Note: White-Tailed Deer Impacts and Forest Management," Natural Resources Conservation Service, USDA, 2012, https://njaudubon.org/wp-content/uploads/2019/09/White_Tailed_Deer_and_Forest_Management_Tech_Doc_NJAS.pdf.

39. Thomas P. Rooney and Donald M. Waller, "Direct and Indirect Effects of White-Tailed Deer in Forest Ecosystems," *Forest Ecology and Management* 181 (2003): 170.

40. Thomas J. Rawinski, *White-Tailed Deer in Northeastern Forests: Understanding and Assessing Impacts* (2014; repr., Newtown Square, PA: USDA Forest Service Northeastern Area, January 2016), 2.

41. Rawinski, 2.

42. Rawinski, 2–3.

43. C. Meine, *Aldo Leopold: His Life and Work* (Madison: University of Wisconsin Press, 1988), 5, quoted in Rawinski, "Impacts of White-Tailed Deer," 5. The quote dates to 1944.

44. Henry David Thoreau, "Walking," *Atlantic Monthly*, June 1862, available at Walden Woods Project, https://www.walden.org/wp-content/uploads/2016/03/Walking.pdf.

Index

Page numbers in italics refer to figures.

Walls Point Creek, 70
wampum: quahog clamshell and, 88;
    whelks as source of, 21
Wander, Wade, 24
warblers, 152–153, 156
Ward, Anson W. and Florence, 106–107
Washington, George, 11–12
water: from aquifers, 94–95; meltwater,
    92, 93–94; toxins in groundwater/
    drinking water, 95
waterlily, 93
water-table lake, 96
waterweed, 100
waves, sand transport by, 13–14
Webster, Daniel, 106
Weis, Judith, 79, 83, 84, 85
Wertheim, Maurice, 107
Wertheim National Wildlife Refuge, *103*,
    107
West Connecticut River. *See* Carmans
    River
Westhampton, 14; groins at, 30
Westhampton Beach, beach erosion and,
    30
West Nile virus, mosquito spraying and,
    84
wetland restoration plans, 89–91
wetlands, 17; role in ecosystem, 88–89
Weymouth, George, 43, 55
whale meat, as cold food, 54–55
whales, 51–59; beached, 52–54, 56, 57; in
    Hudson Canyon, 41, 47; humpback,
    51–52; inshore, 51–52; minke, 51, 52;
    North Atlantic right whale, 54–55,
    57–59
whaling, shore, 55–58
whelk egg case, 21
whelks, 10, 21, 24, 41
When Dinosaurs Roamed New Jersey
    (Gallagher), 10

White, Alfred T., 80
White Island, 89
white oak, 150
white perch, 96
white pines, old-growth, 145–147
white-tailed deer, 2, 129, 130; effect of
    overbrowsing by, 153–156
Whitman, Walt, 35, 121, 123
Wild, Scenic and Recreational River,
    Carmans as, 107
wilderness preserve, 103
wildflowers, 125; spring ephemerals,
    156–157
wild indigo, 125
wild strawberry, 156
willets, 72, 83
Wilson, Alexander, 25
Wilson, Marillyn, 145
Wilson's Grove, 14–147
wind, dunes created by, 16
Wood, William, 108–109, 110
wood anemone, 156
woolly mammoths, 2
World Wildlife Fund, 50
worms, 40
wrack, 21, 38
Wyandanch: land gift of, 98; right to
    beached whales and, 53–54

Yaphank/Carmans River, *6*
Yellow Bar Hassock, 82
yellow-crowned night-heron, 70, 71,
    86
yellow eels, 111–112
yellowfin tuna, 47, 51
yellow perch, 96
yellow warbler, 156

Zeckendorf, William, 124
zooplankton, 10, 40, 59

About the Author

Betsy McCully has frequently written and lectured about New York's natural and environmental history, from its ancient geological origins to its human developments. Her previous book is *City at the Water's Edge: A Natural History of New York*. For forty years, she has explored and documented the region's natural worlds. Her discovery of Long Island's richly diverse habitats, and her witnessing of our human impact on those habitats, led her to write this book on Long Island. She taught writing and American literature at Kingsborough College of the City University of New York for twenty years, where she founded the award-winning Eco-Festival. Now retired from a university teaching career that spanned forty years, she lives with her husband on Long Island.